Wages in the Business Cycle

Wages in the Business Cycle

An Empirical and Methodological Analysis

Jonathan Michie

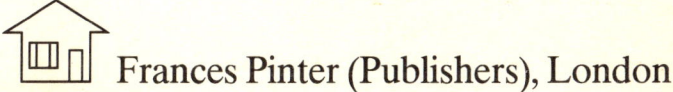 Frances Pinter (Publishers), London

© Jonathan Michie 1987

First published in Great Britain in 1987 by
Frances Pinter (Publishers), Limited
25 Floral Street, London WC2E 9DS

All rights reserved. No part of this
publication may be reproduced,
stored in a retrieval system, or
transmitted by any means without
the prior written permission of the
copyright holder. Please direct
all enquiries to the publisher

British Library Cataloguing in Publication Data
Michie, Jonathan
   Wages in the business cycle: an empirical
   and methodological analysis.
   1. Wages—Effect of business cycle on
   I. Title
   331.2'15   HD4906
ISBN 0-86187-686-5

Typeset by Joshua Associates Limited, Oxford
Printed by Biddles of Guildford, Limited

Contents

1. Introduction — 1
  1. The 'stylized fact' of cyclical wages — 1
    1.1. The belief in counter-cyclical real wages — 2
  2. Theory, facts and falsification — 3
    2.1. Falsification and the methodological responses — 4
    2.2. Falsification and the individual responses — 6
  3. Inference — 6
  4. Structure of the book — 12

2. The Theoretical Background — 15
  1. Neoclassical assumptions — 15
  2. Alternative assumptions — 16
    2.1. Technology shocks — 17
    2.2. Quantity rationing — 21
    2.3. Kalecki — 23
  3. Generalized model — 25
  4. Pro-cyclical wage movements — 27
    4.1. Logical possibility — 28
    4.2. Causal mechanism — 28
  5. Conclusion — 30

3. A Survey of the Literature — 32
  1. The Literature — 32
  2. From Keynes (1936) to Keynes (1939) — 33
    2.1. Accuracy and uniformity — 34
    2.2. Real and product wages — 35
    2.3. Marginal user cost — 35
    2.4. Shape of cost curves — 36
    2.5. Mark-up — 36
  3. Methods — 37
    3.1. Wage equations and labour demand schedules — 39
    3.2. The existence of cycles — 41
    3.3. Cyclical variable — 43
    3.4. Wage series and the role of materials — 44
    3.5. Lags — 46
    3.6. Detrending — 47
    3.7. Data coverage — 49

	CONTENTS	
	4. Results	50
	5. Conclusion	56

4. International Results 57
1. Product wages 57
2. Lags and leads 59
3. Materials costs 62
4. Wages and materials costs 63
5. Wages, materials costs and output 67
6. Total direct costs 69
7. Comparison with other studies 71
8. Parameter stability 73
9. Conclusion 74

5. Employment 79
1. Methods 79
   1.1. The specification of the correlation to be tested 79
   1.2. The estimation of the correlations 80
2. Results 81
   2.1. Wages and employment 81
   2.2. Materials costs and total direct costs 83
   2.3. Employment conditional on output 83
   2.4. Number employed 87
3. Discussion 87
4. Conclusion 90

6. Phases of the Cycle 91
1. Methods 91
   1.1. Phase Average Trend 91
   1.2. Dependent and independent variables 92
2. Results 92
   2.1. Cycle phases 95
   2.2. 1952 III to 1967 III 96
3. Conclusion 96

7. Individual Industries and the Aggregate Economy 99
1. Methods 100
2. Results 100
3. Aggregate output and industry wage 102
4. Wage–output correlation and the aggregate cycle 108
5. Conclusion 110

CONTENTS

8. The History of the Cyclical Wage Debate — 111
   1. Historiography — 112
      1.1. Comparison with Dunlop and Keynes — 115
      1.2. Materials and total direct costs — 120
   2. 1920–1939 — 121
   3. Conclusion — 124

9. Conclusion — 126
   1. The cyclical wage debate — 127
   2. The three levels of the debate — 128
      2.1. The search for a stylized fact — 128
      2.2. Theory, facts and falsification — 130
      2.3. Inference — 132
   3. Government economic policy — 133

Appendix 1. Using Alternative Price Deflators — 135
Appendix 2. Construction of Total Direct Cost Index — 137
Appendix 3. Statistical Tests — 141
Appendix 4. Data — 148
Appendix 5. The Phase Average Trend Technique — 176
Appendix 6. Seasonal Adjustment — 177

Bibliography — 178

Author Index — 191
Subject Index — 193

For my mother, Anne

Acknowledgements

I am grateful for help and criticisms from family, friends and colleagues. Particular thanks to Andrew Glyn and Ann Logan.

1
Introduction

In 1938 Dunlop challenged the assertion made by Keynes (1936) that real wages moved counter-cyclically. This prompted a debate which has continued to the present day. The debate on the cyclical movement of wages[1] is an important economic controversy which deserves serious study as an episode in the history of economic thought. This is pursued in Chapter 2 of this book, which reviews the theoretical issues, and Chapter 3 which reviews the empirical work. To understand this history, however, requires some analysis of the meaning and significance of the debate. This can be examined at a number of levels.

1. The 'stylized fact' of cyclical wages

At one level the debate can be interpreted as the search for a 'stylized fact': that is, the search for a general empirical observation that real wage movements are counter- (or pro-) cyclical. This is apparently an empirical question, and is of some interest in its own right. Indeed, there has been renewed interest in this empirical question since the mid-1970s.

One aim of the work reported in this book is to contribute to that empirical literature, using data for various countries, time periods, cycle phases and industries to examine whether there is any such systematic cyclical pattern in wage movements. For comparability, this empirical analysis will be conducted using the procedures adopted by the participants in the debate. The status of these procedures is discussed further below.

However, even at this simple level of a search for a stylized fact, the empirical question (are wage movements pro- or counter-cyclical?) is not well defined until there is agreement on how to characterize the cyclical pattern of the economy with which wage movements are being compared; but within economics there is no such agreement. The cyclical pattern can be defined in terms of some general reference cycle, or as innovations relative to rational expectations of the variable, or in terms of the correlation of wages with some cyclical variable such as output or employment. There is also considerable controversy about

---

[1] Definitions of 'real' and 'product' earnings are discussed in Chapter 2.

the separation of trend from cycle and the allowance for extraneous influences. The sensitivity of the results to these issues is examined in the empirical analysis.

The conclusion of the empirical analysis reported in this book (and of some but not all of the recent literature) is that there is no evidence of a systematic empirical regularity in the cyclical pattern of wage movements. There does not appear to be a stylized fact to be found, which is perhaps a part of the reason why the search and the controversy have proceeded for so long. The other necessary part of such an explanation for the durability of the controversy would need to explain why the *non*-cyclical pattern has not yet been generally accepted. The answer may be twofold. First, and more fundamentally, is the belief held by some that there *should* be a cyclical pattern. Second, the two (cyclical output and wage) series do appear to be related, only not directly and the resulting correlation is not a stable one. There may be a perfectly determinate (and explicable) relation between these two economic variables, reflecting, even, a stable structure of the economy; and yet that statistical correlation between the two time series may vary over time as a result of the other variables and relations in the economy. Nevertheless, the appearance of temporary correlations between the two series has encouraged the claim of a cyclical pattern to continue to be made at the level of theory and empirical prediction.

1.1 *The belief in counter-cyclical real wages*

It might appear strange to put such emphasis on the empirical side of the cyclical wage debate. An examination of the 'stylized fact' of real wages being counter-cyclical might be thought methodologically redundant (as meaningless without properly identified assumptions to be estimated) and/or already empirically disproved. The former question is considered separately, below. As for the latter, this is not the case: there are at least three groups of writers who imply that real wages actually are counter-cyclical.

First, there are passing references made from outside the cyclical wage literature, including in textbook presentations of the diminishing marginal product of labour curve, which imply, or even state, that real wages do move counter-cyclically. For example, an article by Stanley Dennison (1984, p. 64) claims that 'Keynes himself...fully accepted the "orthodox" analysis', citing Keynes's (1936, p. 17) statement that 'an increase in employment can only occur to the accompaniment of a decline in the rate of real wages. Thus I am not disputing this vital fact which the classical economists have (rightly) asserted as indefeasible'. As discussed in Chapter 3, Keynes in 1939 dissociated himself from this view. The point here is that Dennison appears to believe what Keynes did in 1936, namely that real wages do, empirically, move counter-cyclically.

Second, and most important for the empirical work reported later, there are some participants in the cyclical wage debate itself who report having found that real wages are, indeed, counter-cyclical. An example would be Otani (1978). This, and the other studies, are discussed in Chapter 3.

Third, last, and most topical are the economic and political commentators, from Samuel Brittan in the *Financial Times*, to the Chancellor of the Exchequer, Nigel Lawson, who imply that a cyclical reduction in real wages is necessary and/or sufficient for a cyclical expansion in employment and output. A typical such article by Samuel Brittan appeared in the *Financial Times* on 26 July 1984:

> real wage growth would need to slip below two per cent per annum and probably below one per cent and stay there for several years if unemployment were to be reduced in the remainder of the 1980s.
> Unemployment is being swollen by ... high real wages ...
> ... If a rise in real wages is associated with a fall in employment for a given capital stock, labour productivity will rise ... the economy has moved up the demand curve for labour to a lower employment level.

Brittan's article was based on Symons (1984) which argued that 'the fall in manufacturing employment since 1978 is entirely consistent with an operative neoclassical demand for labour schedule' (Symons 1984, p. 1), and continued: 'What these calculations do at least show is that the data do not contain an *obvious* refutation of the proposition that the real wage is too high' (Symons 1984, p. 9, emphasis in original).

2. Theory, facts and falsification

Despite the views illustrated in the previous section, it is not surprising that there is no simple cyclical pattern to real wages. This point has been made in reply to the current government claims referred to above, for example by Nickell (1985). Chapter 2 also shows that even the assumption underlying much of the counter-cyclical wage viewpoint— the shape of the marginal product of labour, and cost, curves—has long been open to dispute.

At a second level, then, the cyclical wage debate was, and is, a theoretical one. The controversy generated such heat because the empirical observation that wages did not move counter-cyclically was thought to falsify a prevailing theory. The perceived theoretical significance of the result is discussed in Chapter 2. What is particularly interesting about the debate at this level is the light it sheds on the response of economists to apparent falsification.

2.1 Falsification and the methodological responses

Behind the different responses of economists to apparent falsification lie different methodological beliefs as to the status of falsificationism, and what the response of theory *should* be.

First a working definition of what is meant by 'falsificationism' is needed:

> *Falsificationism*. A methodological standpoint that regards theories and hypotheses as scientific if and only if their predictions are, at least in principle, empirically falsifiable; naïve falsificationism holds that theories can be refuted by a single test, whereas sophisticated falsificationism holds that it requires a large number of tests to refute a theory (Blaug 1980, p. 266).

The methodological approach most impervious to falsificationism would be apriorism:

> If a contradiction appears between a theory and experience, we must always assume that a condition pre-supposed by the theory was not present, or else that there is some error in our observation. The disagreement between the theory and the facts of experience frequently forces us to think through the problems of the theory again. But so long as a rethinking of the theory uncovers no errors in our thinking, we are not entitled to doubt its truth. (Mises 1933, p. 30 in 1960 edition. Cited in Katouzian 1980, pp. 38–40).

The strongest counter-influence to the philosophical approach typified by this passage from von Mises would be from the falsificationists of the Popper school. Blaug, in advocating falsificationism, acknowledges Duhem's argument that no individual scientific hypothesis is conclusively falsifiable since the particular hypothesis is always tested in conjunction with auxiliary statements, hence we can never be sure that we have confirmed or refuted the hypothesis itself rather than the auxiliary statements (Duhem 1954). Thus Blaug describes the view that a single test alone could refute a hypothesis as 'naïve falsificationism'. He also argues that Popper's whole methodology was conceived to deal with this difficulty:

> In point of fact, no conclusive disproof of a theory can ever be produced; for it is always possible to say that the experimental results

are not reliable, or that the discrepancies which are asserted to exist between the experimental results and the theory are only apparent and that they will disappear with the advance of our understanding' (Popper 1959, p. 50; cited in Blaug 1980, p. 18).

The arguments here about the reliability of experiments are not actually the crucial ones for Duhem's irrefutability hypothesis, the latter being explicitly discussed elsewhere in Popper (1959) and more fully in Popper (1963):

> Now it has to be admitted that we can often test only a large chunk of a theoretical system, and sometimes perhaps only the whole system, and that, in these cases, it is sheer guesswork which of its ingredients should be held responsible for any falsification; a point which I have tried to emphasise—also with reference to Duhem—for a long time past (Popper 1963, p. 239).

The relevance of this to the argument of this book is that the results from estimating a model will depend not only on the data, but also on the prior specification of the model. It also leads to the difficulty of deciding when a disproof becomes conclusive. In Popperian terms this is a matter of setting methodological limits on strategems which might be adopted to safeguard theories against refutation.

How individual participants, and particularly Keynes, reacted to the apparent falsification is considered in the following section. First it can be indicated what 'immunizing strategy' was, historically, adopted in defence of the neoclassical diminishing marginal product of labour hypothesis (against the challenge that its prediction of counter-cyclical real wages had been refuted empirically). Paraphrasing the passage from Popper cited above, it has been argued that the reported results are not necessarily reliable. In addition, there has been a 'Lakatosian' tendency to treat the neoclassical diminishing marginal product of labour hypothesis as an increasingly 'hard core' belief surrounded by a protective belt of auxiliary assumptions. The most extreme example, discussed in Chapter 3, is that of Tatom.

It might be objected by modern economists that the interconnection of labour and product markets, the possibility of supply or demand shocks, and so on, do not imply a counter-cyclical real wage hypothesis, regardless of whether the diminishing marginal product of labour hypothesis is valid or not. There would, therefore, be no need for a protective belt of auxiliary assumptions around such a belief protecting it from actual cyclical patterns of real wage movements. In other words there are enough indispensible assumptions, without which the model would be misspecified, to produce an agnostic prediction for real wages. The point, however, is that such a view of the economy, with its agnostic view as to the cyclical pattern of real wages, was not the view held in the 1930s: hence Keynes's assertion (or unthinking acceptance) of the *requirement* for real wages to move counter-cyclically (and hence for real wages to decline in the boom). It was *this* (diminishing marginal product of labour) model of the economy, and *this* empirical prediction (of counter-cyclical real wages) that was confronted in the 1930s by apparent falsification. Today's theory, and cyclical wage predictions, have developed out of that 1930s version and the resulting 'immunizing strategy' adopted by that version of neoclassical theory in the face of apparent falsification.

2.2 *Falsification and the individual responses*

The responses of Keynes (1939) to the apparent falsification of the theory held by Keynes (1936) was particularly striking in terms of the methods used to immunize theories against such falsification. He responded with three defences. First, he makes clear that he had not intended his assertion (regarding the counter-cyclical behaviour of real wages) as a scientific prediction to be tested: 'I complain a little that I in particular should be criticised ... as if I was the first to have entertained the fifty-year-old generalisation that, trend eliminated, increasing output is usually associated with a falling real wage' (Keynes 1939, pp. 50–1). It is ironic in this context, though, that his original (1936) statement regarding the counter-cyclical behaviour of real wages was worded in terms of an empirical task to be undertaken. Second, Keynes suggests that possibly 'the experimental results are not reliable' (to quote from the above passage from Popper). Third, Keynes argues that even if his hypothesis had been falsified it would not affect his general theory of employment, other than to strengthen it.

These responses from Keynes are considered in greater detail in the survey of the literature (Chapter 3), as are the other contributions. Keynes ended his 1939 article with an appeal for more empirical work (which would be the Popperian approach to overcoming Duhem's irrefutability theorem—despite Keynes's other, anti-Popperian, responses). It is striking, however, that following one empirical study by Richardson (1939) the subsequent two contributors, Ruggles (1940) and Tobin (1947), far from attempting any such work, instead raised further doubts as to the reliability of the work which had been undertaken by Dunlop (1938), Tarshis (1939) and Richardson (1939).

3. Inference

A third level of the debate, then, which was rarely explicitly discussed, is the issue of inference: the question of how observations related to theories. Keynes tended to treat theory as prior, attacking 'pseudo natural science' procedures which did otherwise. His response to theory being confronted with empirical results was, far from viewing theory as being inferred from such empirical observations, close to the extreme apriorism of von Mises cited above.

Stewart (1979, p. 122) distinguishes between apriorism of the von Mises school, on the one hand, and, on the other hand, Keynes's methodology which he labels 'analytical':

> Quite often in methodological literature, writers fail to make any distinction between the analytical and apriorist schools, using either one of the labels to describe both approaches. But there is a clear and significant difference between the two. The analytical account does not assert that the propositions of economic theory are materially true a priori. What is being argued, instead, is that these are propositions about empirical reality—that they are *capable* of being set against factual observation—but that they are so obvious to commonsense that they do not *need* to be 'tested' by inductive-statistical means (emphasis in original).

Similarly in his classic *Essay on the Nature and Significance of Economic Science*, Robbins (1935, pp. 115–16) refers to the 'analytical' school to mean the standard, orthodox tradition of economics; and describes the analytical school's use of prior beliefs as follows:

> These are not postulates the existence of whose counterpart in reality admits of extensive dispute once their nature is fully realised. We do not need controlled experiments to establish their validity: they are so much the stuff of our everyday experience that they have only to be stated to be recognised as obvious (Robbins 1935, p. 79).

The 'Law of Diminishing Returns' is stated by Robbins (1935, pp. 76–7) to be one of these prior beliefs that 'have only to be stated to be recognised as obvious': a prior belief of some importance in establishing the belief that cyclical returns to labour in an expansion must diminish. The distinction is an important one: between those (like von Mises) who hold prior beliefs independent of experience, and those (like Robbins and Keynes) who hold prior beliefs which, while being so obviously true that they do not need to be tested, nevertheless could be so tested, and, more importantly, are considered to derive from experience. Rather than use Stewart's terminology of apriorism and the analytical school, the fact that the latter do, in practice, hold prior beliefs, can be indicated by using the distinction in Klant (1984) between 'rationalistic apriorism' (corresponding to the philosophical school of apriorism) and 'empirical apriorism'.

Keynes's criticism of the idea that economists should, empirically, discover the 'real values' for the variable functions in economic models is best known from his writings on Tinbergen's work. Similar sentiments are voiced in the following letter to Roy Harrod:

> It seems to me that economics is a branch of logic, a way of thinking; and that you do not repel sufficiently firmly attempts *à la* Schultz to turn it into a pseudo-natural science. One can make some quite worthwhile progress merely by using your axioms and maxims. But one cannot get very far except by devising new and improved models. This requires, as you say, a 'vigilant observation of the actual working of our system'. Progress in economics consists almost entirely in a progressive improvement in the choice of models...
>
> But it is of the essence of a model that one does not fill in real values for the variable functions. To do so would make it useless as a model. For as soon as this is done, the model loses its generality and its value as a mode of thought. That is why Clapham with his empty boxes was barking up the wrong tree and why Schultz's results, if he ever gets any, are not very interesting (for we know beforehand that they will not be applicable to future cases). The object of statistical study is not so much to fill in missing variables with a view to prediction, as to test the relevance and validity of the model.
>
> Economics is a science of thinking in terms of models joined to the art of choosing models which are relevant to the contemporary world. It is compelled to be this, because, unlike the typical natural science, the material to which it is applied is, in too many respects, not homogeneous through time. The object of a model is to segregate the semi-permanent or relatively constant factors from those which are transitory or fluctuating so as to develop a logical way of thinking about the latter, and of understanding the time sequence to which they give rise in particular cases.
>
> Good economists are scarce because the gift for using 'vigilant observation' to choose good models, although it does not require a highly specialised intellectual technique, appears to be a very rare one.
>
> In the second place, as against Robbins, economics is essentially a moral science and not a natural science. That is to say, it employs introspection and judgements of value (Keynes 1973, pp. 296–7; cited by Blaug 1980, pp. 90–1).

Presumably Keynes cites Robbins as believing economics to be a natural science because Robbins argues for 'delimiting the neutral area of science from the more disputable area of moral and political philosophy' (Robbins 1935, p. 151). Nevertheless, following on from the passage cited above, Robbins (1935, pp. 99-100) does go on to conclude that:

> In the light of all that has been said the nature of economic analysis should now be plain. It consists of deductions from a series of postulates, the chief of which are almost universal facts of experience present whenever human activity has an economic aspect, the rest being assumptions of a more limited nature based upon the general features of particular situations or types of situations which the theory is to be used to explain.

Robbins also argues (1935, pp. 108-10) that, while the coefficients derived from observation are useful, they cannot be compared to 'statistical laws' of natural science. And he criticizes Mitchell's attempts to generalize from statistical data. Thus Robbins would accept Keynes's objection to inferring theory from observation: that economic relations are not stable over time, (an objection with which Popper would also agree). Hence, Keynes argued, it was not methodologically acceptable to infer economic 'laws' as applying to data other than those from which the inference was made (in which case they would lack generality and would not be laws).

In so far as this criticism is made against any attempt to infer a theory of cyclical wages from observations, it would receive support from the empirical results reported in this book. These show that where such theories have been inferred, they fail to account for data other than those on which the inference was based. To this methodological point modern economics would object that to attempt such an inference would be the result of misspecification but that it is possible to specify underlying stable relations (albeit with structural breaks) which would not be falsified by observed cyclical wage behaviour. Nevertheless, not only have inferences of cyclical wage behaviour been attempted, but the fifty-year-old generalization accepted by Keynes originally came not from a prior belief but from, precisely, such an invalid inference from observations taken from one, single atypical, cycle (as described in Chapter 8).

Modern economists would emphasize the need for identifying assumptions before estimates could be used to test hypotheses in the context of a simultaneous equations system. In this framework, there is no reason to expect any systematic reduced form regularity to emerge; and even were it to emerge, its implications for the theory would be ambiguous in the absence of non-data-based identifying assumptions. Of course, there are considerable differences in methodological approach within modern economics. A currently standard econometric textbook (Koutsoyiannis 1977, pp. 22-5) distinguishes between the 'orthodox approach' and the 'experimental approach', the latter being described as less rigid in sticking to a priori assumptions than the former. Hendry & Wallis (1984, Preface) state that their book 'reflects the change of emphasis from estimation to modelling', and contrast the role of theory in such modelling as follows:

> Theories are designed to highlight the features of importance in an analysis, and are necessarily highly idealized abstractions. Often the variables of the theory are not directly observable, or even have no clear measurable counterparts ... The 'correct' formulation of the econometric model is not just highly uncertain, it may not even be a sensible concept.
>
> In empirical econometrics, however, the emphasis is placed squarely on the operational—is the model adequate for the purposes to which it will be put? One does not ask an engineer if the 'correct' bridge was built, but rather if it will fulfil its functions satisfactorily; when the functions alter (carrying tanks rather than pedestrians) so will the adequacy (Hendry & Wallis 1984, pp. 3–4)

Marshall (1885, p. 159) used a similar analogy to make the same point:

> The theory of mechanics contains no statement of fact as to the greatest strain which bridges will bear. Every bridge has it peculiarities of construction of material: and mechanics supplies a universal engine, which will help in determining what strain any bridge will bear. But it has no universal dogmas by which this strain can be determined without observation of the particular facts of the case.

It is not an original point that, while a bee would put many a human architect to shame by the construction of its honeycomb cells, what distinguishes the worst of architects from the best of bees is that the architect raises the structure in their imagination before erecting it in reality. So not only is theory necessary for empirical work, but the results of that work will depend in part on the prior assumptions. Thus, for example, Hendry & Wallis (1984, p. 8) state that 'theories are themselves part of an iterative strategy, formalising and abstracting the salient features of existing evidence in a coherent framework, summarising current understanding and seeking to predict or explain new phenomena, and this emerges clearly from Nickell's account', where 'Nickell's account' refers to Nickell (1984). This study assumes that firms face no quantity constraints, one of the results being that cyclical fluctuations in employment are only possible through the influence of the real interest term in labour supply: 'Thus a rise in government expenditure can, if it raises the real interest rate, both raise employment (and hence output) and lower the real wage' (Nickell 1984, p. 17).

While some such modern studies claim direct relevance to the cyclical wage literature (particularly the various studies by Symons), that literature (including recent contributions) tends to adopt a different methodological approach. Instead of specifying and estimating structural equations, the reduced form correlation of the two (wage and cyclical variable) series is tested for. Bernanke & Powell (1984, p. 1) explicitly state that:

> The methodology of this study follows that of the traditional Burns & Mitchell (1946) business cycle analysis... we have not formulated or tested a specific structural model of labour markets during the cycle but instead concentrate on measuring qualitative features of the data. As did Burns & Mitchell, we see descriptive analysis of the data as a useful prelude to theorising about business cycles. Thus, although the research reported in this paper permits *no* direct structural inferences, it should be useful in restricting the class of structural models or hypotheses which may subsequently be considered (emphasis in original).

It is also the reduced form correlation (rather than structural model) which is tested for in the empirical chapters of this book; and a more explicit explanation than occurs in any of the cyclical wage studies should be given of why such an approach is followed. First is the point (discussed in Chapter 3, Section 3.1) that omitting those regressor variables uncorrelated with the cycle would not be expected to bias the regression coefficient of wages on cyclical output. Hence nothing is lost by omitting them. As for the other omitted regressor variables—those which are correlated with the cycle—it is only by omitting them that the cyclical output variable can be forced to proxy for all cyclical influences, hence the only way the coefficient on that regressor can be made to reflect the actual cyclical pattern of wages. Second, fully specified and estimated models at present allow contradictory cyclical wage patterns. Hence, for example, Layard & Nickell (1983, p. 881), replying to a criticism from Whitley & Wilson (1983) of their (1980, p. 53) assertion that the current state of the art in economics renders it impossible to analyse policy effects in the context of a fully dynamic model, stated that:

> What we meant by this was not that we consider the existing UK macro models to be unsuitable but that there exists no theoretical dynamic macro model which commands wide enough support among economists to enable us to generate dynamic reponses which would convince more than a small proportion of the profession. This absence of consensus does, in fact, spill over into the empirical models as well in the sense that with the key wage-equation, for

example, the difference in specification across the various large models is very large indeed and generates very different responses to certain types of policy, particularly in the short run.

The reason for this is that, first, as E. H. Carr (1962, p. 11) put it in his criticism of empiricism (and of Popper in particular), 'a fact is like a sack—it won't stand up till you've put something in it'; and, second, that the results inferred from such facts will then depend in part on what 'you've put ... in'. Hence the interest in looking at simple direct relationships not embedded in a more specific model, as a way of abstracting from the assumptions of a model, assumptions which in each case would not necessarily be generally accepted.

To conclude on the question of inference, then, few would go along with von Mises' view that 'The economist need not displace himself; he can, in spite of all sneers, like the logician and the mathematician accomplish his job in an armchair' (Mises 1962, p. 78; cited in Klant 1984, p. 73). The reaction of Keynes to the cyclical wage question showed that he was not opposed to statistical work in principle. The reference made above to Robbins's criticism of Mitchell was not for compiling descriptive statistics, but for attempting to generalize from them. However, while naming no names, the criticism from Burns & Mitchell (1946, p. 8) of the theorist who 'often stops before his work is finished, leaving "inductive verification" to others, who may or may not take on the job' is a reasonable description of Keynes's approach to the cyclical behaviour of wages (leaving aside the now outdated reference to 'inductive verification'). Thus the differences in the methodological approaches of participants in the cyclical wage debate to the question of inference are displayed not just by what they say but by what they do.

4. Structure of the book

This book uses the history of the cyclical wage debate and the empirical analysis to illustrate the themes of observation, theory and inference. The theoretical assumptions underlying the cyclical wage literature are surveyed in Chapter 2 *not* to identify various possible mutually incompatible theories for each possible empirical outcome but, on the contrary, to develop a more general framework within which to consider the real wage–cyclical output relation. Of course, whether any correlation would be expected at all depends on how each (cyclical output and cyclical wage) series is thought to be generated: in which markets and what the relation is thought to be between the relevant markets. The models considered in Chapter 2 (and the generalized model there developed to consider the possible relation between competing assumptions over the course of the cycle in capacity utilization) merely set some constraints (or not) on the limits within which the outcome of the labour-market and product-market price fixing processes must operate to be compatible with cyclical output (and productivity). It is these latter constraints, as opposed to the former mechanisms, with which the cyclical wage literature has been concerned. Indeed, Keynes's 1936 pronouncement on the necessity of counter-cyclical wages was based on the acceptance that the neoclassical diminishing marginal product of labour constraint operated and hence the assumption that the price fixing processes in the labour and product markets must conform to those constraints. The resulting literature, on the actual empirical behaviour of cyclical wages, is surveyed in Chapter 3. The remaining chapters then report the results of testing for the wage–output (and wage–employment) correlation across countries, time, cycle phases and industries.

One problem underlying the theory, and investigation, of the cyclical behaviour of earnings is whether output or employment is the appropriate cyclical indicator. The business cycle refers to the output cycle, and so a consideration of the cyclical behaviour of earning must establish whether there exists any systematic relation between earnings and this output cycle. It is this task which the work reported in this book attempts. Chapter 4 reports the results of such an investigation on post-Second World War international data.

At the same time, however, the neoclassical theory of counter-cyclical (product) earnings derives from hypothesized variations in the marginal product of labour as employment varies over the cycle. Thus it is this cyclical behaviour of employment which is directly associated with cyclical earnings. This question, then, of whether there exists any systematic relation between earnings and cyclical employment is considered in Chapter 5.

A more detailed look at the cycle, testing for the possibility of different behaviour in different phases of the cycle is carried out for quarterly UK data as reported in Chapter 6.

Industry-level UK disaggregated data are tested for in Chapter 7, both as a comparison with the aggregate results and to allow further tests of the neoclassical marginal product of labour theory of cyclical wages.

Chapter 8 reports comparisons with pre-Second World War UK data; and these data are used to trace the empirical basis from which earlier writers (Marshall and Keynes) drew their conclusions.

At the level of observation and the search for the 'stylized fact' of cyclical wage behaviour, the empirical work reported in Chapters 4–8 find no such stylized fact. Real wages are found to be non-cyclical. The results there reported are believed to be comprehensive enough finally to close the door on this empirical literature. While it is always possible to extend the data base and improve the statistical techniques, neither would alter the failure of the data tested for in this work to indicate any such cyclical wage pattern.

The methodological implications of this work, taken in this sense as a 'case study' in economic methodology, are drawn together in the concluding chapter.

2
The Theoretical Background

1. Neoclassical assumptions

The elements of the neoclassical model relevant to the cyclical behaviour of product wages[1] are, first, that in order to have positive profits the feasible range of output corresponds to the marginal product of labour (mpl) being less than the average product of labour (apl); and, second, competitive assumptions assure that the product wage will be equal to the mpl. Hence in Figure 1, with the real wage ($W = w/p$) on the vertical axis and employment (L) on the horizontal, at wage W_1, employment will be at L_1.

The addition of standard neoclassical full market clearing would not, however, be compatible with fully fledged cycles. Neoclassical assumptions do not involve cyclical output behaviour. The starting point in this chapter for discussing the economic theory behind hypothesized wage–output correlations is the debate in the 1930s to which the arguments of the Treasury and Keynes (1936) referred. These were based on the application of neoclassical assumptions to a situation already *without* full market clearing. That is, real wages are too high because of a failure of labour markets to clear (Treasury), or because of insufficient aggregate demand (Keynes 1936). This is historically and intellectually the framework within which the debate developed.

These economic assumptions, which imply counter-cyclical real wages (or, at least, an inverse wage–output correlation as the economy adjusts back to equilibrium from a disequilibrium position) in both their (Treasury and Keynesian) forms, are also compatible with

---

[1] The term 'real wage' is used in this book in the general sense of the nominal wage deflated by a price index, without specifying what price index. When the term 'product wage' is used it is in the generally accepted sense of the nominal wage having been deflated by an index of the price received by the employer for the products produced by the worker whose money wage is being referred to. When the term 'real wage' is used specifically as an alternative to the product wage then it refers to the nominal wage deflated by an index of prices of consumer goods. However, the term 'real wage' is also used in the broader sense when the context is clear.

The real wage is what is of interest to the worker. The product wage is what is of interest to the employer. It is this product wage with which this book is concerned.

Similarly the terms 'earnings' and 'wages' are used interchangeably to mean the amount actually received on average per hour. Further distinctions, between wage rates and earnings, for example, are discussed with reference to data sources in the empirical chapters.

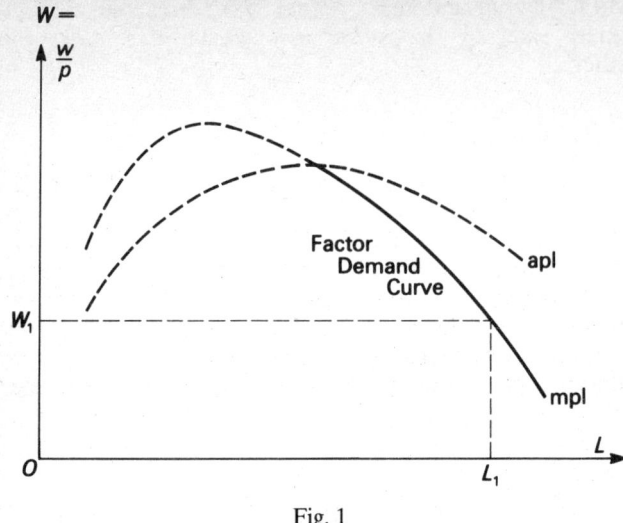

Fig. 1

imperfect competition. In this case the labour demand curve would not be the mpl curve but would be a function of it reflecting the degree of monopoly. If the degree of monopoly was invariant to the cycle the wage would be equal to some constant proportion of the (counter-cyclical) mpl and hence would itself be counter-cyclical.

Such assumptions implying counter-cyclical wages are not, however, the only logically coherent ones by which a study of cyclical wage behaviour can be informed. Different assumptions involve different (pro- or non-) cyclical wage behaviour. Thus an empirical investigation into cyclical wage behaviour need not have a priori beliefs to which the data must either conform or else be regarded as 'perverse'.

2. Alternative assumptions

This section sets out some alternative assumptions which, in contrast to the 'standard' neoclassical ones, would allow the possibility of pro-cyclical wages. Such alternative assumptions are set out in three categories, each successively more 'radical', representing successively more fundamental breaks with the 'standard' neoclassical assumptions.

The first category maintains both the neoclassical assumptions that, first, the mpl diminishes as employment expands, and, second, the product wage will be equal to the mpl. The second category, quantity rationing, introduces a distinction between the notional and effective demand for labour and hence the notional and actual mpl. The third, Kaleckian, category drops the assumption of a diminishing mpl altogether.

2.1 Technology shocks

Of the three categories of theoretical assumptions which break the neoclassical requirement of counter-cyclical real wages (and, therefore, of real wages to decline in order to return to full employment equilibrium), the first, least radical, category consists of those involving the mpl curve itself shifting up to the right in the boom, as in Figure 2. Such a mechanism might be referred to as a supply shock or technology shock. Several possible causes have been put forward in the literature, and others come to mind, although none appear particularly convincing.

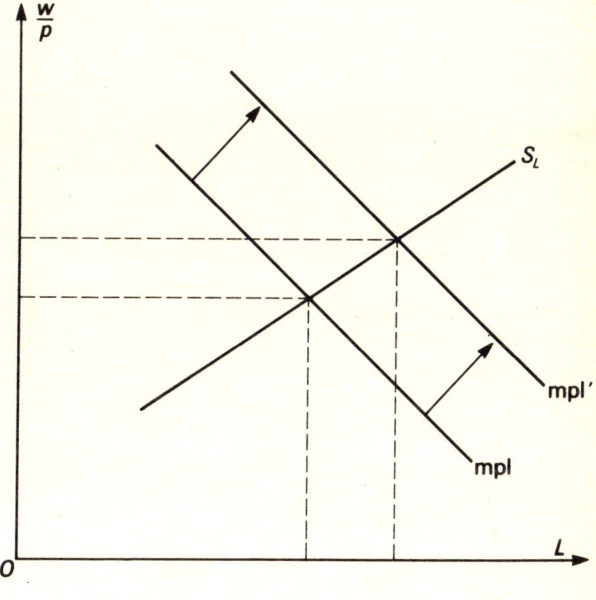

Fig. 2

First, changes in non-labour material input prices might shift the net mpl. The role of such non-labour inputs is considered extensively in this book, although the sort of cyclical variation in relative labour and non-labour components as would result from this suggested mechanism does not appear to hold.

Second, fluctuations in the rate of capital accumulation over the cycle would introduce such a pattern cyclically. However, Bowers, Deaton & Turk (1982, p. 15) argue that, in so far as one can meaningfully measure capital stock, its cyclical variation is negligible. They cite Panic (1978) for a capital stock series in manufacturing thus: 'The coefficient of variation of the deviation cycle of this series is 0.28 per cent which is negligible compared with those for output and employment.' (Bowers *et al.* 1982, p. 15 n. 1).

Two possibilities put forward in the literature have been changes in capacity utilization, as discussed by Tatom (1980); and the price-theoretic approach of Lucas and Barro. In the latter, general (pro-cyclical) price increases are mistaken for being relative increases in the prices of the products of the immediate producer (or wage earner if it is the price of labour). Thus the economic agents concerned work harder and output increases, until they learn that their relative prices have not risen, and hence the boom ends.

Ackley (1983) argues that such a price theoretic version of the business cycle cannot apply to a world with firms and hired employees because the inflation would have to fool people in opposite directions: employers believing that product prices had risen relative to wages, workers believing that wages had risen relative to product prices. While it might be argued that logically this *could* occur, despite Ackley's objections, because of the possibility of workers and employers within each firm or industry (mistakenly) thinking that prices and wages in their firm or industry had risen more than in other firms or industries, nevertheless it remains rather far fetched as a theory of the business cycle. Barro, at least, appears to have abandoned such a causal hypothesis, rejecting it as being inconsistent with time-separable preferences. Instead business cycles are generated by 'disturbances to technology' (Barro & King 1984, p. 818). However, such technology shocks, allowing pro-cyclical real wages within what is still a neo-classical framework, would ordinarily imply *counter-cyclical* prices (as more output is produced from given inputs). This latter implication might itself, however, be thought to throw doubt on such a category of explanations.

Tatom (1980) states that real wages and productivity are pro-cyclical, but that the diminishing returns to labour theory still holds true. The diminishing returns to labour theory has only been thought contradicted by the above facts because of a misspecification: because the cyclical pattern of factor employment has been ignored.

If we denote capital utilization by k, then $k = cK$, where K is capital stock and c is the capacity-utilization rate. Tatom finds that during recessions, the ratio of capital to labour employed declines. An mpl curve shows what the marginal product of any level of employment services would be with that, given, level of capital services. In recessions, the level of capital services declines so that instead of moving back up the mpl curve, we shift down onto a lower mpl curve corresponding to the new, lower, level of capital services. Thus, in Figure 3, instead of moving from *a* to *b*, we move from *a* to *c*.

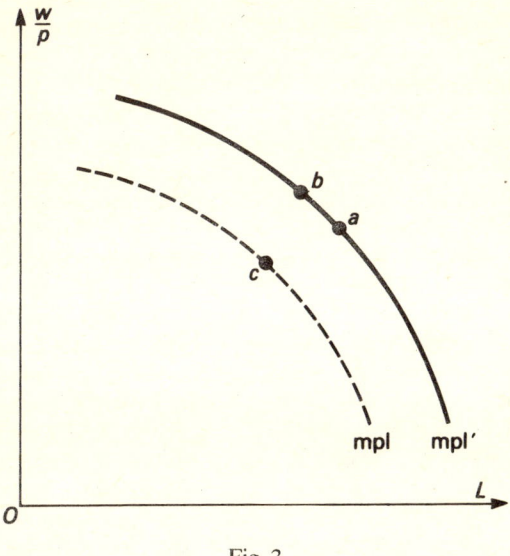

Fig. 3

The converse applies in an expansion: instead of moving down the mpl curve from *a*, resulting in a lower mpl and hence a lower product wage (implying counter-cyclical productivity and real wages), we will move up on to a new, higher mpl curve representing a higher flow of capital services. Hence productivity and the product wage are pro-cyclical.

Boddy (1985) argues that Tatom's results, which imply a negatively sloped (constant capacity utlization) mpl curve, are specious; and are due to biased and inconsistent estimators resulting from an incorrect use of the capacity utilization index such that the dependent variable appears on both sides of his estimating and test equations. Estimates of a corrected specification 'do not support the hypothesis of diminishing returns to labour' (Boddy 1985, p. 187). The literature on the 'empirical relationship between labor and output' is considered by Fay & Medoff (1985) and in Section 2.3 below. The argument of this section is different: that Tatom's attempt to save the idea of the neo-classical mpl curve is at the expense of redefining it. The neoclassical mpl curve is normally drawn for a given capital stock (K), so that an increase in employment (L) with constant K results in moving to the right down the mpl curve, while increased L with increased K results in the mpl curve shifting up to the right. This allows the distinction to be drawn between short-term fluctuations along a curve, and the longer-term necessary for altering the capital stock. Tatom's definitions do not allow this distinction: no period is too short for a change in capital services. Indeed, any change in labour services would very likely be accompanied by a change in capital services so that any movement requires a move on to a new mpl curve. The mpl curve which Tatom wished to defend no longer exists to either side of the point we happen to be on.

The standard textbook idea of moving along the mpl curve is of varying L while not affecting the level of utilization of capital services: 'Implicitly we assume here a constant rate of utilisation of capital stock so that there is a one-to-one relationship between capital stock and machine-hour input' (Branson 1972, p. 209). A vintage model, on the other hand, does not have a given capital stock. Rather, capital in use is explicitly allowed to vary with different vintages being brought into, or dropped out of, use. A vintage model would then explain the declining marginal product of labour in an expansion as being caused by the older, less efficient, vintages being brought into use. This increased capacity utilization, however, far from increasing the mpl will mean— assuming efficient rationing so that employment expands on successively less productive plants—reduced mpl in the boom and hence reduced real wages.

To conclude, neoclassical assumptions involve the necessity of real wages falling towards equilibrium. If the mpl curve itself shifts up to the right, this can allow a return to (a different) market clearing equilibrium without the necessity of any reduction in real wages. This category of explanations involving such a mechanism therefore avoids the neoclassical requirement of counter-cyclical real wages while remaining closely within the neoclassical model.

Some of the implicit contract literature assumes such a modified model of the cycle with 'bad times' (slumps) involving a lower mpl than 'good times' (booms); (see, for example, Oliver Hart 1983). The implicit contract idea can thus be used to explain *why*, when the economy is knocked off equilibrium by a negative technology shock, market clearing fails to establish a new equilibrium. The reason is that stable wages have been 'guaranteed' in the implicit contract, hence preventing market clearing and leaving involuntary unemployment, until such time as 'good times' return, returning the economy to (the previous) equilibrium.

Without such implicit contracts markets would clear and there would be no involuntary unemployment, but wages would then be pro-cyclical, not counter-cyclical as in the 'pure' neoclassical model. It is this pro-cyclical pattern, not the neoclassical counter-cyclical pattern, of wages which implicit contracts distort (flatten). Put another way: the point is that implicit contracts cause involuntary unemployment by raising wages above what they would otherwise be in the slump, and (as the other half of the contract, to compensate the employer) reduce wages, relatively, in the boom. This is the precise opposite effect from the one in which we are interested, namely, modifications (or alternatives) to neoclassical assumptions which allow for higher wages in the boom (and lower in the slump) than would be generated by 'pure' neoclassical assumptions.

2.2 Quantity rationing

The neoclassical prediction of reduced real wages with increased output (indeed, the theory that the reduced real wage is a necessary concomitant of the increased output) follows from the belief that, first, the mpl curve slopes down to the right and, second, the wage is equal to the marginal product of the marginal worker.

A quantity rationing model, such as Barro & Grossman (1971) avoids the neoclassical conclusion by denying that the firm, industry or economy is necessarily constrained by a diminishing mpl (or, more generally, by relative prices). Instead there may be quantity (demand) constraints. Hence in a recession the wage may be below the marginal product of the marginal worker so that, in an expansion, the real wage can increase towards the (decreasing) mpl. Thus in Figure 4 the *effective* demand for labour is denoted by D_{L^e}, a vertical line at L_1 determined by Y, where $Y > Y_s$.

Unemployment in the neoclassical model can also be described by Figure 4, being caused by the real wage, W_0, being too high, thus causing unemployment $= (L_0 - L_1)$. If the real wage is reduced to W_1, we move down the marginal product of/demand for labour curve to point a, where full employment, L_2, is achieved. With quantity rationing, however, cutting the real wage from W_0 to W_1 would move us, not down the demand for labour curve (D_L), but down the *effective* demand for labour curve (D_{L^e}), i.e. down bc not ba. Thus there is no effect on employment. But we are no longer on the marginal product of labour curve and hence there is no necessity for the real wage to fall. Instead, we can move from c to a with no reduction in the real wage. Alternatively, if the wage had been reduced to W_2 (thus eliminating unemployment while maintaining employment unchanged), then W moves up the S_L curve from d to a, thus rising from W_2 to W_1. Thus increased output is accompanied by increased real wages. The analysis

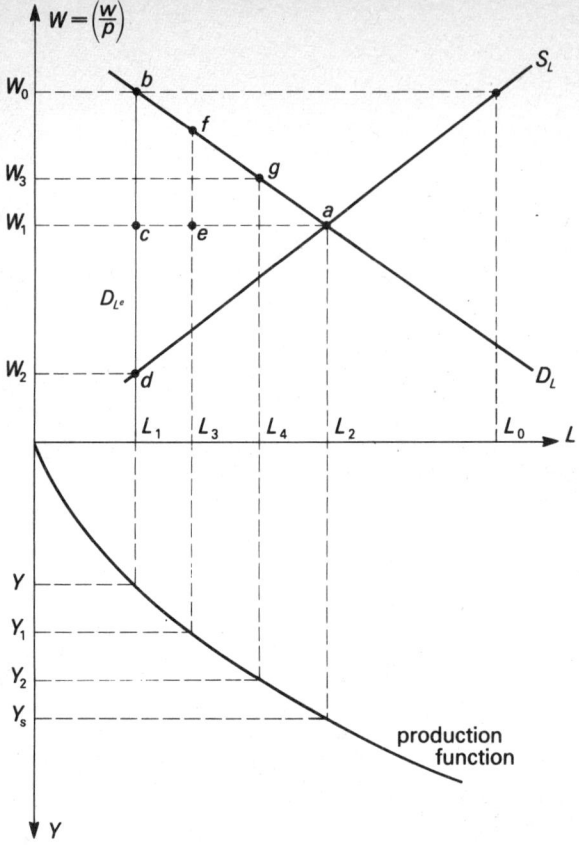

Fig. 4

can be taken further to show that (it is at least logically possible for) an increase in real wages to *cause* an increase in output. This depends on the cause of the initial rationing (i.e. the reason for Y being less than Y_s. If this is due to an insufficient level of effective demand, then increasing real wages from W_2 to W_1 may increase Y to Y_s, hence increasing L from L_1 to L_2 and moving from d to a.

Even if the effect is less dramatic, we may have a period of increasing real wages causing increased employment, before hitting the demand for labour curve (D_L), at which point increased employment will only occur with reduced real wages. The wage increase from W_2 to W_1 in Figure 4 may increase the level of (demand-constrained) income from Y to Y_1. This will increase employment from L_1 to L_3. Since the corresponding point e is still below point f (the point on the demand for labour curve corresponding to employment level L_3), this process can continue. In this case, increasing the real wage even beyond W_1 will, if it continues to increase the level of (demand-constrained/quantity-rationed) income, also continue to increase employment, beyond L_3. This process, then, can continue until we are back on our (non-quantity-constrained) demand for labour curve (D_L), for example at point g, where the increase in the real wage from W_1 to W_3 increased income from Y_1 to Y_2, hence increasing employment from L_3 to L_4.

Since the economy is now on the D_L curve, further increases in the real wage will move us back up the D_L curve to the left, hence reducing employment. But if Y_2 is still our quantity ration, then the remaining unemployment is of the quantity rationing type whereby reduced real wages will not increase employment and may, if it sets off the above process in reverse, reduce employment.

To summarize: Section 1 above sets out the standard neoclassical assumptions requiring counter-cyclical wages. Alternative assumptions (Section 2) allow other cyclical wage patterns. Technology shocks (Section 2.1) allow neoclassical assumptions to predict pro-cyclical wages (by shifting the mpl curve). Quantity rationing (Section 2.2) preserves the counter-cyclical pattern of productivity, but allows any pattern of wage movements. The more fundamental break of assuming horizontal productivity and cost curves (Section 2.3) was suggested by Sraffa (1926) but used most extensively as an operating framework by Kalecki.

2.3 *Kalecki*

Kalecki's model can be drawn in output–price space (Figure 5). Oa is the wage, ab is other prime costs, so that Ob is total prime costs; price, Oc, is a (here constant) mark-up over prime costs. The average cost curve (AC), incorporating overhead costs (including overhead labour) therefore slopes down to the right. Denoting output by Q, if $Q > Q_1$ (full capacity utilization), then marginal cost climbs steeply so that it is unprofitable to produce much past Q_1. The firm will then sell at price c, as much as it can, which will be determined by the demand curve DD: in this case Q_0, so that the surplus left is $bcde$, of which $bfge$ goes to pay overheads, leaving $fcdg$ as net profit.

Such a diagram can be inverted and drawn in employment–output space (Figure 6), thus corresponding to the previous diagrams. Marginal product is considered constant, and is also, therefore, the average product for direct workers. Assuming that non-wage prime costs are a constant fraction of total prime costs, then the real wage is some proportion of the (constant) marginal product.

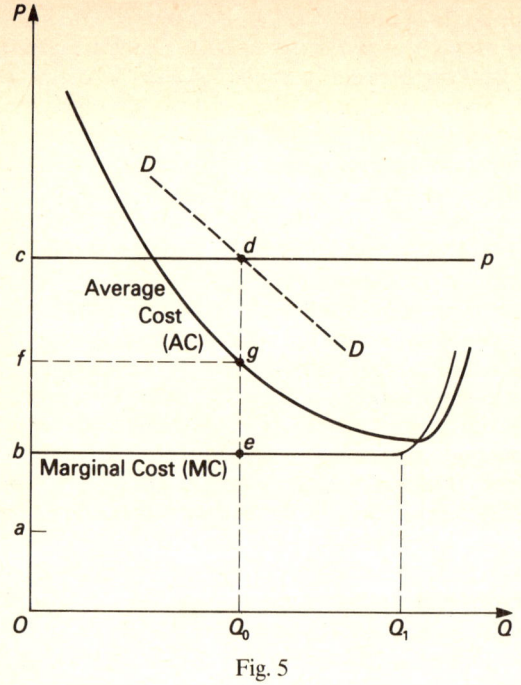

Fig. 5

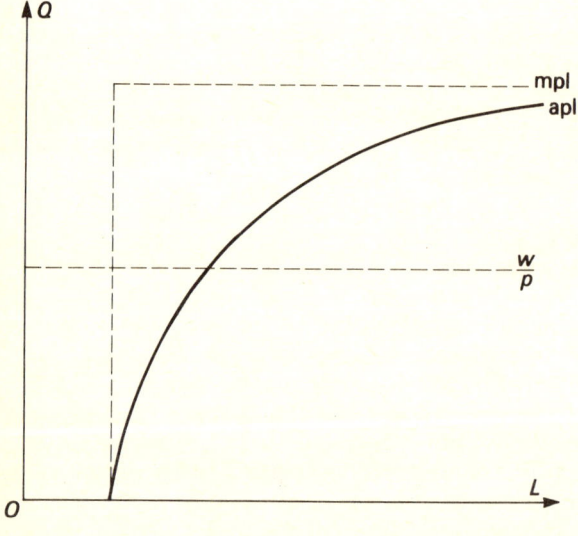

Fig. 6

Such Kaleckian assumptions are considered further, below. For present purposes it is clear enough that the neoclassical requirement of counter-cyclical wages is completely broken. There is no requirement, within such a framework, for real wages to, of necessity, rise or fall. Firms simply produce as much as they can sell. The greater the resulting capacity utilization the more are overhead costs spread. The resulting pattern of prices, profits and real wages then depends on only two other factors: the behaviour of (non-labour, materials) input prices; and the degree of monopoly (or mark up). Kalecki expected these two factors to influence wages in opposite directions over the cycle. First, he expected the ratio of the price of raw materials to wages to be pro-cyclical, so that a constant mark-up over total direct costs would result in a counter-cyclical tendency for real wages. Second, however, he expected the mark-up itself (the 'degree of monopoly') to be counter-cyclical, resulting in a pro-cyclical tendency for real wages. 'Thus the rise or decline in real wages depends on the relative weight of the two opposite tendencies. It is very likely that the resulting changes in real wages are generally rather small' (Kalecki 1969, p. 54) and 'the direction of the changes in real wages cannot be foreseen' (Kalecki 1969, p. 61).

Theoretically, the possibility of different cyclical patterns for input and output prices is introduced by the differential price formation mechanisms for 'cost-determined' and 'demand determined' groups of commodities (Kalecki, 1943). Empirically, the cyclical pattern of non-labour input prices is investigated in the later, empirical, chapters of this book.

As for the mark-up, Kalecki had no theoretical *requirement* for this to conform to any particular cyclical pattern despite his expectation for it to be counter-cyclical. Layard & Nickell (1985a) similarly echo Kalecki in analysing different possibilities for the cyclical behaviour of the mark-up (but within a framework of diminishing marginal productivity).

3. Generalized model

The generalized model is one which incorporates the area of the economy that the neoclassicals consider to be relevant (declining marginal and average productivity) with the area that Kalecki considered to be relevant (constant marginal productivity). In Figure 7, OL_0 is overhead labour. Thus to the left of L_0 there is no output. OL_1 is the lowest level of employment at which total product meets the wage bill (of both production and overhead workers). The loss is, then, precisely equal to non-labour overhead payments. At some output, say that corresponding to OL_2, the surplus precisely meets the non-labour

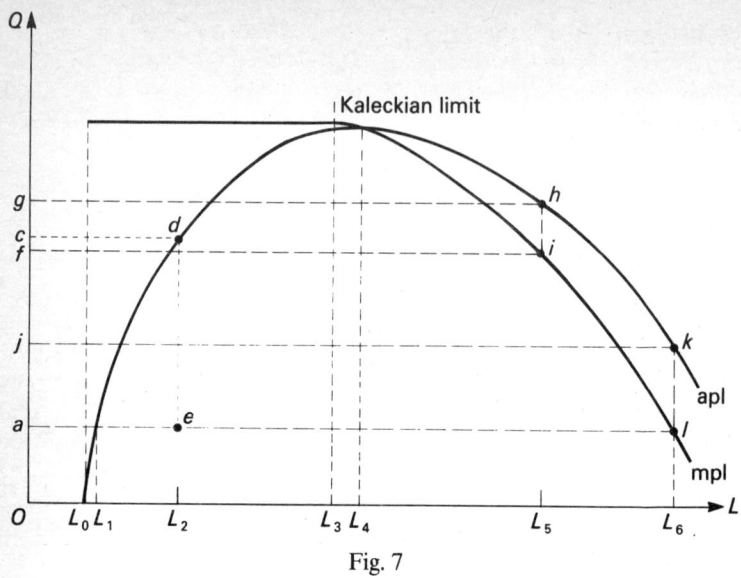

Fig. 7

overhead costs, both of which are, then, equal to *acde*. Net profits are then zero (or, if normal profits are included with overhead costs, then normal profits precisely are earned). OL_3 is considered by Kalecki the practical limit beyond which marginal productivity falls so rapidly (i.e. marginal costs rise so rapidly) that production to the right of L_3 would be unprofitable. In other words, OL_3 would be followed immediately by OL_6 (which is the point where mpl first falls below the Kaleckian real wage). For neoclassical economics the wage is determined by the marginal product of the marginal worker. To the left of OL_4 this is above the *apl* and hence total product would not even meet the wage bill. At OL_4, apl = mpl = (w/p). Thus total product is precisely equal to total wage bill. The losses (negative profits) are then equal to total non-labour overhead costs. There is then some point, say OL_5, where (apl − mpl)L is equal to total overheads (including 'normal' profits), in this case equal to *fghi*. To the right of L_5 profits will be greater than normal, and to the left, less than normal.

It can now be seen how the alternative models envisage the business cycle. For the neoclassical model, normal profits are earned at L_5. In an expansion, L increases beyond L_5, but this is only profitable if the real wage falls. The economy faces a dimishing mpl, and the wage is equal to the marginal product of the marginal worker. Thus in an expansion the real wage must fall. This can occur via reduced money wages, or via increased prices, the latter being advocated by Keynes (1936). Profits will increase. Thus if the expansion involves employment increasing from L_5 to L_6, profits will increase from (*fghi* − non-labour overheads) to (*ajkl* − non-labour overheads). Thus if overhead costs are, indeed, constant, profits increase by (*ajkl* − *fghi*).

In a recession, employment will contract from L_5. Real wages rise and profits fall below normal. If employment falls below L_4, the marginal product of labour continues to rise, but now the average product of labour is falling rather than rising. For Kalecki, fluctuations occur between L_0 and L_3, with the real wage given.

The purpose of developing this generalized model has been to show that, logically at least, the seemingly opposed models of, on the one hand, the Kaleckian type, and, on the other hand, the neoclassical type may be (accurately) describing different possible states of the economy corresponding to different levels of economic activity. The result is that if, for example, we want to describe an economic expansion, it may be that no simple conclusion can be reached applicable to all phases of the expansion. On the contrary, an expansion (if it involves wide enough fluctuations in capacity utilization) may pass through various phases: both Kaleckian (with no particular cyclical requirement for product wages) and neoclassical.

Initially the expansion may proceed with no fall in the marginal product of labour (although this assumes that the product wage is not, therefore, equal to the mpl, and in the following description is assumed constant at the 'Kaleckian' level, *a* in Figure 7). In this case not only profits, but total surplus (out of which overhead costs are met) may be negative. As output expands, surplus will approach zero and then grow as (negative) profits approach zero and, in turn, become positive and grow. At some point the mpl will begin to fall, thus falling below the average product which will, therefore, itself begin to fall. Profits will, however, continue to increase, although after the point at which the mpl and apl curves intersect (ignoring overhead costs and overhead labour) less than proportionately with L, until mpl falls to equal the real wage (still assuming this to have been at the 'Kaleckian' level). Beyond this point, profits will fall back towards normal as the expansion continues, and, if the expansion continues further with no cut in the real wage, profits will fall below normal towards zero.

Such a model allows different wage–output relations over different phases of the cycle.

4. Pro-cyclical wage movements

Having indicated various non-neoclassical assumptions which would allow the avoidance of the neoclassical result of counter-cyclical wages, this section considers both the logical possibility, and possible causal mechanisms, for *pro*-cyclical wage movements.

4.1 Logical possibility

In a Kaleckian model, profits increase in an expansion at a *constant* product wage, so that it is quite possible for a part of this increase to go on *higher* wages. This result is also allowed in a neoclassical model if, for whatever reason, we are off our mpl and apl curves, so that, in an expansion, we move up to the right towards them. In either case—Kaleckian or modified neoclassical—it is therefore logically possible for increased real wages to cause an expansion (and hence increase employment).

Of course, for a wage increase also to lead, via an expansion of the economy, to increased profits, requires increased non-wage spending (investment and/or consumption of non-wage goods) in order for the increased profits to be realized. Indeed, it was Kalecki who made the point that 'workers spend what they get, and capitalists get what they spend'. Simple models can be constructed which, while satisfying Kalecki's behavioural description or workers and capitalists, also allow increased wages to increase profits, the increased realization of profits coming from capitalist consumption being dependent in part at least on potential profits, or investment being dependent, in part at least, on output (or the rate of increase of output).

4.2 Causal mechanism

A possible causal mechanism for pro-cyclical real wages, considered by Lucas (1970) follows from Marris's (1964) study of shift-working. The pro-cyclical occurence of overtime working, along with the existence of overtime rates, allows pro-cyclical wage movements. An ironic aspect of Lucas's paper, as well as that of Solow & Stiglitz (1968), is that in the face of empirical evidence it abandons the neoclassical insistence on counter-cyclical real wage movements, while still assuming counter-cyclical productivity movements. In fact, though, the empirical evidence pointing to pro-cyclical productivity movements is much stronger than the evidence pointing to pro-cyclical real wage movements.

The causal mechanism which our model would suggest is that the increased profits in an expansion reduce the necessity to match increased money wages with increased prices, i.e. that the mark-up falls.

Coutts *et al.* (1978), however, find a constant mark-up as far as wage rates are concerned. Even accepting their findings, though, there are three possible mechanisms which would still cause pro-cyclical wage movements. First, increased money wages could lead to wages becoming an increased share of normal costs. Thus normal costs, and hence prices, would not increase in the same proportion as had money wages. Cowling (1982) considers this, however, and finds no evidence of it happening. Second, 'normal' costs may be a lagged function of actual costs, so that the firm's idea of what is normal is affected by past experience. Thus as actual unit costs fall, this may have a dampening effect on 'normal' costs, and hence on prices. Third, Coutts *et al.*'s normal earnings series 'has been purged of its reversible cyclical component' (Coutts *et al.* 1978, p. 26), and that component is pro-cyclical. It is not clear, however, how any of these would be able to explain a 'profit-squeeze' nor, given a profit squeeze, how they would operate.

Cowling (1981) suggests three reasons for price increases being less than money-wage increases, all of which could operate under a profit squeeze. The first is balance of payments constraints, which devaluation would be unable to overcome. The second is political pressure leading to price controls, subsidies of wage-goods and so on (Cowling 1981, p. 213–4). The third (Cowling 1981, p. 197) is if the level of concentration, and thereby the mark-up, falls in the boom.

The first factor, namely balance of payments constraints, would seem unlikely to be a general explanation, and certainly Cowling does not provide any hypothesis for why it should operate as such. The second factor appears unlikely to have operated in many, if any, cases. The third factor, of the changed mark-up forced on firms by reduced concentration, is a more fundamental point. Indeed, the basic theoretical point of such a discussion goes wider than simply allowing a possible causal mechanism for pro-cyclical real wages.

The idea of a direct, necessary, causal link between productivity and product wages and any resulting cyclical wage requirement, ceases to hold when the possibility is introduced of variations in the mark-up of prices over wages (or direct costs). However, simply pointing out the existence of this pricing process, mediating between productivity and product wages, is not in itself sufficient cause to reject the neoclassical claim that if the marginal product of labour is counter-cyclical then so must be the product wage. Unless there is some reason to suppose that the mark-up will vary, then the neoclassical hypothesis holds. If, however, there are reasons to suppose that non-cyclical factors do, in practice, alter the mark-up, the pattern of product wage movements becomes that much less cyclical.

To the extent that the mark-up is assumed to move counter-cyclically, acceptance of no observable cyclical pattern in product wage movements can be accompanied by the retention of neoclassical assumptions which would otherwise require the empirical observation of counter-cyclical product wages. If such an assumption of a counter-cyclical mark-up is introduced simply to overcome inconsistencies between other assumptions in the model then it is clearly a fairly weak procedure unless some convincing explanation is made as to, first, why the mark-up is assumed counter-cyclical and, second, why the other assumptions (those which require the mark-up assumption to introduce consistency with what is believed to be the actual movement of product wages) are retained. Kalecki himself did not introduce the mark-up for such purposes. He assumed horizontal marginal product curves and hence no requirement for product wages to move cyclically in response to cyclical productivity. He did, as reported above, believe there to be a counter-cyclical pattern to the mark-up; but he also believed there to be a pro-cyclical movement of non-labour direct costs, and hence did not believe that the mediating role of the mark-up process between cyclical productivity and cyclical product wages would determine the behaviour of the latter.

5. Conclusion

This chapter began by setting out the theoretical background to the neoclassical proposition of counter-cyclical wages. Alternative assumptions, consistent with wages *not* being counter-cyclical, were then considered. These were categorized in terms of how fundamentally they differed from the neoclassical assumptions. First is the movement of, rather than movement *along*, the mpl curve. Second are those who maintain the idea of the marginal productivity of labour diminishing with increased employment, but argue that quantity rationing prevents this from necessarily being a constraint on output, hence removing the necessity of counter-cyclical wage movements. Such ideas are common to all quantity rationing models, and to authors such as Malinvaud, and Solow & Stiglitz. To limit the chapter's length, the discussion of such models was limited to the example of Barro & Grossman. Finally, and most 'radically', are the ideas of Kalecki which do not involve a diminishing mpl and hence imply no presumption at all for wages to move counter-cyclically.

Having set the scene for the empirical investigation, with rival assumptions allowing different expectations as to the evidence on cyclical wage behaviour, the argument in the chapter then posed the possibility of a wage increase, in addition to being *compatible* with a cyclical expansion of output, actually *causing* such an increase, and such (demand-stimulating) real wage increases actually leading to increased profits.

THE THEORETICAL BACKGROUND 31

Having set out different assumptions allowing for different empirical patterns for cyclical wage behaviour, the remainder of the book attempts to establish what that pattern is. How theory confronts data, and therefore how the models outlined in this chapter would confront the results reported in the following chapter, and developed in the empirical chapters, is a methodological question the answer to which would differ between different methodological schools. These schools of thought differ over how interesting such descriptive empirical work is; and also over how such work relates to theory. These methodological issues are left to the concluding chapter.

3
A Survey of the Literature

The cyclical behaviour of real wages, productivity, and labour's share has been explored in a vast number of econometric studies in the past 40 years. It is fair to summarise the consensus as finding no detectable significant pattern in real wages. Meanwhile, the pro-cyclical pattern of productivity movements has been solidly established in dozens of empirical studies (Okun 1981, p. 16).

While the pro-cyclical pattern of productivity movements is, indeed, generally accepted, the number of econometric studies on the cyclical behaviour of real and product wages is far from vast (although several have been published since Okun's statement). There is not, as yet, the consensus Okun suggests. Recent econometric studies, surveyed in this chapter, have come to contradictory conclusions.

1. The Literature

Keynes (1936) and Keynes (1939) are turning points in this field. Keynes (1936) presented the accepted belief of counter-cyclical real wages, and presented the accepted theoretical marginal-productivity arguments behind the accepted belief. Because, perhaps, of the manner in which this accepted theory and its corresponding predictions were made, in the form of suggested research, it provoked statistical investigations by Dunlop (1938) and Tarshis (1939) which seemed to contradict the accepted prediction, instead finding pro-cyclical real wages.

This contradiction between accepted theory and the new statistical findings provoked Keynes (1939) to suggest possible modifications to the theory. At the same time, he suggested that the new findings were inconclusive and that further statistical work was necessary to determine the actual cyclical behaviour of the real (product) wage.

Far from carrying out this work, Ruggles (1940) and Tobin (1947) threw further doubt on the little statistical work in existence. It was not until 1969 that an attempt was made, by Bodkin, to directly tackle this question. His (weakly pro-cyclical) results were questioned by the counter-cyclical results of Neftci (1978) and Sargent (1978), the generality of which has, in turn, been questioned by Geary & Kennan (1982a) who report no cyclical correlation.

This latter conflicts with the counter-cyclical results of Otani (1978) and Sachs (1979), and is directly challenged (for not including the cost of materials as an explanatory variable) by Symons & Layard (1984) and Symons (1985) as well as (for the choice of deflator) by Layard & Nickell (1984). The robustness of the alternative results reported in these latter two studies is questioned by Wadhwani (1985a) after respecifying the demand for labour equation. Bernanke & Powell (1984) find rather more pro-cyclical results than Geary & Kennan, although their explanation of the different results is not entirely satisfactory. The issue appears, then, to be further from a consensus than ever.

2. From Keynes (1936) to Keynes (1939)

Keynes (1936) assumes real wages to be counter-cyclical. He postulates an inverse relationship between the real wage and the money wage, thus taking the money wage to be a proxy for output movements. He also assumed employment to be a proxy for output movements. His argument goes as follows:

> It would be interesting to see the results of a statistical enquiry into the actual relationship between changes in money wages and changes in real wages. In the case of a change peculiar to a particular industry one would expect the change in real wages to be in the same direction as the changes in money wages. But in the case of changes in the general level of wages, it will be found, I think, that the change in real wages associated with a change in money wages, so far from being usually in the same direction, is almost always in the opposite direction... This is because, in the short period, falling money wages and rising real wages are each, for independent reasons, likely to accompany decreasing employment; labour being readier to accept wage cuts when employment is falling off, yet real wages inevitably rising in the same circumstances on account of the increasing marginal returns to a given capital equipment when output is diminished (Keynes 1939, p. 34, citing Keynes 1936, pp. 9–10).

Dunlop (1938) and Tarshis (1939) attempted the statistical enquiry which Keynes had expressed an interest in. But they did not find what Keynes had thought they would. Dunlop found, for Britain, that when money wages are rising, real wages have usually risen also whilst, when money wages are falling, real wages are no more likely to rise than to fall. Tarshis obtained similar results for the United States.

Keynes (1939) begins by stating that the studies by Dunlop and Tarshis clearly indicate that a common belief to which I acceded in my *General Theory of Employment* needs to be reconsidered ... I was accepting, without taking care to check the facts for myself, a belief which has been widely held by British economists up to the last year or two (Keynes 1939, p. 394).

He then traces this view to Marshall (1926) and the evidence he gave before the Gold and Silver Commission in 1887 and the Indian Currency Committee in 1899. This historiographical aspect of Keynes's article is considered further in Chapter 8. The relevance of Keynes's article to this chapter is its comprehensive review of the literature up to that date, which there is little point in repeating here. He also discusses the neoclassical theory underlying predictions about real wages being counter-cyclical.

The important pointer for any future research is where Keynes suggests five areas for further statistical investigation 'with a view to discovering at what points the weaknesses of the former argument emerge', where 'former' refers to the neoclassical argument. These five areas are as follows. First, accuracy and uniformity: 'First of all, are the statistics on which Mr Dunlop and Mr Tarshis are relying sufficiently accurate and sufficiently uniform in their indications to form the basis of a reliable induction?' (Keynes 1939, p. 41). Second, real and product wages: 'It is important, therefore, if we are to understand the situation, that the statisticians should endeavour to calculate wages in terms of the actual product of the labour in question.' (Keynes 1939, p. 44). Third, marginal user cost: 'Has the identification of marginal cost with marginal wage cost introduced a relevant error?' (Keynes 1939, p. 44). Fourth, shape of cost curves: 'Is it the assumption of increasing marginal real cost in the short period which we ought to suspect? Mr Tarshis finds part of the explanation here; and Dr Kalecki is inclined to infer approximately constant marginal real cost.' (Keynes 1939, p. 44). And finally, mark-up: 'There remains the question whether the mistake lies in the approximate identification of marginal cost with price, or rather in the assumption that for output as a whole they bear a more or less proportionate relationship to one another irrespective of the intensity of output.' (Keynes 1939, p. 46). These five issues are now dealt with in turn.

2.1 *Accuracy and uniformity*

Keynes (1939, p. 41) questions whether the statistics on which Dunlop and Tarshis rely are 'sufficiently accurate and sufficiently uniform in their indications to form the basis of a reliable induction'. He gives, as an example, the findings of Meade (1938) on counter-cyclical real wages in both the depression starting in 1929, and the following recovery. Such conflicting results can emerge from inaccurate statistics, and we will see that there are debates in the literature, up to and including current articles, which question which statistics are the appropriate ones. The other point, however, on uniformity, is rather different. It has been argued in Chapter 2 that, depending on the economic assumptions thought appropriate, it is quite possible for the actual behaviour (as opposed to the imperfectly measured behaviour) of real wages in the cycle to differ from one period to another and/or from one country to another. In this case, the lack of uniformity of the statistics is not necessarily a basis for doubting the reliability of any induction but, rather, a basis for defining the induction as only necessarily being applicable to the country and time period to which the statistics referred. The Meade study which Keynes quotes as contradicting the Dunlop–Tarshis prediction, by finding falling real wages in the 1930s recovery, itself finds that no such fall took place in the United States or France.

2.2 Real and product wages

Keynes recognizes that different conclusions may result using real wages rather than product wages. That said, Keynes (1939, p. 44) recognizes the importance of testing any results for product wages: 'It is important, therefore, if we are to understand the situation, that the statisticians should endeavour to calculate wages in terms of the actual product of the labour in question'. It is ironic, therefore, that the only previous (albeit crude) attempt to do this, where Rueff (1925) divided money wages by the wholesale price index (WPI) instead of by the consumer price index (CPI) is criticized by Pigou (1933) for having done so, and further, Keynes (1939, p. 39) seems to accept that Rueff has somehow made a mistake by writing that 'Pigou *points out* that these statistics are vitiated by the fact that M. Rueff divided money wages by the wholesale index instead of by the cost-of-living index' (emphasis added). The issue of what is the relevant wage series is considered further in Section 3.4.

2.3 Marginal user cost

Keynes (1936, p. 66) defines user cost as:

> $A + (G' - B') - G$, where A is the amount of our entrepreneur's puchases from other entrepreneurs, G the actual value of his capital equipment at the end of the period, and G' the value it might have had at the end of the period if he had refrained from using it and had spent the optimum sum B' on its maintenance and improvement.

He concludes that this factor could not explain a divergence of marginal wage costs away from a counter-cyclical movement of the marginal product of labour (pro-cyclical marginal costs). On the contrary:

> marginal user cost is likely to increase when output is increasing, so that this factor would work in the opposite direction from that required to explain our present problem, and would be an additional reason for expecting prices to rise more than wages. Indeed, one would, on general grounds, expect marginal total cost to increase more, and not less, than marginal wage cost. (Keynes 1939, p. 44).

The role of that component of user cost constituted by non-labour direct costs ('materials')—as distinct from the role of depreciation—is considered in Section 3.4 below, and is investigated in the empirical chapters.

2.4 Shape of cost curves

The first two of Keynes's comments—on the accuracy and uniformity of the data, and on the importance of measuring product wages—are points to be borne in mind when trying to establish the actual behaviour of wages in the cycle. Keynes's third comment, on the shape of cost curves, relates to possible explanations for empirical findings suggesting that the real wage/product wage is *not* counter-cyclical.

This third comment concerns the range of capacity utilization to be discussed. Keynes suggests that Kaleckian assumptions may hold over some phases of the business cycle, but that they may be superseded over other phases. It is this importance of considering the whole range of capacity utilization fluctuations, and the behaviour of cost/productivity curves over different levels of capacity utilization, and hence over different phases of the business cycle, which I tried to present diagramatically in Chapter 2 (Figure 7, p. 26).

2.5 Mark-up

Again, this section is simply suggesting a logically possible reason why the real/product wage might be pro-cyclical: that is, because the mark-up is counter-cyclical. Keynes does not necessarily accept, however, that the real/product wage *will* be pro-cyclical. At the time of his writing, this had still to be statistically tested satisfactorily. He concludes, therefore, by appealing for further such statistical enquiry and, in particular, that such enquiry seek to determine:

> (i) How the real hourly wage changes in the short period, not merely in relation to the money wage, but in relation to the percentage which

actual output bears to capacity output [in other words, to determine the relation between changes in the real wage and changes in capacity utilization];

(ii) How the purchasing power of the industrial money wage in terms of its own product changes when output changes [in other words, how the product wage changes when output changes]; and

(iii) How gross profit per unit of output changes
    (a) when money costs change
    (b) when output changes (Keynes 1939, p. 51).

Up until 1936, then, economists were generally agreed that a statistical study would reveal counter-cyclical real wage movements, and were agreed that this was due to counter-cyclical productivity movements. Keynes (1936) restated both beliefs.

The studies of Dunlop and Tarshis claimed to find the opposite of this. Their studies seemed to show pro-cyclical real wage movements. But neither study attempted to also overturn accepted theory. This left the economics profession with a contradiction between accepted theory (counter-cyclical real wages) and evidence (pro-cyclical real wages).

Keynes (1939) did not claim to solve this contradiction, but tried to suggest the logically possible ways of reuniting accepted theory with accepted fact. On the one hand, the studies of Dunlop and Tarshis could be questioned on technical grounds, so that there were not, as yet, any definite statistical conclusions. On the other hand, the theoretical underpinnings of the previously agreed conclusions could also be questioned. His only definite conclusion was that further work was required.

3. Methods

Keynes's call for further work was first taken up by Richardson (1939) who supported the traditional counter-cyclical position. Reviewing the debate, however, Ruggles (1940, p. 137) found that all three studies, those of Dunlop, Tarshis and Richardson, were 'of doubtful significance'. Nevertheless, his article does not attempt any such study itself, simply concluding that 'statisticians and theorists should unite in studying the cyclical relationships of the above variables' (Ruggles 1940, p. 149). Again, Tobin (1947, p. 577) simply cites Ruggles to the effect that the above investigations were statistically inconclusive. And again, he simply concluded that further theoretical and statistical work was necessary (Tobin 1947, p. 587) and simply repeated Keynes's call for someone to do the necessary statistical investigation.

The call was not taken up until 1960, and even then not explicitly, when Hultgren published *Changes in Labour Cost during Cycles in Production and Business*, followed in 1965 by *Cost, Prices and Profits: Their Cyclical Relations*. In tracing the source of the well-known tendency for profits of manufacturing concerns to rise and fall with the volume of sales, Hultgren finds that margins (profits per dollar of sales) also rise and fall with sales; prices do not regularly rise and fall with sales (at least since the Second World War); and unit costs tend to move inversely with sales. The two major drawbacks of Hultgren (1965) are, first, that he does not try to isolate the cyclical from the secular movements, and second, that he only considers money wages. This results in Hultgren finding that his earnings measure was higher at the peak of the output cycle than at the trough in every quantity expansion; and that they were also higher at the trough that at the peak in all but two contractions.

The only post-Ruggles (1940) work which Okun cites, with reference to the quote from Okun (1981) at the head of this chapter, are Kuh (1966) and Bodkin (1969). Kuh's article does not, in fact, report any statistical tests. An appendix records real wage data in manufacturing which indicates that, over long stretches of time, the real wage increases rather steadily with acceleration or retardation. Kuh (1966, p. 240) therefore concludes that there appears to be slight systematic relation between real wages and short term fluctuations in output and employment. Remarkably, then, the 30 years following Keynes's call for further research saw little work on the subject; reflecting, perhaps, the general acceptance by the profession of 'Keynesian' assumptions which implied that the cyclical behaviour of product wages was of little importance. Bodkin (1969) begins his article by pointing out that there was more than a quarter of a century of data available to him since the last published statistical examination of whether real wages tend to increase or decrease with increased utilization of labour over the course of the business cycle. As we shall see, Bodkin's article remained the only published study until 1978, since when this topic has become an area of active economic investigation.

The resulting literature is not yet developed enough to have reached any generally accepted conclusions. More than this, however, the investigative techniques to be used are still subject to dispute. The various published results have been challenged on the grounds of incorrect techniques. In surveying this literature, then, it is necessary to go into some detail about the techniques used by each study, including the form of the equation, the dependent variable, the independent variable(s), the price deflators, countries covered, whether lags are used, the statistical tests employed and so on. We will raise each of these issues, concentrating attention on the only paper aknowledged in all other studies: that of Bodkin. This will give us the list of issues in the light of which all subsequent papers can be viewed. Finally, we summarize the techniques used by each study in a table.

3.1 Wage equations and labour demand schedules

The cyclical wage literature is concerned not with a full causal explanation of wages and product prices via a simultaneous system, but simply with the net result of the various forces which are at work on the direction of movement of these variables, and with the resulting cyclical behaviour of product wages. All the tests, and regressions, within this literature could have been conducted instead with a properly specified wage equation, the construction of which could be based on any number of such reported equations. The reason why such an approach has not been adopted by these studies is that the issue in question is how the wage moves *in relation to cyclical output*. A wage equation attempts to pick up not simply the effect of output on wages but also the effects of other explanatory variables on the wage, part of which might produce cyclical fluctuations in the wage series additional to that picked up directly by the output term. Thus suppose a wage equation were estimated with, as explanatory variables, the terms of trade (TT), level of unionisation and rate of change of unionisation (TU, TU^*), the level of unemployment and rate of change of unemployment (U, U^*), as well as the cyclical behaviour of output (Q), thus:

$$W = aQ + bTT + cTU + dTU^* + eU + fU^* \qquad (3.1)$$

then the coefficient on cyclical output Q—a—is no longer measuring what is wanted, because other explanatory variables may have a cyclical pattern so that the effect of those coefficients on W will be to move W in a cyclical way. The direct effect which a given increase in output in a boom will have on cyclical wages, other things being equal, is what the coefficient a shows in the above formulation. But other things are *not* equal in a cyclical upturn. The literature is concerned to establish how the cyclical wage series will behave given that the cyclical expansion of output may have effects on the wage (or at least be associated with changes in the cyclical wage series) which are captured only partly in the coefficient a, and are also captured in part by the coefficients on the other explanatory variables.

Thus, equation (3.1) can be rewritten as:

$$W = aQ + bZ + dX \qquad (3.2)$$

where Z comprises all those explanatory variables uncorrelated with the output cycle and X comprises those which are so correlated, so that in:

$$Z = cQ \qquad (3.3)$$
$$X = eQ \qquad (3.4)$$

the expected value of c, $E(c)$, is O. The procedure of simply running regression tests on:

$$W = a'Q \qquad (3.5)$$

will involve a reparameterization such that $a' = a + cb + ed$. Now $E(cb) = 0$, so if a large number of regressions are run (as in the tests reported in this book) then there will be no reason to suppose that dropping the Z regressors will bias the results. On the other hand, the cyclical correlation coefficient describing the actual cyclical pattern of wages will not be a, but the reparameterized $a + ed$, the estimation of which is therefore the desirable consequence of dropping the X regressors.

By eliminating all explanatory variables other than the cyclical output variable, clearly the resulting regression may have a low explanatory power. But that remaining cyclical variable will be forced to act as a proxy for the cyclical components of the eliminated variables. This may constitute only a small proportion of non-trend movements of wages. That proportion may even be zero. Nevertheless, it is that proportion which the literature has set out to establish: how, if at all, are non-trend fluctuations in wages associated with the output cycle?

This has indeed been the approach adopted in most of the literature (e.g. Bodkin 1969; Geary & Kennan 1982a; Bernanke & Powell 1984). There is, however, a rather different literature which attempts to estimate a labour demand schedule (e.g. Symons & Layard 1984). The relevance of the latter to this survey of the cyclical wage literature arises because (if for no other reason) authors such as Symons have themselves implied such relevance: implied, that is, not only that the sign of the coefficient on the price of labour in a labour demand schedule represents the actual historical pattern of wages over the output cycle; but also that studies in the cyclical wage literature which suggest a pattern other than this are therefore at fault.

The question of whether the appropriate cyclical variable is output or employment is a separate one from the basic differences in method between the two branches of the literature, and is considered in Section 3.3 below.

The point on method is that a coefficient in a wage equation, or labour demand schedule, does not represent (i.e. is not 'picking up') the same information as the ultimately reduced form correlation between historical movements in the two, output and wage, series. That the labour demand schedule is indeed estimating something other than the historical, empirical pattern of wages over the output cycle is indicated by the use such studies have been put to in the Treasury (1985) survey to indicate that a cut in wages would increase employment over several subsequent years. To say that for a *given* output there is an inverse real-wage–employment relation does *not* necessarily imply that an actual reduction in the real wage would increase employment, because it may be that the reduction in the real wage would, via reduced product demand, reduce output. Whether or not there is such a negative wage–employment relation for a given output is a (logically) separate question from whether such wage cuts have occurred in cyclical expansions in the past. Indeed, the Treasury paper indicates that such wage cuts have not occurred in the past due to trend influences in the various series. No attempt is made, however, to detrend such series. There may be reasons in economic theory to expect a cyclical decline in wages to lead to a cyclical expansion in employment (although as indicated in Chapter 2, such assumptions are certainly not as universally accepted as might be implied by the Treasury discussion). Even were this so, however, there may be other, logically consistent assumptions which allow for increases in cyclical output (and employment) for reasons *other* than reductions in cyclical wages, *and* (perhaps) for such cyclical expansions in output to lead to a cyclical expansion in wages. Thus the former hypothesized relation between wages and employment, while logically coherent, may not be the determining one when it comes to the actual behaviour of real wages over the cycle. Whether this is so or not is what the cyclical wage literature aims to establish.

3.2 *The existence of cycles*

The very idea of the existence of cycles is, of course, 'conditional' on the view of the world from which the empirical investigation is being conducted. This whole literature on cycles, and the cyclical behaviour of wages is, of course, set within a view of the world which sees the description 'cyclical' as valid, and hence can look at series in terms of their trend movements, their cyclical fluctuations, and other fluctuations. Thus Zarnowitz (1985, p. 525) argues that 'The term "business cycle" is a misnomer insofar as no unique periodicities are involved, but its wide acceptance reflects the recognition of important regularities of long standing'.

Certainly different views of the world can be compared, and empirical evidence can have some bearing on such comparisons. Such competing views of the world could perhaps be divided between two categories. On the one hand are different assumptions which can be compared and tested within the framework adopted for the research. Thus the discussion in subsequent chapters is, where possible, put in terms theoretically capable of encompassing such different assumptions (for example 'associated with' rather than 'caused by' or 'causes'). On the other hand, the broad framework of the work reported in this literature—cyclical relations—within which it is possible to discuss and compare certain alternative theoretical models, itself is conditional on the theory that the deviations from trend in time do represent cyclical movements. The results, including those of comparing different models, are therefore conditional on that general view of the world. The latter can only then be compared with the alternative, that there is no such cyclical behaviour, in much more general terms of the apparent usefulness of looking at events in that way—from that 'window'.

So while objections could be made to looking at everything in cyclical terms, the tide is rather in the other direction, of increasing attention being focused on cyclical behaviour, and neoclassical/new theory being criticized for being inconsistent with empirically observable cyclical behaviour. As a corollary of this, neoclassical/new classical theory itself is increasingly discussing cyclical fluctuations; although of course such economists look at the cyclical data with very different prior beliefs. Hence Keynes's criticism of orthodox theory's attempts to account for cyclical behaviour, in a letter to Beveridge dated 28 July 1936:

> I am indeed arguing that the orthodox theory is in effect based on the assumption that there is no such thing as cyclical fluctuation. That is to say, although orthodox economists purport to be discussing it, they are discussing it on the basis of assumptions which, if valid, mean that it is non-existent (Keynes 1973, p. 56).

To conclude: the starting point of the cyclical wage literature is, of course, that output cycles do, empirically, occur. The literature is not only looking at detrended series for output and wages: it is looking at how the wage series does or does not move with the output cycle. To investigate the empirical regularities, or lack of them, over cycles is to investigate the effect on an economic variable (product wages) of all the entangled relations involved. Those economic relations (and the corresponding correlation coefficients) may themselves vary over the cycle: it may be, for example, that the constraint on employment varies, in some circumstances being relative input prices (the resulting employment level hence determining output levels), and at other times being product demand. If firms were constrained in this way—output being determined by 'the short end of the market'—then both the labour demand equation and the production function may play distinct roles.

Whether or not they do is not here the point at issue; rather it is to test the ultimately reduced form correlation of cyclical movements in the product wage series with movements in the cyclical output series.

3.3 Cyclical variable

Bodkin (1969, p. 356) describes the purpose of his paper as: 'primarily to have a fresh look at the issue of whether real wages tend to fall or rise with an increased utilisation of the labour force, over the course of the business cycle'. The cyclical variable is unemployment (although he uses an employment variable in two cases, with similar results). Thus in terms of Bodkin's results 'pro-cyclical' or 'counter-cyclical' movements of earnings do not technically refer to the movement of earnings over the business (output) cycle, but over the employment cycle. Clearly the employment cycle is closely related to the output cycle, although the cyclical relation itself may change over time. In addition, the employment–unemployment relation may change over time.

The implications of his introduction on the possible cyclical behaviour of earnings is that employment and earnings are related in two separate ways. First, there is a causal link whereby unemployment inversely affects the real wage. Hence with pro-cyclical employment one obtains pro-cyclical earnings. Second, there is the contemporaneous effect of a change in output on both unemployment and the real wage. This output effect on real wages operates both counter-cyclically, via pro-cyclical price movements (and a money-wage adjustment coefficient with a value of less than one); and pro-cyclically via a profit-level effect whereby increased profits in the upswing allow increased wages.

Bodkin then tests for the resulting behaviour of earnings over the cycle using unemployment as the cyclical variable. When interpreting the results of such tests it should be borne in mind that 'unemployment' has entered the story in two separate ways. First, as having a direct effect on wage levels. Second, as a proxy for the output cycle: a cycle which affects wages through three channels, one of which is unemployment itself (the other two being pricing and profitability).

When a variable is described as pro-cyclical, this is normally interpreted to mean that it rises in the (output) boom and falls in the (output) slump. That is, it is positively correlated to the *output* cycle. Yet the important variable for the cyclical behaviour of earnings (dictated, for example, by a negatively sloped mpl/D_L curve) might be thought to be employment (rather than output). Hence the lack of clarity within and between studies about whether we are measuring wage changes against output changes or employmet changes.

Otani (1978), Geary & Kennan (1982b), and Bernanke & Powell (1984) use output directly, while the other studies (including Geary &

Kennan 1982a and 1982b) use employment and/or unemployment. There are two points with regard to the choice of output and/or employment. First, we should include whichever our model suggests *should* be correlated, and if there are independent reasons for *both* output *and* employment to cause changes in earning, as suggested by Bodkin, then both variables should be included (although Bodkin, as we have seen, does not include output). Second, if we are interpreting the coefficient on employment, we should make clear that any 'pro-cyclical' relations are with respect to employment, and the behaviour of earnings over the (output) cycle will be mitigated by the output–employment relation.

The former point generalizes to which variables are to be included and which are not. Some studies have earnings as the dependent variable, dependent on one or more cyclical variables, while a rather separate body of work is related, rather, to labour demand schedules and hence specifies employment as its dependent variable.

Such labour demand schedules have then been interpreted as equivalent to the tests on the cyclical behaviour of earnings. Thus Symons (1985) (and Symons & Layard 1984) interpet labour demand schedule tests as contradicting Geary & Kennan's (1982a) findings of no significant reflection of the real wage on the level of employment. If the results of the labour demand schedule studies (such as Symons) are to be compared with the results of the cyclical behaviour of earnings studies (such as Geary & Kennan), as Symons does, then the distinction should be made explicit. That Symons's negative coefficient on the real wage (implying an elasticity of around one) may contain information other than simply the effect of the output cycle on earnings is also suggested by Symons's negative coefficients on input prices (in real terms) and strikes. These latter two are not (in that study) interpreted to mean that input prices and strike behaviour are counter-cyclical.

To conclude on the question of using output and/or employment as the cyclical variable, the two are dealt with separately in this book in Chapters 4 and 5 respectively, Chapter 5 then considering further the separate and joint correlations these two series might have with cyclical earnings.

3.4 *Wage series and the role of materials*

Bodkin's wage series are average hourly earnings of production workers (payment to non-production workers is included in one case), deflated alternatively by the consumer price index and wholesale price index, for both manufacturing and the total private economy, for operatives (and in one case all workers), including overtime, but straight time for the historical Canadian data. Thus he tests a number of series for both the United States and Canada.

Given the dependent variable, the question remains of which independent variables should be included. Geary & Kennan (1982a) is criticized by Symons (1981) for not including non-labour input costs. Symons estimates a simple demand for labour schedule for the British manufacturing sector: $EM = EM(RW, FL, KS, NH, ST, RE)$ where EM is employment in manufacturing; RW is the product wage (equals nominal wage divided by PR, wholesale prices of domestic sales); FL ('fuel') is real input costs (nominal input costs, FN, divided by PR); KS is capital stock; NH is normal hours; ST is strikes; and RE is the relative price of exports, (export unit values divided by PR). He finds an elasticity of employment with respect to the real wage of around -1; and with respect to the real price of inputs of around -0.5. If input costs are excluded from the model he finds only the weak relationship found by Geary & Kennan (1982a).

The difference between the two (cyclical wage, and labour demand) approaches has been discussed above. That non-labour costs should be included in such studies does, nevertheless, seem correct for both, although for different reasons. In Symons's case of estimating a labour demand schedule, then clearly if non-labour material input prices is a genuine explanatory variable then it must be included as such. In the case of the cyclical wage literature, on the other hand, the interest in non-labour material input prices would be different. The theoretical underpinnings for expectations as to the cyclical behaviour of wages, discussed in Chapter 2, implicitly assumed no cyclical pattern of non-labour direct costs so that, for example, Kalecki's horizontal marginal cost curve was taken to be equivalent, over the cyclical fluctuations in capacity utilization, to a horizontal marginal labour cost curve. If, however, there were some cyclical pattern to non-labour inputs then the assumption as to the cyclical constraints on total direct costs would impose some reciprocal constraints from the non-labour input price fluctuations on to the possible behaviour of the cost of labour. Thus investigations of cyclical wage costs must investigate the behaviour of total direct costs, and of labour costs within that. This point, of the importance of considering non-labour inputs, and of total direct costs, is developed further in the empirical chapters.

To conclude on the question of materials costs, it should be pointed out that Symons's criticism applies equally to all studies in the cyclical wage literature, not just to that of Geary & Kennan (1982a).

Since we are concerned with labour costs, we should start with average hourly earnings, rather than wage rates; include all payments including overtime payments; and adjust for other costs to the employer of paying wages (such as national insurance (NI) contributions in Britain).

Whether actual average hourly earnings (including overtime) or only 'straight time' should be used appears to be in dispute: Symons & Layard (1984), for example, use 'straight time', while Bodkin uses actual hourly earnings (except for his Canadian historical series). It is the actual earnings, including overtime differentials, which the employers pay, and so it is this series which is used in the tests reported in this book. Note, however, that by averaging these costs of employing a marginal hour of labour in the upswing out over all hours worked, the cost of the marginal hour is still made to appear less pro-cyclical (more counter-cyclical) than is in fact the case.

The other crucial factor in constructing our earnings series is what price index is used to deflate the money-wage series. Sachs (1983, p. 268 n. 8) argues that the

> most important problem with the Geary–Kennan analysis is that the wage is measured relative to the wholesale price index (WPI), rather than to Pv (the price of value added). This procedure is treacherous in a period of supply shocks, which raise WPI relative to Pv. It appears that the real wage has decreased when measured as W/WPI, when in fact it has *increased* when measured as W/Pv (emphasis added).

We have already agreed with Symons that non-labour direct costs should be included in any analysis of the cyclical behaviour of labour costs. In this case the WPI, rather than the value-added price (VAP) (or Pv in Sachs's terminology) *is* the appropriate price deflator. It is only if non-labour direct costs have not been included that the VAP becomes a more useful price deflator, for reasons explained below. All the major empirical investigations are subject to this two-point criticism. Only Sachs so far has used VAP and only Symons has included material costs (where references to Symons includes the extension to international data with Layard). In the absence of a non-labour material cost index being included in such tests, however, the use of VAP remains treacherous, albeit not to the same extent as is the use of the WPI. The implications of using one or other of the two possible price deflators for constructing a *product* wage is discussed in Appendix 1.

3.5 *Lags*

The insistence on the necessity of testing for *lagged* relations has not been challenged, and hence casts doubts on the pre-1978 results. But none of the studies to date has adequately discussed the interpretation of coefficients on lagged variables, particularly when the lagged effect is over a time-scale which makes a nonsense of the picture of a 'pro-cyclical' series. When the wage series is not claimed to move, say, counter to the output series but, instead, to be negatively related to lagged output then it raises the question of what the meaning is of 'pro-cyclical' or 'counter-cyclical' descriptions in the presence of lags. For example, Symons (1981, p. 47) reports that 'it is about seven quarters before half the effect is felt ... Sargent estimates a similarly slow response of employment to the real wage in his 1978 *JPE* paper' and that 'The real wage has a powerful but slow-acting negative effect on the demand for labour: long-run elasticity is about 2 and the mean lag is over 18 months' (Symons 1985, p. 37). Neftci (1978) cites the lack of lags as causing Bodkin to miss the counter-cyclical (dynamic) relation, although Otani (1978) finds just that relation *without* the use of lags, and *with* the use of lags Geary & Kennan (1982a) find no such relation.

Certainly, if we have reason to believe that some relation is lagged then such lags should be tested for. For example, if we hypothesize that an increase in output *caused* by an increase in demand reduces the marginal productivity of labour, *necessitating* eventually a reduction in the product wage, and that this will be brought about by price changes which may take up to a year to be implemented, then we would test with four quarterly lags to pick up such lagged behaviour. We would expect to have some idea about such lag lengths.

A specific example of this lack of discussion about the meaning of lagged coefficients is the citing by Neftci (1978) of a negative sum of lagged coefficients as proof of a counter-cyclical relation. In their criticism of Neftci's result, Geary & Kennan (1982a) do not question this approach, but, rather, repeat the exercise of adding the 24 (monthly) lagged coefficients of alternative regressions (with different price deflators and samples). The point is that a 24-month lag is fairly long in relation to (say) a four-year cycle, at least if we are trying to reach conclusions as to pro- or counter-cyclical movements. If a study reported finding counter-cyclical wage movements, this would normally be interpreted as implying that wages will rise during the recession. Since, however, the recession often lasts twelve months, if this 'counter-cyclical' movement only operated significantly over a distributed lag of more than twelve months, the description of wage movements as 'counter-cyclical' might not be very informative.

3.6 *Detrending*

Bodkin (1969) reports sometimes using an arithmetic trend and other times using a semilog trend. In most cases, the period was broken into sub-periods so that the fitted trend would fit the real wage better. As this is all the detail reported it is impossible to comment on the technique used. However, it seems that the actual percentage unemployment figure was taken as the final form of this variable, rather than deviation from trend. The assumption, presumably, is that there is no trend component in unemployment. While this may be true of Bodkin's data, it would not necessarily be an acceptable procedure to apply to more recent data, where there is a possibility of a trend movement in unemployment, nor to European data, where likewise there have been trend movements in unemployment even over Bodkin's sample: 'In Britain and to a slightly lesser extent in other European countries the fundamental unemployment problem is the inexorably rising trend upon which the business cycles are superimposed. This trend is barely apparent in the United States' (Nickell 1982, p. 51).

To test for the *cyclical* behaviour of variables we must use *cyclical* data. Bodkin's deviation-from-trend measure has not been criticized, and yet it has not been repeated. Otani (1978) simply uses percentage changes. But this is not really a satisfactory *cyclical* measure. Does a 2 per cent increase in output correspond to a cyclical expansion or a cyclical contraction? The answer, of course, is that we cannot say: in the 1950s or 1960s it may have corresponded to a cyclical contraction, being below trend, while today it might be above trend, and hence correspond to a cyclical expansion. Put another way, it may be that, historically, percentage changes in output of 4, 5 and 6 per cent are accompanied by percentage changes in real wages of 9, 8 and 7 per cent; while at another period percentage changes in output of 0, 1 or 2 per cent are accompanied by percentage changes in real wages of around 5, 4 or 3 per cent. We may, therefore, pick up a (positive) trend correlation rather than the negative cyclical one. Similarly Symons's use of logarithms of the original series may not totally isolate the cyclical behaviour or the series from trend behaviour.

The detrending method used by Geary & Kennan (1982a), and by Alogoskoufis (1982) is to take 'innovations' of the series. The definition of an innovation (Alogoskoufis 1982, p. 4) is a deviation from a variable's 'rational forecast' conditional on information available up to the end of the previous period. But a variable's rational forecast conditional on information available up to the end of the previous period might itself contain a cyclical factor which would not, then, be included in the innovation. Certainly the standard deviations of Geary & Kennan's univariate innovations are all less than the corresponding standard deviations in their 'trend and seasonal components removed' data. Indeed the average 'innovation' is less than half the fluctuation in the 'trend and seasonal removed' series.

Alogoskoufis (1982, p. 4) actually makes the following qualification concerning the use of innovations: 'Our results are opposite to the Dunlop–Tarshis–Bodkin results, although it has to be said that they were concerned with actual wages and employment, not innovations.'

It seems that since we want to test for deviations from trend, then that is the series we should use. For testing between cycle-phases (Chapter 6) clearly the turning points in such a series are crucial. We will, therefore, use deviations from trend as calculated by the 'phase average trend' technique, originally developed at the National Bureau of Economic Research. The results reported in other chapters use a simple moving average trend.

3.7 Data coverage

Only Otani (1978), Geary & Kennan (1982a), and Symons & Layard (1984) have attempted comprehensive international studies. Otani uses no lagged relations and has not generally been referred to in subsequent studies. Some of the criticisms of Geary & Kennan's methods would, however, apply to Otani's study. The discussion of this issue is easy to summarize: that research cannot be generalized from one country. It is desirable to test any proposition using data from a range of countries.

Bodkin (1969) hints at the importance of testing against disaggregated data, and Geary & Kennan (1982a) mention other work in passing. Bernanke & Powell (1984) (and Burda 1985) report results of such work on American data. In general we should be wary of accepting conclusions based solely on studying aggregated data because of the dangers involved in aggregation. What we would actually expect from such disaggregated work would depend on our assumed model; and specifically, on what we think the causal mechanism is behind any earnings results. Alternative mechanisms might be best captured by different price deflators. Thus a labour demand curve idea would hinge on the product wage and movements in this. A wage bargaining model, on the other hand, might predict the real wage to be the one with cyclical tendencies (in which case it is particularly ironic that Neftci (1978) and Sargent (1978) use the CPI). If such a real wage relation were found, then whether or not it would survive at a disaggregated level would depend, presumably, on whether it was the result of factors such as cyclical bargaining strength, in which case it might not survive (given the difference between the output cycles for industry as a whole on the one hand and for individual industries and firms on the other), or whether it was the spin-off from some product wage relation, in which case we would expect it to survive.

These questions are considered further in Chapter 7 where British disaggregated (and aggregate) data are tested.

4. Results

Bodkin's weakly pro-cyclical results were challeged in 1978 by Otani, by Neftci, and by Sargent, all of whom reported counter-cyclical results for real wages. These results (and the methods used in the latter two studies) were challenged by Geary & Kennan (1982a). Their paper has, in turn, been criticized by Sachs (1983) and by Symons (1985). Both have made specific criticisms which they report as allowing the Geary & Kennan result and which, when corrected for, show counter-cyclical earnings. Both criticisms (not having included material prices and, alternatively, not having used the Pv rather than the WPI as the price deflator) apply equally to all other studies.

Bernanke & Powell (1984) consider their results from frequency and time domain tests respectively (and the differences from each) as explaining why Geary & Kennan (1982a) find independence of wages over the cycle rather than pro-cyclical wages (as do Bernanke & Powell). They make this statement with respect to real wages, however, rather than the product wage series considered by Geary & Kennan (and by Bernanke & Powell elsewhere in their paper). Also Bernanke and Powell use only American data which, according to the results reported in Chapter 4, tend to be more pro-cyclical than data taken from other countries. Burda (1985), on the other hand, reports a negative wage–employment correlation for American data but does not report (or discuss) whether the correlation is statistically significant, and does not attempt to account for the contrast with other studies.

Starting, then, with Bodkin's (1969) regression results, these suggest that, since the Second World War, real wages have moved pro-cyclically in the United States, and non-cyclically in Canada. The results for different tests are summarized in Table 3.1. It does seem strange for Bodkin to report regression results with such poor Durbin–Watson statistics, varying from 0.24 to 1.42. In the one case where the regression gave different conclusions to the χ^2 tests (USA, WPI, manufacturing) when autocorrelation is corrected for, the significant result disappears. However, of the eight post-war American regressions, all show pro-cyclical earnings, and all show autocorrelation of the error term. He only corrected for two of the regressions, and simply reports that the coefficients remain significant. He does not report any regression results with satisfactory Durbin–Watson statistics, that is, after autoregressive transformation.

Otani (1978) confirms that there is no statistically significant relation between changes in product wages and changes in output for either Canada or the United States. (Otani refers to 'real wages', but had

Table 3.1 Bodkin's (1969) results summarized

Price deflator	Country		Coefficient on U	
			sign	significant
CPI	Canada	historical	−ve	no
		post-war	+ve	no
	USA	historical	−ve	yes
		post-war	−ve	no
WPI	Canada		+ve	no
	USA	economy	−ve	yes
		manufacturing	+ve	yes*

* but insignificant after correcting for autocorrelation of the residuals, indicated by the Durbin–Watson statistic for this original regression.

divided by the WPI to achieve his wages variable, in order, explicitly, to approximate product wages. It was when Bodkin divided the money-wage by the WPI that he, too, found no relation.) His data are only annual, over about 25 years. His method of detrending is simply to use percentage changes. However, Otani goes on to test for a total of 14 countries. Three of them showed positive coefficients between the product wage and output, but none of these were significant. The other 11 showed negative correlations, of which six were significant. Only six out of 14 countries, then, showed a statistically significant coefficient at the 5% level.

Counter-cyclical earnings are found by Neftci (1978), Sargent (1978), and Sachs (1979). Sachs simply cites Otani's (1978) results, and reports briefly on similar findings. Neftci, on the other hand, introduces his paper as finding the relationship between real wages and employment to be *significantly* different from the one reported in Bodkin. When the appropriate distributed lags are estimated, argues Neftci, employment and real wages are negatively correlated. This response is non-contemporaneous and statistically significant. The sum of coefficients in the distributed lag is negative for employment and positive for unemployment. The only significant coefficient which has the 'wrong' sign is the contemporaneous one.

Similar results are reported in Sargent's estimation and testing of a dynamic linear demand schedule for labour. He argues that the simple contemporaneous correlations that formed the evidence in the Dunlop–Tarshis–Keynes exchange and after are *not* sufficient to rule on the question of whether we are on the demand schedule for labour. His results, on the other hand, support the view that employment–real wages observations lie on a negatively sloped labour demand schedule.

The major difference in method between Sargent and Neftci (both finding counter-cyclical real wages) and Bodkin is their use of lags. They also distinguish between overtime payments and straight time rates. Their use of straight time rates will bias their results in favour of neoclassical results, since straight time rates underestimate the average hourly costs of labour in a boom.

Geary & Kennan (1982a) contrast these recent studies, finding couter-cyclical real wages, with the older empirical work which suggest that real wages and employment are statistically independent over the cycle. They conclude that it is difficult to reject the latter hypothesis using data for 12 countries. They explain the difference between their findings and those of Neftci and Sargent as due to different price deflators and sample periods.

Symons & Layard (1984) report a negative 'real wage effect' on employment; ask 'Why have other researches (and especially Geary & Kennan) not found results like ours for the real wage effect?'; and answer that 'The basic reason is that they have not simultaneously included real input prices' (Symons & Layard 1984, p. 796). Thus Symons & Layard pose their results as contradicting the non-cyclical conclusions of Geary & Kennan, and as proving instead that wages are counter-cyclical. As already indicated, however, Symons & Layard's 'real wage effect', found in their demand for labour schedule, does not in itself prove that wages are counter-cyclical. The demand schedule for any commodity would be expected to show a negative coefficient on its own price, but that does not mean that simply because the demand is pro-cyclical the price must be counter-cyclical. On the reported results themselves, Symons & Layard appear in any case to overstate their (counter-cyclical) conclusions. Of the 25 wage terms (current and four lagged, on each of five countries) almost half have positive coefficients, and in either case the majority of wage terms prove insignificant. The large elasticities quoted are due to large coefficients on the lagged dependent variable of labour demand (1.23 to 1.45 on l_{t-1} and -0.57 to -0.32 on l_{t-2}). This of course results in very large long-run effects for the other regressors.

Symons's work, as already mentioned, is cited by the Treasury (1985) as indicating an inverse wage–employment relation. However, the Treasury is *not* concerned with unemployment in general, but only that part 'due to' wages being 'too high'. The remainder may well, therefore, be due to 'other' (cyclical) factors which, if eliminated in a cyclical expansion of output, might well have a quite different relation to wages than that claimed for the wage–employment relation discussed in the Treasury paper.

Wadhwani (1985a) demonstrates that such econometric results are in any case notoriously unreliable. He finds that the result, of increased real wages reducing the aggregate demand for labour is not robust when the equation is respecified by the addition of variables: 'we suggest that the higher (in absolute terms) real wage elasticities obtained by previous researchers (e.g. Symons [1985], Layard & Nickell 1984) might simply result from omitting other relevant variables'. He also recalls that Symons's result depends on stopping at the second quarter of 1977, and that re-estimating to the fourth quarter of 1980 gives a *positive* (although statistically not significant) estimate of the wage elasticity. This breakdown is discussed by Symons (1985, p. 44). Another worry with Symons's work in terms of the cyclical wage literature has already been discussed, namely the fact that 'the mean lag is over 18 months' (Symons 1985, p. 37).

Bernanke & Powell (1984) use frequency domain and time domain techniques to consider US (disaggregate and aggregate, pre- and post-war) data. On the question of lags they state that 'there is some dispute over whether the contemporaneous correlation of the real wage and output (or employment) is an interesting measure of the real wage's cyclical pattern' (Bernanke & Powell 1984, p. 7). They define pro-cyclical as contemporaneous, and counter-cyclical as a lagged relation with the lag being half the cycle length (Bernanke & Powell 1984, p. 18). Using their frequency domain technique they find that real wages lagged output pre-war, and were pro-cyclical post-war. They do not report the results for product wages. Using their time domain technique they find real wages to be independent of other variables, although the pre-war data suggest that a wage shock would lead to a decline in output and employment, whereas post-war data suggest the opposite effect (Bernanke & Powell 1984, pp. 29–30). They then cite the differences between the frequency and time domain results to explain why Geary and Kennan (1982a) find independence (as Bernanke & Powell themselves do with their time domain technique). However, this is in relation to the real wage in their tests while Geary & Kennan use a product wage. Bernanke & Powell's results differ as between their two techniques, their two (pre- and post-war) data samples, and their two (real and product) wage measures. Taken as a whole, however, their results suggest that if there is any cyclical wage relation, then it is a pro-cyclical one.

One study not yet referred to is Schor (1982). This reports pro-cyclical wages for 1955–70, followed by counter-cyclical, for nine OECD countries. These results are not, however, directly comparable with the cyclical wage literature since, first, Schor's units of observation are business cycle turning points, rather than chronological units; and, second, changes in acceleration and deceleration of wages are investigated, rather than rates of change themselves. However, the reporting of these results in Schor (1985) is presented as a hypothesis for explaining the different findings reported in the different contributions to the cyclical wage literature (Schor 1985, p. 454). While different data samples can account for some of the differences between reported results (as shown, for example, in Geary & Kennan's discussion of Neftci's results), they do not account for the whole of such differences, and other factors (such as different price deflators, accounting or not for non-labour inputs, lags, and so on) can be shown to account for some discrepencies between reported results. Further, using the methods of the cyclical wage literature (as in Chapters 4–8 below) does not produce the same results as do Schor's; hence the results of the latter can not account for discrepencies within the former.

Finally, in a short note Burda (1985, p. 283) asserts:

> That the covariation of real wages and employment is positive over the business cycle remains a central, relatively undisputed 'stylized fact' since its identification in the 1930s by Dunlop (1938), Tarshis (1939) and Keynes (1939), and continues to influence theoretical and econometric research in aggregative economics.

Burda's short note finds negative 'wage–employment relationships for aggregate and disaggregated US manufacturing data for the period 1949–1978'. The statistical significance, or otherwise, of the correlations is not reported or discussed. The appearance of this article is of more interest, then, as an illustration of the methodological point being argued in this book: that to understand the cyclical wage debate as an episode in the history of economic thought requires some analysis of the meaning and significance of the debate. Thus Burda's article is presented as a contribution to the debate (involving Dunlop, Tarshis and Keynes) over the stylized fact of cyclical wages, but with no explanation for, or discussion of, the 46-year gap between Keynes (1939) and the paper's response to Keynes's call, and no mention of Bodkin, and hence no attempt to compare the reported results with the post-1930s literature.

Thus Burda's paper illustrates one of the conclusions of the work reported in this book: that the comeback being made by the neoclassical labour demand equation is not due to a change in the 'facts', nor even to a more accurate observation of the facts being achieved, but rather to an attempt to overthrow the Keynesian theoretical assumptions implicit in the bulk of applied macro-econometric work up to the late 1970s (see Chapter 9, Section 2.2).

We conclude this section with a summary of techniques used by the various studies we have examined (Table 3.2).

Table 3.2 Summary of studies' methods and results

	Bodkin (1969)	Otani (1978)	Sargent (1978)	Geary & Kennan (1982a)	Geary & Kennan (1982b)	Symons & Layard (1984)	Bernanke & Powell (1984)
Tests	R^1, χ^2	R^1	$R(FIML)^1$	$R^1, S \& F$ tests	innovations	R^1	time & frequency
Lags	no	no	yes	yes	yes	yes	yes
Detrending	dev. from trend	% change		innovations		none (t trend)	log diff
Overtime	yes	yes	no	nc^2	nc^2	no	not known
NI costs	no	no	no	no	no	yes	
Deflator	CPI & WPI	WPI	CPI	WPI	WPI	WPI	CPI & WPI
Materials[3]	no	no	no	no	no	yes	no
Cyclical Variable	$U \& L$	Q	L	L	Q, L	D_L	Q
Countries	2	14	1	12	5	6	1
Disaggregated	no (calls for)	no	no	no	no	no	yes
Results	weakly pro	counter	counter	non	non	counter	non, pro

[1] Regression
[2] Not consistent
[3] Non-labour input costs (inclusion allows WPI to act as product-wages price deflator)

5. Conclusion

As seen in Chapter 2, when it appeared that the data did not fit the simple neoclassical model, modifications to that model, and alternative models, were developed to fit with the data. Strangely, then, there is no agreement on what the data show. Strangest of all are those articles which explicitly set out to modify the simple diminishing mpl model to fit with the evidence of pro-cyclical earnings (such as Tatom 1980) when the most recent studies have tended to come down, out of the three possible options, on the side of one or other of the other two options—non-cyclical or counter-cyclical. Tatom refers to other publications, but to no empirical investigations.

Three points have been made about what has to be incorporated in any such study. These are: incorporation of lagged relations (Neftci 1978, Sargent 1978); incorporation of non-labour costs (Symons 1985); and application to international data (Otani 1978, Geary & Kennan 1982a). Symons & Layard (1984) is the only published study to date attempting to cover all these points, although, as argued above, their study is not directly comparable, being an attempt to estimate a demand for labour schedule. Their article is therefore unlikely to be accepted as answering the question with which the literature is concerned, namely: what is the cyclical pattern of earnings? The literature is likely therefore to continue its current growth until such an answer is considered to have been established. Meanwhile, to the three above requirements for work aimed to establish the empirical facts a fourth could be added: that the data series are clearly measuring *cyclical* behaviour. The results of such an empirical investigation incorporating the above points, are reported in the following chapters.

4
International results

This chapter reports the results of performing the tests which the previous chapter suggested as appropriate for testing the cyclical behaviour of wages. Annual data from after the Second World War are taken for six countries: the United States, Canada, Japan, France, West Germany and the United Kingdom. The data are all set out in Appendix 4, and the sources and data construction methods discussed, as are the statistical methods used. As a general rule data on which regression and other statistical tests were performed were first plotted. The international post-Second World War data on output, employment, nominal and real wages, are all, of course, dominated by the strong upward trends of the post-war boom.

1. Product wages

To investigate possible cyclical, as opposed to trend, correlations between output and wages, the percentage deviation from trend was taken of all data series, where trend was taken as a five-year moving average of the series in question. The wage series was hourly compensation in manufacturing industry, in product terms, i.e. deflated by producer prices. The compensation data were on a national currency basis, and were adjusted to include changes in employment taxes that are not compensation to employees, but are labour costs to employers. All data series were for 1950–82 with two years being lost at either end in constructing the trend.

These series of the percentage deviation from trend of product earnings were plotted against time, along with the percentage deviation from trend for output. The resulting plots are reported and discussed in Michie (1985). While there were no immediately striking correlations, the diagrams did suggest different patterns between countries. The time series plot for Japan, for example, did suggest that the two series move, if anything inversely; and this was also borne out when the two series were graphed against each other, with almost all the cases of output above trend being correlated with wages below trend.

To investigate further, the percentage deviations from trend of product earnings were regressed on the output deviations. The original regressions, using ordinary least squares, indicated serial correlation of the error terms, so all reported regression results are from the Hildreth–Lu (HILU) method. This loses a further observation in constructing ρ. Observations were also lost when lags and leads were introduced, as discussed below.

The results are reported in Table 4.1. The same basic statistical methods, and presentation format, are used in all the tables of results, so the following comments will not be repeated for each table of results. Each set of six figures corresponding to each country, for each regression, refers to, first, the value of the coefficient on the regressor, in this case the deviation of output from trend; second, the absolute value of the corresponding t-statistic; third, the value of the R^2 statistic adjusted for degrees of freedom; fourth, the Durbin–Watson test statistic; fifth, the standard error of the regression; and sixth, the F-statistic; thus:

| value of coefficient | $\bar{R}^2$ | SER |
| (absolute t-statistic) | DW | F-statistic |

A constant term was included and was in all cases not significant (except where indicated). Where a t-statistic indicates a coefficient

Table 4.1 Product wage regressed on output

	Coefficient on Q (absolute t-stat.)	$\bar{R}^2$ DW	SER $F(1,26)$
US	0.16* (2.29)	0.135 1.75	1.54 5.22†
Canada	−1.10 (0.81)	−ve 1.52	1.97 0.66
Japan	−0.32** (3.28)	0.265 1.62	2.50 10.8‡
France	−0.82 (1.61)	0.055 1.89	4.18 2.58
Germany	−0.10 (1.09)	0.007 1.67	1.40 1.18
UK	−0.28 (2.00)	0.100 2.34	2.22 4.01

* Significant at the 5% level; ** 1% level.
† Significant at the 5% level: ‡ 1% level.
HILU 1952–80; DW statistics indicate non-autocorrelation; constant term insignificant.

being statistically significant at the 5% level the coefficient is marked with an asterisk; and when statistically significant at the 1% level, with a double asterisk. These refer to the two-tailed test since any a priori expectations regarding the sign of the coefficients of the economic relationships being tested in this chapter are not sufficiently established to allow the use of the one-tailed test.

The cyclical wage behaviour in each country, set out in Table 4.1, vary considerably. Of the six countries, the coefficients are negative in five cases, positive in one. The only two countries with significant coefficients are the United States and Japan, although these are significantly pro-cyclical and significantly counter-cyclical relations, respectively. This contrast in results across economies suggests that there is no necessary cyclical behaviour of wages in 'free market' economies.

2. Lags and leads

The different wage behaviour between countries was considered further by repeating all regressions, adding the deviation of output from trend lagged one year as a second explanatory variable. The results are reported in Table 4.2. As can be seen, the results confirm the different wage patterns, with no convergence towards a norm being produced by the addition of the lagged variable.

In the case of the United States, the relation between the current wage and lagged output is different from the contemporaneous one, the coefficients on the output variables being equal and opposite (negatively and positively related respectively). This suggests that two quite different correlations are being picked up with, for example, increased (cyclical) output being associated (causing?), with a lag, cyclically lower wages; while a cyclical increase in wages is associated (perhaps via increased demand effects) with an increase in cyclical output.

In the case of Japan the two coefficients have the same sign and the contemporaneous (negative) relation appears strengthened. For Canada a relation now appears (being a lagged one), while for France, although the regression explains a little more, the coefficients on contemporaneous and lagged output are, as with the United States, opposite in sign. The addition of the lagged variable does nothing for the regression equation on German or British data other than lose it degrees of freedom.

To conclude: the introduction of lagged output to the regression tends to confirm the separate patterns suggested by the original regression rather than explain the differences as being due to similar economic mechanisms working with different time-lags in the different countries.

Table 4.2 Product wage regressed on current and lagged output

	Coefficient on		$\bar{R}^2$ DW	SER $F(2,24)$
	Q_t (t-stat.)	Q_{t+1} (t-stat.)		
US	0.14* (2.07)	−0.15* (2.13)	0.221 1.90	1.46 4.70†
Canada	−0.15 (1.59)	−0.45*** (4.75)	0.456 1.70	1.47 11.9‡
Japan	−0.35** (3.58)	−0.09 (0.93)	0.297 1.62	2.55 6.50‡
France	−0.89 (1.74)	−0.93 (1.84)	0.168 1.84	4.05 3.62†
Germany	−0.10 (1.10)	0.06 (0.60)	−ve 1.95	1.40 0.78
UK	−0.27 (1.77)	−0.08 (0.57)	0.068 2.28	2.29 1.95

* Significant at the 5% level; ** 1% level; *** 0.1% level.
† Significant at the 5% level; ‡ 1% level.
HILU 1952–80; DW statistics indicate non-autocorrelation; constant term insignificant.

One possible theory of cyclical wage behaviour which might imply a lagged relationship would be a bargaining model whereby changes in the deviation of output from trend changed the relative bargaining position of agents in production, with information lags and/or structural delays in the bargaining and/or price setting processes tending to create a lag in the mechanism working through to wage levels. A neoclassical model might suggest a lag working in the opposite direction, with a reduction in the wage being a necessary precondition for expanding output, or an increase in the wage necessarily leading to a reduction in output, so that there might be a relation between current wage levels and future output. This sort of hypothesized correlation lies behind much current policy debate, with wage cuts being advocated in order to allow increased output. To test for this possibility, the deviation of product wages from trend was now regressed on the deviation from trend of both current and future output. The results of these regressions are summarized in Table 4.3.

Table 4.3 Product wage regressed on current and future output

	Coefficient on		$\bar{R}^2$ DW	SER $F(2,24)$
	Q_t (t-stat.)	Q_{t+1} (t-stat.)		
US	0.17* (2.57)	0.17* (2.53)	0.283 1.66	1.38 6.13‡
Canada	−0.07 (0.61)	0.30* (2.65)	0.183 1.64	1.72 3.90†
Japan	−0.26** (3.18)	0.17* (2.11)	0.365 1.77	2.17 8.46‡
France	−1.24*** (4.15)	2.24*** (7.47)	0.714 2.02	2.37 33.5‡
Germany	−0.11 (1.09)	0.05 (0.51)	−ve 1.65	1.44 0.71
UK	−0.29 (2.00)	0.08 (0.52)	0.073 2.30	2.29 2.02

* Significant at the 5% level; ** 1% level; *** 0.1% level.
† Significant at the 5% level; ‡ 1% level.
HILU 1952–79; DW statistics indicate non-autocorrelation; constant term insignificant.

With the notable exception of France, the addition of future output as a second regressor does not significantly alter the statistical significance of the contemporaneous relation. However, two results of this exercise are worth noting: first, in the case of both countries where a statistically significant relation had been found previously (the United States and Japan), and in the case of France and Canada, there is a statistically significant (positive) correlation between the deviation from trend of product wages in time t and the deviation from trend of output in time $t + 1$; and, second, in all six cases this coefficient is positive. This result is the precise opposite of what would be expected according to the theory which prompted the test to be made.

The latter test has, again, confirmed the different contemporaneous wage–output relations existing across countries but has, at the same time, revealed a positive relation, statistically significant in four of the six countries, between current wage and future output levels (in cyclical terms). These results appear to lend weight to the argument that wage cuts would be associated with *reduced* future output, and that increases in future output would be correlated with *increased* current real wage levels (working, presumably, through demand effects).

The striking results from the French data suggest two separate effects being picked up, one contemporaneous, the other lagged. Thus, for example, increased output might, via increased prices (of the six countries the French data produced the largest positive coefficient when prices are regressed on output, although as with the positive coefficients in each case, not statistically significant) be contemporaneously correlated with reduced wages; while at the same time 'exogenous' wage increases might, via increased demand and with a lag, lead to increased future output (again, of the six countries tested for by Symons & Layard (1984)—the same six as in this book—France was the only one for which employment appeared to respond positively to increased demand from either government spending or world trade).

3. Materials costs

The case for including non-labour costs in any such investigation has already been made (as reported and discussed in Chapter 3), particularly for any post-oil price shock study. This conclusion was actually reached independently when the first set of data was analysed: the UK quarterly series discussed in Chapter 6 and, in particular, the behaviour of the real wage series over the first cycle. This was one of only two cycles for which earnings were below trend at the output peak. This quarter actually witnessed a lower level of product earnings than any of the other 127 quarters covered by the data. This was the result of a fall in product earnings of more than 20 per cent over less than two years leading up to the second quarter of 1951, caused by a surge in the WPI (of more than 38 per cent over the corresponding seven quarters). These initial results first suggested the necessity of constructing a non-labour direct cost series ('materials'), which could then, in addition, allow the cyclical behaviour of total costs to be considered.

The marginal decision of whether or not to hire another worker will depend not only on what is happening, over the cycle, to the cost in product terms of employing that worker but also on what is happening to the price of the materials (to the employer, i.e. in product terms) which that worker will use. Any cyclical investigation of earnings should, therefore, test also for the cyclical behaviour of the price of materials. Price indices were therefore constructed for non-labour direct costs ('materials'), and were weighted through time by a moving average of output per hour to construct a 'cost of materials used per hour' index. This was deflated by producer prices to give material costs in product terms (MC). Further details are given in Appendix 2.

This series for the cost of materials used per hour in product terms was plotted against time, along with the output series, both detrended. The data suggested a pro-cyclical relation, particularly in the cases of Canada, France, and West Germany. Other countries suggested some cyclical influences at work, but not consistent ones over the whole sample period. The United States, for example, displayed an initially negative correlation followed by a positive correlation. The positive correlation suggested by the British data, on the other hand, did not survive the violent fluctuations in materials costs of the 1970s.

The deviation from trend of these material costs were then regressed on the deviation of output from trend. This component of direct costs might be expected to behave more consistently across countries than the labour component, given the relatively fewer institutional, non-free-market, forces at work in their supply; and to the extent that such factors are at work, the less country-specific form they take (in contrast to, say, the trade union, bargaining, structure). This is confirmed by the results reported in Table 4.4. Only in Japan does there appear to be no contemporaneous correlation. For the other five countries there is a positive coefficient on output, statistically significant in four cases.

The results reported in Table 4.5 show that *lagged* output, when added as a regressor, while not having a statistically significant coefficient itself (with the exception of the United States where lagged output was significant at the 5% level, though not at the 1% level as is contemporaneous output in both regressions) does tend to confirm the previous pattern. Positive coefficients are found for five countries, raising the explanatory power of the regression equation for the United States, Canada and the United Kingdom. The regression continues to be totally independent of the regressors in the equation for Japanese data. Adding the deviation from trend of output with a one year *lead* shows no relation, except in the case of the UK. The statistical significance of these regression equations on future output is not improved by the savings in degrees of freedom involved in dropping current output.

4. Wages and materials costs

There are two conflicting pressures on the relation between product wages and product materials cost, which each lead to different a priori expectations as to the sign of the coefficient we would expect when the deviation from trend of product wages is regressed on the deviation from trend of material costs. On the one hand, given a constant mark-up

Table 4.4 Material cost (in product terms) regressed on output

	Coefficient on Q (t-stat.)	$\bar{R}^2$ DW	SER $F(1,26)$
US	0.59** (3.08)	0.239 1.86	4.09 9.46‡
Canada	0.70** (3.10)	0.242 1.74	3.41 9.62‡
Japan	−0.04 (0.17)	−ve 1.78	5.18 0.03
France	1.27** (2.94)	0.221 2.00	3.55 8.64‡
Germany	0.20* (2.75)	0.196 1.82	1.10 7.57†
UK	0.46 (1.46)	0.041 1.42	4.63 2.14

* Significant at the 5% level; ** 1% level.
† Significant at the 5% level; ‡ 1% level.
HILU 1952–80; DW statistics indicate non-autocorrelation except UK which is indeterminate; constant term insignificant.

over total direct costs to form prices, the labour and non-labour (materials) components of direct costs would tend to be negatively related. On the other hand, any change in the mark-up over total direct costs would affect both components of that total direct costs in the same direction, thus leading to the opposite a priori expectation, of a positive coefficient. This latter effect refers to an exogenous change in the mark-up, not an endogenous one caused by a modification of the former effect in which the mark-up does not remain constant but is reduced to absorb some proportion of the rise in nominal terms of the element of direct costs which increased. In this case, the reduction in the mark-up would not simply imply a positive coefficient relating the two direct cost components in product terms, but, rather, would reduce the former negative effect (with the increased cost of the one direct cost component representing a larger increase in product terms, while the direct cost component which is unchanged in nominal terms translates into a smaller reduction in product terms).

Plotting the deviations from trend of the two components of direct

Table 4.5 MC regressed on current and lagged output

	Coefficient on		$\bar{R}^2$ DW	SER $F(2,24)$
	Q_t (t-stat.)	Q_{t-1} (t-stat.)		
US	0.64** (3.60)	0.43* (2.48)	0.392 1.92	3.71 9.39‡
Canada	0.76** (3.40)	0.22 (1.00)	0.288 1.77	3.34 6.25‡
Japan	−0.08 (0.35)	0.07 (0.30)	−ve 1.66	5.33 0.11
France	1.31** (2.86)	−0.37 (0.80)	0.194 2.06	3.64 4.12†
Germany	0.20* (2.59)	0.01 (0.17)	0.154 1.72	1.14 3.37
UK	0.45 (1.46)	0.38 (1.23)	0.060 1.60	4.49 1.83

* Significant at the 5% level; ** 1% level.
† Significant at the 5% level; ‡ 1% level.
HILU 1953–80; DW statistics indicate non-autocorrelation; constant term insignificant.

costs—labour and materials—only the plots for Japan and Germany indicated a consistent correlation, in both cases negative. Regressing the deviation from trend of product wages on the deviation from trend of materials costs in product terms (MC) confirmed these patterns, with significant coefficients in two of the six countries—Japan and Germany—both being negative, as reported in Table 4.6.

In contrast to the positive coefficient which would be expected from an 'exogenous' change in the mark-up, which would affect both components of direct costs simultaneously thereby generating a contemporaneous positive coefficient, the effect of a change in one component on the other may operate through lags (and leads). The negative relation caused by the constant mark-up may be reflected in the coefficient on the contemporaneous or one-year lagged variable, depending on the lags involved in marking up to final prices.

The results of adding lagged material costs in product terms (MC) are reported in Table 4.7. The coefficients on the American and Canadian lagged series are both significant and negative. In no cases are

Table 4.6 Product wage regressed on MC

	Coefficient on MC (t-stat.)	$\bar{R}^2$ DW	SER $F(1,26)$
US	0.04	−ve	1.67
	(0.54)	1.66	0.30
Canada	−0.11	0.016	1.94
	(1.20)	1.57	1.43
Japan	−0.29**	0.234	2.49
	(3.04)	1.77	9.26‡
France	−0.19	−ve	4.30
	(0.91)	2.00	0.82
Germany	−0.75***	0.431	1.06
	(4.66)	2.09	21.7‡
UK	−0.11	0.030	2.31
	(1.35)	2.23	1.83

** Significant at the 1% level; *** 0.1% level.
‡ Significant at the 1% level.
HILU 1952–80; DW statistics indicate non-autocorrelation; constant term insignificant.

the coefficients on contemporaneous MC significantly affected, those for the United States and Canada remaining statistically insignificant.

The strong negative relation in Japan and Germany implies that workers do not/cannot offset increased material costs in increased earnings. The lag in the American and Canadian negative correlations suggests a lagged mark-up effect of one of the components of direct costs, via the output price, on the other component (in product terms).

It should also be noted that even complete absorption of changes in real material costs by wages would produce a coefficient less than one, since earnings represent a greater proportion of total direct costs than do material costs. Thus the results for West Germany, for example, suggest that the extremely pro-cyclical pattern of non-labour direct costs represents something other than (or at least additional to) any compensating mechanism operating between the two components of total direct costs. Otherwise, for the other five countries, the largest absolute value attained by any of the coefficients on (lagged and contemporaneous) material costs was 0.32, suggesting that cyclical

Table 4.7 Product wage regressed on current and lagged MC

	Coefficient on		$\bar{R}^2$ DW	SER $F(2,24)$
	MC_t (t-stat.)	MC_{t-1} (t-stat.)		
US	0.05 (1.50)	−0.30*** (8.16)	0.716 1.75	0.88 33.7‡
Canada	−0.09 (1.18)	−0.32*** (4.44)	0.432 1.43	1.50 10.9‡
Japan	−0.29** (2.95)	0.04 (0.42)	0.207 1.80	2.58 4.40
France	−0.22 (1.02)	−0.16 (0.75)	−ve 2.04	4.42 0.78
Germany	−0.72*** (4.32)	−0.01 (0.07)	0.392 1.92	1.08 9.37‡
UK	−0.12 (1.19)	0.02 (0.16)	−ve 2.23	2.40 0.75

* Significant at the 1% level; *** 0.1% level.
† Significant at the 5% level; ‡ 1% level.
HILU 1953–80; DW statistics indicate non-autocorrelation except Canada which is indeterminate; constant term insignificant.

fluctuations in the two cost series were absorbed partly by each other and partly by the price mark-up over total direct costs.

Having constructed an index for non-labour direct costs, and considered its relation to labour direct costs, the next section considers the role which this 'material costs' index plays in the correlation (or lack of it) between the output cycle and the deviation of product wages from trend.

5. Wages, materials costs and output

Adding this index of the deviation from trend of non-labour direct costs ('materials costs') in product terms to the regression equations of wages on output confirms the different behaviour patterns across countries. Comparing the results of these regressions, given in Table 4.8, with the results of regressing on output alone (Table 4.1), it

Table 4.8 Product wage regressed on MC and output

	Coefficient on		$\bar{R}^2$ DW	SER $F(2,25)$
	MC (t-stat.)	Q (t-stat.)		
US	−0.06 (0.85)	0.20* (2.36)	0.122 1.82	1.55 2.76
Canada	−0.10 (0.88)	−0.04 (0.25)	−ve 1.58	1.98 0.69
Japan	−0.30*** (4.34)	−0.33*** (4.58)	0.581 1.80	1.93 18.9‡
France	−0.06 (0.24)	−0.74 (1.25)	0.20 1.89	4.26 1.22
Germany	−0.83*** (4.39)	0.06 (0.79)	0.426 2.14	1.07 10.6‡
UK	−0.07 (0.93)	−0.25 (1.79)	0.096 2.30	2.22 2.33

* Significant at the 5% level; *** 0.1% level.
‡ Significant at the 1% level.
HILU 1952–80; DW statistics indicate non-autocorrelation, constant term insignificant.

can be seen that there is very little change at all in the value or the significance of the coefficient on output.

For the Japanese data, and to some extent the UK data, the combination of both MC and output, as regressors, does improve the significance of the correlations. Taken as a whole these results suggest that the cyclical output–product wage relation is *not* dominated by cyclical fluctuations in non-labour direct costs. The two elements of direct costs should, however, by combined to test if the cyclical output–product wage relation is repeated for total direct costs. It is this latter index, rather than labour costs alone, which neoclassical theory should consider to be constrained by, and to constrain, cyclical output.

The index of the cost of materials used per hour was, therefore, combined with the index of the cost of labour per hour to produce an index of total direct costs used per hour. The same weights were used as had been derived from the quarterly UK data, as reported and discussed in Appendix 2; and were here applied to the average of all 33 observations per country.

6. Total direct costs

This index of total direct costs used per hour, in product terms, was plotted over time, along with output, both detrended. The American data suggested a pro-cyclical movement. The cyclical behaviour of the index from Canadian data appeared unstable, as did the index for France. The West German index showed no particular cyclical activity for direct costs; while for the United Kingdom a generally pro-cyclical pattern appeared to be replaced over time by a counter-cyclical one. Finally, the Japanese data moved counter-cyclically. The percentage deviation from trend of this total direct cost index (DC) in product terms was then regressed on output (Table 4.9), current and lagged output (Table 4.10), and current and future output (Table 4.11). Comparing the behaviour of this total direct cost index with, first, the behaviour of wages alone, the insignificant correlation of wages with the output cycle found for France, West Germany and the United Kingdom remains, with no cyclical behaviour at all for total direct costs.

Table 4.9 Direct costs regressed on output

	Coefficient on Q (t-stat.)	$\bar{R}^2$ DW	SER $F(1,26)$
US	0.30***	0.422	1.46
	(4.55)	2.02	20.7‡
Canada	0.12	0.015	1.53
	(1.19)	1.70	1.42
Japan	−0.23***	0.398	1.44
	(4.34)	1.79	18.8‡
France	−0.13	−ve	2.98
	(0.35)	1.91	0.12
Germany	−0.02	−ve	0.83
	(0.31)	2.02	0.10
UK	−0.09	−ve	1.88
	(0.70)	1.85	0.49

*** Significant at the 0.1% level.
‡ Significant at the 1% level.
HILU 1952–80; DW statistics indicate non-autocorrelation; constant term insignificant.

Table 4.10 Direct costs regressed on current and lagged output

	Coefficient on		$\bar{R}^2$ DW	SER $F(2,24)$
	Q_t (t-stat.)	Q_{t+1} (t-stat.)		
US	0.31*** (4.42)	0.02 (0.33)	0.408 1.84	1.50 9.95†
Canada	0.14 (1.49)	−0.26** (2.80)	0.229 1.85	1.37 4.87†
Japan	−0.25*** (4.74)	−0.04 (0.82)	0.441 1.94	1.45 11.3‡
France	−0.04 (0.10)	−0.74* (2.08)	0.090 1.90	2.83 2.28
Germany	−0.01 (0.18)	0.04 (0.77)	−ve 2.06	0.84 0.31
UK	−0.10 (0.75)	0.02 (0.16)	−ve 1.90	1.94 0.29

* Significant at the 5% level; ** 1% level; *** 0.1% level.
† Significant at the 5% level; ‡ 1% level.
HILU 1953–80; DW statistics indicate non-autocorrelation; constant term insignificant.

The two countries which did show significantly cyclical wage costs now show even more marked cyclical behaviour for the composite index: for the United States, more pro-cyclical, for Japan more counter-cyclical (although with a smaller coefficient, albeit more satistically significant). These relations between the wage index and total direct cost index are also borne out when lagged output is included, as well as when future output is included.

For the UK and Germany, then, direct costs show no cyclical pattern. For France there is no contemporaneous relation, although there is a weak (negative) correlation between direct costs and lagged output, and a strong (positive) correlation with future output. In Japan direct costs and output show a significant negative correlation while in the US there is the opposite, significantly positive correlation. The Canadian data on total costs are negatively correlated with lagged output and positively correlated with future output.

Despite the generally positive correlation of total direct costs with future output, there appears a lack of any persistent relation between

Table 4.11 Direct costs regressed on current and future output

	Coefficient on		$\bar{R}^2$ DW	SER $F(2,24)$
	Q_t (t-stat.)	Q_{t+1} (t-stat.)		
US	0.30*** (4.23)	0.04 (0.54)	0.386 2.15	1.50 9.16‡
Canada	0.13 (1.56)	0.21* (2.46)	0.207 1.99	1.28 4.40†
Japan	−0.23*** (4.08)	0.07 (1.28)	0.413 1.77	1.45 10.2‡
France	−0.39 (1.60)	1.49*** (6.08)	0.579 1.95	1.94 18.9‡
Germany	−0.02 (0.31)	0.01 (0.07)	−ve 2.01	0.87 0.05
UK	−0.07 (0.52)	−0.13 (1.02)	−ve 1.96	1.90 0.68

* Significant at the 5% level; *** 0.1% level.
† Significant at the 5% level; ‡ 1% level.
HILU 1952–79; DW statistics indicate non-autocorrelation; constant term insignificant.

the two series. Total direct costs, in product terms, appear to bear no necessary relation to the business cycle.

7. Comparison with other studies

The results from regressing wages on output are similar to those reported by Otani (1978), who also finds a positive contemporaneous relation for the United States, and negative coefficients for Canada, the United Kingdom and Japan, in order of increasing significance. The order is not the same for the remaining two countries, with Otani's coefficient on output for the West German data being (the most) positive, rather than negative; and for the French data the most negative, rather than the third most. Thus, ranking the country results from the tests in this chapter, Otani (1978) and Symons & Layard (1984), starting with the most pro-cyclical and ending with the most counter-cyclical (the relation being negative after the '*****', and positive before), and with countries for which the correlation is statistically significant being asterisked, gives:

Otani	Above tests	Symons & Layard
Germany		
US	US*	US
*****	*****	*****
Canada	Canada	
	Germany	Germany
	France	France
		Japan
UK*	UK	UK*
Japan*	Japan*	Canada*
France*		

It is not clear why Otani should have got a different ranking for France (although having used different sample periods it is perhaps not surprising). The Durbin–Watson statistic for Otani's regression on West German data indicates autocorrelation of the errors, which would prevent too much weight being put on the different ranking West Germany's coefficient has in the international results table. The results of testing for total direct costs give the same international ranking, although the coefficient on cyclical output for the Canadian data, while remaining statistically not significant, becomes positive.

As indicated in the previous chapter, none of the other studies provide similar comparable descriptive statistics indicating the cyclical pattern of product wages, and the statistical significance of any apparent pattern. Geary & Kennan (1982a) test the null hypothesis of no relation, but do not investigate whether the alternative hypothesis, of a cyclical movement, would be pro- or counter-cyclical. The studies within the demand for labour schedule approach (Symons 1985; Symons & Layard 1984; Layard & Nickell 1985b) tend to test for correlations between employment and a number of other variables, rather than testing for an ultimately reduced form correlation of product wages with the output cycle; and while material prices are included in such 'demand for labour schedules', no comparable index for total direct costs is tested. While not, therefore, directly comparable, Symons & Layard's results are nevertheless reported above. The two differences with the results reported in this chapter are the reversal of the positions of the United Kingdom and Japan, and the more negative correlation for Canada. In both cases Otani's results correspond to those found for the data tested in this chapter.

It should be stressed that the different ranking (and statistical significance) reported by Symons & Layard is not necessarily surprising. They are conducting a quite different test. Indeed, a more negative correlation for Canada is reported in the following Chapter (Table 5.3) when product wages were regressed on employment as well as a separate cyclical output variable the role of which may have been played to an extent by Symons & Layard's demand variables.

The above comparisons have been considered on the basis of the R^2 statistic (adjusted for degrees of freedom), t-statistics, deviation of the Durbin–Watson statistic from two, and F-tests of the significance of the regressor variables, other than the constant term, taken together. The following section, and Appendix 3, consider more elaborate tests (not directly reported by TSP version 3.5, the package on which the regressions were run).

Section 8 discusses the question of parameter stability, and reports the results of running Chow tests on selected equations. The results of testing for heteroscedasticity (using the Goldfeld–Quandt test), and for higher order serial correlation, are reported in Appendix 3.

8. Parameter stability

We would not necessarily expect the coefficients in any of the above tests to be stable over the entire data sample, particularly because of the events of 1973. The data series were, therefore, divided into two samples: the first including all data up to 1970 (the final deviation from trend figure being from a trend taking account of data only up to 1972), and the second including only post-1971 data. The regression equations were then re-estimated, this time separately against each of the two samples respectively, and an F-ratio was constructed in order to perform the test suggested by Chow (1960)[1]:

$$F^* = \frac{(\text{RRSS} - \text{URSS})/(k+1)}{\text{URSS}/(n_1 + n_2 - 2k - 2)}$$

where RRSS stands for the restricted sum of squares, that is the sum of squared residuals from the regression equation being estimated with the restriction that the parameters are stable over the entire data sample; URSS stands for the unrestricted sum of squares, that is the addition of both sums of squared residuals from the two regression equations being estimated without the restriction; k is the number of regressors, excluding the constant term; n_1 is the number of observations in the first of the two sub-samples; and n_2 the number of observations in the other, so that F^* has an F distribution with degrees

---

[1] Maddala (1979) points out that the test was derived by others before Chow, and argues, therefore, that in view of this, it is better not to attach any name to the test (p. 198n). The test is only referred to above as the 'Chow' test to fit with common usage, rather than to imply authorship.

of freedom $(k + 1)$, $(n_1 + n_2 - 2k - 2)$. Table 4.12 reports the calculated value of this F^* for each of the six countries on nine regression equations (all previously reported above), along with the F-distribution degrees of freedom, and the theoretical value of $F_{0.05}$ and $F_{0.01}$ corresponding to each of these degrees of freedom.

In order to calculate the statistics reported in Table 4.12, the regression equations were all estimated over both sub-samples as well as over the entire sample. Rather than report the sub-sample results for each equation, Tables 4.13 and 4.14 report these results for two selected equations: W on Q, which the Chow test had shown to be stable across sub-samples; and DC on Q and lagged Q, which the Chow test had shown not to be stable on data from the United States, Canada and the United Kingdom. As expected, the economic relationships being studied change over time, specifically before and after the early 1970s.

The extent to which the two samples give different relationships varies between the correlations being considered. Specifically, the correlations between materials costs and either output or wages differ significantly between samples, while the wage–output correlation does not, indeed is the only one of the nine regressions to display parameter stability against data from every country. The lag structures, in particular, appear to have changed over time. Thus while the parameter of W on MC shifts significantly for three of the six countries, five of the six show a significant shift in the correlation between W and current and lagged MC.

The main conclusions from these tests of parameter stability are, then, that the oil shock (for want of any other generally acceptable phrase to describe the breakdown of the post-war boom) affected different economies in different ways—the correlations reported in Tables 4.13 and 4.14 becoming more pro-cyclical in the United States but more counter-cyclical in the United Kingdom—and that the lack of uniformity between countries seems even more pronounced after 1971.

9. Conclusion

The past few years have seen increasingly sophisticated econometric approaches to investigating the cyclical pattern of wages. This increased sophistication has not, as yet, established a consensus view of the facts. This is due, in part at least, to the different studies, from the 1930s to the present, not only using different degrees of econometric sophistication, but also using different data samples, series and sources, as discussed in Chapter 3. To attempt to establish the facts of cyclical wage behaviour requires a study which, at least, tests for data drawn

Table 4.12 Chow test for parameter stability
$(k+1), (n_1 + n_2 - 2k - 2); F_{0.05}, F_{0.01}$

	US	Canada	Japan	France	Germany	UK
W on Q 2,23; 3.42, 5.66	3.26	0.66	3.25	0.43	1.47	2.65
W on Q, MC 3,21; 3.07, 4.87	5.85‡	1.14	4.52†	4.26†	2.52	2.47
W on MC 2,23; 3.42, 5.66	1.22	1.25	2.89	4.06†	4.24†	0.24
W on MC_t, MC_{t-1} 3,20; 3.10, 4.94	10.1‡	3.50†	3.56†	3.00	3.24†	0.26
W on Q_t, Q_{t-1}, MC_t, MC_{t-1} 5,16; 2.85, 4.44	8.06‡	4.39†	2.10	1.96	2.65	4.28†
MC on Q 2,23; 3.42, 5.66	7.46‡	4.59†	0.03	2.25	1.63	1.15
MC on Q_t, Q_{t-1} 3,20; 3.10, 4.94	4.02†	5.20‡	0.82	4.75†	1.78	1.05
DC on Q 2,23; 3.42, 5.66	19.9‡	1.34	3.13	0.26	2.27	4.45†
DC on Q_t, Q_{t-1} 3,20; 3.20, 4.94	12.1‡	7.70‡	1.99	1.20	2.25	3.70†

† Signifies rejection of the null hypothesis at the 5% level of significance.
‡ Signifies rejection at the 1% level.
To reject the null hypothesis is to accept that the two samples give different relationships.

Table 4.13 Sub-samples for W on Q

	Coefficient on Q (t-stat.)	$\bar{R}^2$ / DW	SER / F-stat.
Pre–1971; $N = 18$, $F(1,16)$			
US	0.05 (1.07)	0.010 / 1.24	0.74 / 1.15
Canada	−0.07 (0.73)	−ve / 2.08	1.01 / 0.54
Japan	−0.27** (3.39)	0.381 / 1.50	1.77 / 11.5‡
France	−0.93 (1.27)	0.035 / 1.82	3.82 / 1.62
Germany	−0.08 (0.91)	−ve / 1.52	1.14 / 0.83
UK	0.05 (0.44)	−ve / 1.48	1.04 / 0.19
Post–1971; $N = 9$, $F(1,7)$			
US	0.37 (2.11)	0.302 / 2.14	2.36 / 4.47
Canada	−0.07 (0.19)	−ve / 1.33	3.36 / 0.04
Japan	−0.32 (1.34)	0.090 / 1.73	3.30 / 1.79
France	−1.17 (1.18)	0.046 / 1.75	5.41 / 1.39
Germany	−0.17 (0.74)	−ve / 1.75	1.85 / 0.55
UK	−0.58 (1.86)	0.236 / 2.60	3.51 / 3.48

** Significant at the 1% level.
‡ Significant at the 1% level.

DW statistics indicate non-autocorrelation pre-1971, except for the US which is indeterminate. For the post-1971 sample the DW statistic is not appropriate to the sample size. The sign patterns of the residuals were therefore examined through contingency tables. The appropriate χ^2 test could not reject the hypothesis of non-autocorrelation.

Table 4.14 Sub-samples for DC on Q_t, Q_{t-1}

	Coefficient on		$\bar{R}^2$ DW	SER F-stat
	Q_t (t-stat.)	Q_{t-1} (t-stat.)		
Pre-1971: $N = 17$, $F(2,14)$				
US	0.02 (0.55)	0.01 (0.22)	−ve 1.91	0.57 0.15
Canada	0.01 (0.06)	−0.19 (1.92)	0.104 1.91	1.04 1.93
Japan	−0.22** (3.22)	−0.04 (0.66)	0.345 1.80	1.45 5.21†
France	−0.12 (0.23)	−1.48* (2.78)	0.281 2.04	2.81 4.12†
Germany	0.01 (0.13)	0.09 (1.62)	0.050 2.00	0.64 1.39
UK	0.15** (3.03)	0.25*** (5.43)	0.730 2.12	0.46 22.7‡
Post-1971: $N = 9$, $F(2,6)$				
US	0.59** (5.73)	−0.05 (0.55)	0.798 1.58	1.56 16.8‡
Canada	0.31 (1.44)	−0.41 (2.06)	0.329 1.77	1.91 2.96
Japan	−0.33* (3.50)	−0.01 (0.01)	0.562 1.86	1.26 6.12†
France	−0.23 (0.44)	−0.53 (1.02)	−ve 1.92	2.96 0.57
Germany	−0.12 (0.91)	−0.06 (0.46)	−ve 1.84	1.07 0.45
UK	−0.40 (1.38)	−0.20 (0.71)	0.043 2.07	3.03 1.18

* Significant at the 5% level; ** 1% level; *** 0.1% level.
† Significant at the 5% level; ‡ 1% level.
DW statistics indicate non-autocorrelation pre-1971. For the post-1971 sample see note to Table 4.13: the appropriate χ^2 test could not reject the hypothesis of non-autocorrelation.

from several countries; and constructs and tests the appropriate data series, taking into account the relevant discussions in, and criticisms of, previous studies. It is the results from such an attempt which have been reported in this chapter.

The results show clearly that there is no necessary cyclical wage behaviour common to advanced capitalist economies, as would be predicted by the neoclassical assumptions outlined in Chapter 2. Those cyclical patterns which are found (for example the conflicting patterns which emerge from the American and Japanese data) do not, therefore, suggest that some necessary relation exists but, rather, that such specific patterns are the product of those institutional and market factors specific to the economy which generated the earnings data in question. Breaking the data series between the post-war boom and the subsequent years does not help to establish a common pattern.

Testing for possible lags and leads simply confirmed the different contemporaneous wage–output relations existing across countries. However, a statistically significant positive correlation was found in four of the six countries between (the cyclical series for) the *current* wage and *future* output levels. Depending on whether terms such as 'pro-cyclical' and 'counter-cyclical' are thought appropriate to describe correlations with the output cycle other than contemporaneous ones, this result might be taken as evidence against a traditional counter-cyclical wage view. That view was associated with the assumption that a (cyclical) expansion in output would be associated with a (cyclical) decline in the real wage. However, these results would be more consistent with a rather contrary view: namely that wage cuts would be associated with *reduced* future output.

While the behaviour of non-labour ('materials') costs may help explain specific fluctuations in real wages, taken as a whole the results from testing jointly for the two component parts of total direct costs suggested that the cyclical output–real wage relation is *not* dominated by cyclical fluctuations in non-labour direct costs (Section 5); and total direct costs, in product terms, appear to bear no necessary relation to the business cycle (Section 6).

5
Employment

One difference in method between the various empirical investigations into the cyclical behaviour of wages not accounted for in Chapter 4 is the difference in the cyclical variable against which the real wage is tested for possible correlation. This chapter therefore compares the results reported in Chapter 4 with the results of using employment, rather than output, as the cyclical variable.

1. Methods

The methods of enquiry pursued in this chapter are similar to those used in Chapter 4, where deviations from trend of product wage series were tested for possible correlation with the output cycle. Points concerning these methods are not, therefore, repeated here; and under the following headings only points new to the method used in this chapter are mentioned.

1.1 *The specification of the correlation to be tested*

Without implying by the word 'dependent' any causal relations, the dependent variable was the same as used in Chapter 4, namely the percentage deviation from trend of product wages. Similarly, the same functional forms and lag structures were used. The only major difference was, therefore, in testing for possible correlations of wages with employment rather than output.

The explanatory variables   The employment series was for total hours in manufacturing, relating to all employed persons (wage and salary earners, the self-employed, and unpaid family workers) in the United States and Canada, and all employees (wage and salary earners) in the other countries, the source being the US Department of Labor, Bureau of Labor Statistics. As with the other series this was transformed into a series for the percentage deviation from trend.

Two points to be mentioned regarding the explanatory variables are, first, that the tests were repeated substituting the above employment series with a series for the total number employed; and that, with both data series, output was also introduced as a second explanatory variable. Also, series for non-labour, and for total direct, costs were introduced. The reason for testing separately for possible correlations with the number employed rather than total employed hours is the possible difference in the cyclical behaviour of the two series, and, further, the possible role wage costs play in this.

The reason the correlations are tested for with the introduction of the output series in addition to the employment series is to be able to indicate the sort of negative correlation which would exist between employment and earnings conditional on output. The correlation of earnings with output conditional on employment is not really relevant. While a change in employment unrelated to any output change is not what would be referred to as a cyclical change in employment (but, rather, a substitution between inputs presumably caused by relative input price shifts), a change in output not accompanied by a change in employment would still be part of the output cycle, and would suggest some additional cyclical factor being at play such as labour hoarding (this discussion being only in terms of cyclical output, not trend changes which clearly could be unaccompanied by employment changes).

All data series are reproduced in Appendix 4.

1.2 *The estimation of the correlations*

The possible correlations between the various cyclical series discussed above were tested for by means of the Hildreth–Lu (HILU) regression technique (Ordinary Least Squares having indicated serial correlation) using annual data between 1950 and 1982 for the United States, Canada, Japan, France, West Germany and the United Kingdom. The various possible correlations to be tested are reported in the following order. First the employment series is considered in relation to wages. Second, non-labour direct costs and a composite total direct costs index are introduced. Third, the correlations are considered with employment conditional on output. Fourth, the different behaviour of number employed and total hours employed over the cycle is considered.

All the theorized correlations discussed above and below were plotted out, both over time and against each other; and lags and leads were tested for in regression equations. In order to restrict the sheer volume of reported results, these are only reported in selected cases.

2. Results

2.1 *Wages and employment*

The deviations from trend of both the employment and earnings series were plotted together over time. The pattern was different across countries, and, in some cases, changed over time. In the United Kingdom, for example, a pro-cyclical pattern appeared to hold up until the early 1970s, following which major out-of-phase fluctuations would be expected to dominate any regression equation estimated over the whole sample. It turns out that the regression result is as hypothesized, as reported in Table 5.1, with a significantly negative coefficient on employment. Graphing the percentage deviation from trend of employment against the percentage deviation from trend of wages in a scatter diagram suggested, however, that this statistically significant inverse correlation was indeed the result of a few outliers. Comparing countries, the time plots (reported in Michie, 1985)

Table 5.1 W regressed on L

	Coefficient on L (t-statistic)	$\bar{R}^2$ DW	SER $F(1,26)$
US	0.12 (1.27)	0.022 1.76	1.63 1.62
Canada	−0.30 (1.80)	0.077 1.65	1.88 3.25
Japan	−0.83*** (4.62)	0.430 1.53	2.16 21.4‡
France	−1.95*** (4.73)	0.441 1.46	3.26 22.3‡
Germany	−0.13 (1.30)	0.025 1.66	1.38 1.69
UK	−0.48* (2.34)	0.142 2.37	2.16 5.49†

* Significant at the 5% level; *** 0.1% level.
† Significant at the 5% level: ‡ 1% level.
HILU 1952–80; DW statistics indicate non-autocorrelation except France which is indeterminate; constant term insignificant.

suggested a possible negative correlation between the two series in Japan and France; while the United States plot suggested, if anything, a (weakly) positive correlation; and the plots for Canada and West Germany suggested no correlation at all. While scatter plots broadly confirmed this picture, the United States correlation appeared to depend on one outlier (corresponding to 1973); and similarly, the scatter for France did not suggest much, were it not for the help of a few outliers.

The possibility of correlations between these two series (in each of the six countries) was then tested for by regressing the series for the deviation of wages from trend (W) on to (a constant and) the series for the deviation of employment from trend (L). The results are given in Table 5.1.

Unless reported otherwise the coefficient on the constant term was not significant. For some regressions a time trend was tested for but, as expected with such percentage deviation from trend series, this was not significant and is not reported. Further econometric tests, for parameter stability, heteroscedasticity, and higher-order serial correlation, are reported for some chosen regressions in Appendix 3.

The regression results reported in Table 5.1 are in line with those suggested by the scatters. Only France and Japan show very definite correlations between the wage and employment series, in both cases a negative one. The negative correlation seen for the United Kingdom data is only just significant (for both the t-statistic and the F-statistic at the 5% level) because of the lack of such correlation in the earlier part of the sample.

These results are broadly similar to the findings for the behaviour of wages over the (output) cycle (reported in Table 14.1). In the case of each country, however, the relation with employment is, as expected, more counter-cyclical/less pro-cyclical. This is because given output, employment and wages would be expected to be inversely correlated. But such correlations between wages and employment which occur with a given output are not 'cyclical' correlations.

Allowing for different speeds of adjustment between countries by adding lagged employment to the regressions did not explain the international differences. While the United States displayed a significant negative correlation between the earnings series and lagged employment, this relation did not appear in the other countries, except for Canada. In the case of both West Germany and the United Kingdom, not only was the coefficient on lagged employment (insignificant and) positive, but the addition of this variable reduced the overall explanatory value of the regressions.

2.2 *Materials costs and total direct costs*

The index of the cost of materials used per hour described previously was now compared with the behaviour of employment. The two series were significantly (positively) related in the United States and West Germany. Grading the six countries from the most pro-cyclical to the most counter-cyclical, the order is almost identical when this materials index is compared with employment as when wages are. The only difference is that France and West Germany swap the last two positions. Thus the (generally not significant) inverse relation between labour and non-labour direct costs reflects itself here in the former being generally negatively correlated with employment while the latter is generally positively correlated, but this does not appear to be part of a process of maintaining fluctuations in total direct costs within limits in relation to employment fluctuations.

Given these results, the addition of non-labour direct costs in the former regressions (which tested for possible correlations between labour costs and employment) would not be expected to explain the different results found across countries. And so it turns out.

Similarly, total direct costs (DC) were compared with the employment series (L) (Table 5.2). This relation, too, differed over countries, and along the same lines as with the wage–employment patterns. The order of countries listed in the type of sequence described above does not alter significantly. The following three further results emerge from comparing the relation of employment to wages with the relation of employment to total direct costs. First, in all six countries the total direct cost index is more positively/less negatively related to employment (in terms of the sign of the coefficient on employment). Second, the difference between countries is, if anything, greater when the behaviour of total direct costs is considered, as the two 'extreme' countries, the United States and Japan, have stronger correlations. Third (and connected with the first), of the five countries showing a negative correlation the coefficients have reduced significance in four cases, and in all cases the absolute value of the coefficients is reduced.

2.3 *Employment conditional on output*

It was argued above that to compare series of (deviations from trend for) earnings and employment would pick up two relations: first, the correlation (or lack of it) due to the output cycle, and the fluctuations in employment related to the output cycle; and second, the relation between deviation from trend of employment not connected with the output cycle, and wages. The earnings series was therefore regressed on both the output and the employment series. This aims to measure the

Table 5.2 DC regressed on L

	Coefficient on L (t-stat.)	$\bar{R}^2$ DW	SER $F(1,26)$
US	0.31** (3.48)	0.292 2.10	1.59 12.1‡
Canada	−0.04 (0.31)	−ve 1.80	1.57 0.09
Japan	−0.60*** (6.83)	0.628 2.08	1.13 46.6‡
France	−1.10** (3.50)	0.294 1.39	2.48 12.3‡
Germany	−0.04 (0.59)	−ve 2.00	0.83 0.35
UK	−0.14 (0.72)	−ve 1.84	1.88 0.52

** Significant at the 1% level; *** 0.1% level.
‡ Significant at the 1% level.
HILU 1952–80; DW statistics indicate non-autocorrelation; constant term insignificant.

correlation between earnings, on the one hand, and fluctuations in employment given output, on the other; as well as the equivalent earnings–output relation. The results of these regressions are reported in Table 5.3.

The results are in line with what had been predicted. The earnings–employment coefficient, given the level of output, is more negative than when it also reflected (by omitting output) employment associated with fluctuations in output. The sign of the employment (conditional on output) series is in all cases negative, significantly so in four of the six cases. Similarly the results on output conditional on employment are more positively correlated than when all output fluctuations, including those associated with similar movements in employment, are tested for possible correlation with earnings.

An obvious problem is that to the extent that the output-cycle variable picks up some of the cyclical employment behaviour, this introduces the problem of multicollinearity. The problem is increased by the instability of the output–employment relation. This latter prevents the possibility of accurately decomposing the employment

Table 5.3 W regressed on L and Q

	Coefficient on		$\bar{R}^2$ DW	SER $F(2,25)$
	L (t-stat.)	Q (t-stat.)		
US	−0.60* (2.63)	0.63** (3.33)	0.295 1.61	1.39 6.39‡
Canada	−0.80* (2.32)	0.41 (1.64)	0.133 1.71	1.82 2.95
Japan	−0.93** (2.98)	0.06 (0.37)	0.411 1.57	2.20 9.99‡
France	−2.41*** (4.30)	0.73 (1.37)	0.435 1.64	3.23 10.9‡
Germany	−0.21 (0.75)	0.08 (0.30)	−ve 1.68	1.41 0.82
UK	−0.42 (1.13)	−0.05 (0.21)	0.110 2.37	2.21 2.56

* Significant at the 5% level; ** 1% level; *** 0.1% level.
‡ Significant at the 1% level.
HILU 1952–80; DW statistics indicate non-autocorrelation; constant term insignificant.

series into the two behavioural series which combine to generate non-trend fluctuations.

These points support the conclusion that the attempt to establish what the 'cyclical behaviour of earnings' is should aim to establish the correlation (or lack of it) between non-trend earnings and cyclical *output*. Such findings would, then, have implications for employment about which the results reported in this chapter would have some bearing.

To test the hypothesis formulated above concerning the different results to be expected when output was, and was not, included in the regression equations, the index for non-labour direct costs was considered. As predicted, the coefficients on employment tended to be more counter-cyclical when the output variable was included. This might have been expected regardless of whether labour or non-labour costs were the instigator of change, given the positive correlation to be expected in the cyclical behaviour of employment and cost of materials used per hour; (while this does not follow from neoclassical theory, it was found, although only weakly, in regression tests). When wages were regressed on the employment and materials indices, both with and without output included, the wage and materials indices were then more negatively correlated when output was included. This would tend to favour the second of the two alternative hypotheses discussed above as to the cause of non-cyclical fluctuations, namely that these are driven by changes in the cost of non-labour direct costs, rather than by changes in wages.

Finally, the results of regressing the total direct cost series on both output and employment are reported in Table 5.4. As predicted, the

Table 5.4 DC regressed on L and Q

| | Coefficient on | | $\bar{R}^2$ | SER |
	L (t-stat.)	Q (t-stat.)	DW	$F(2,25)$
US	−0.23 (0.96)	0.48* (2.41)	0.402 2.13	1.46 9.68‡
Canada	−0.86** (3.53)	0.67** (3.76)	0.313 1.80	1.28 6.87‡
Japan	−0.66** (4.10)	0.03 (0.38)	0.601 1.95	1.15 20.5‡
France	−1.83*** (4.71)	1.09** (3.02)	0.428 1.60	2.22 10.7‡
Germany	−0.13 (0.79)	0.09 (0.62)	−ve 2.02	0.84 0.35
UK	−0.09 (0.25)	−0.04 (0.16)	−ve 1.85	1.92 0.26

* Significant at the 5% level; ** 1% level; *** 0.1% level.
‡ Significant at the 1% level.
HILU 1952–80; DW statistics indicate non-autocorrelation; constant term insignificant.

coefficients on the employment terms tend to be more negative than when the direct cost series is regressed on employment alone; and the coefficients on the output term tend to be more positive. Indeed, these latter coefficients are now positive in five of the six countries, and significantly so in three. The corresponding results reported in Table 4.9, prior to the separate influence of employment being taken out by including such a series in the regression test, had suggested a positive coefficient for the correlation of total direct costs with output in only two of the six countries.

2.4 *Number employed*

Within the movement of total employed hours there are the two composite movements of number employed and hours per person. Similarly with cyclical earnings, there are earnings per person and earnings per hour. Analysis of cyclical earnings refers to earnings per hour, and that is what has been tested for in the work reported in this book. Compared to the results of this, earnings per person would be more pro-cyclical/less counter-cyclical due to the pro-cyclical movement in hours per person. If such earnings series (per hour) are to be compared with cyclical employment (rather than with output directly) then similarly it is total employed hours which is the comparable employment series, and that is what was tested for in the preceding sections. Studies which have used unemployment as the cyclical variable (e.g. Bodkin 1969) are closer to (the inverse of) number employed. There are also implications within theories of cyclical earnings for hourly earnings to be related differently to number employed than to hours employed and, indeed, for the former to be more closely correlated, for example if wage costs have to be reduced in order to take on more employees but do not have to (or cannot) when hours per existing employees are increased. For these reasons all the above tests were repeated using a series for non-trend employment. In all cases the results were similar to those reported with the total employed hours series, and so are not discussed further. Again, for example, the total direct cost series was less negatively related to the employment series alone, and again this meant no relation whatsoever for Canada, West Germany and the United Kingdom; a negative correlation for Japan and France; and a positive correlation for the United States.

3. Discussion

The results reported in this chapter suggest a negative answer to Keynes's assertion/question: 'I should have thought that employment never did fall materially without a rise in the real hourly wage. Is not this one of the best established of statistical conclusions?' (Keynes 1937a, letter to Ohlin dated 29 April 1937, in Keynes 1973, p. 190). Keynes was not here meaning to refer specifically to employment as opposed to output: his statement is made in the context of the cyclical behaviour of wages—not differentiating between the output cycle and the corresponding employment changes. The results of the previous chapter would have the same relevance, then, to this question.

The difference between using output and using employment as the cyclical variable turns out to be small. As expected, the employment–wage correlation is in every case more counter-cyclical (less pro-cyclical) than the output–wage correlation. The significantly pro-cyclical wages of the United States correspond to an insignificant (although positive) wage–employment correlation. Similarly, the non-significant counter-cyclical wages in France and the United Kingdom correspond to significant negative wage–employment correlations.

Reporting this chapter's results, using employment as the cyclical variable, allows comparisons with the other studies which do so, and which are not, therefore, directly comparable with the tests in the previous chapter. Referring to the sample of such studies reported in Table 3.2: Bodkin only tested for the United States and Canada, finding weakly pro-cyclical wages. This is not radically different (given different techniques, data samples and so on) from the results reported here of a positive, although not statistically significant, relation for the US, and a negative, although not statistically significant, relation for Canada.

Sargent's (1978) counter-cyclical results are at odds with those reported here for the US, but are explained away by Geary & Kennan (1982a). Their results of no significant cyclical relations are consistent with the results reported here but largely by default, in that of the six countries from which data are tested in this chapter, the only two with strong wage–employment (negative) correlations are Japan and France, and neither of these countries is included in Geary & Kennan's international sample of 12 OECD countries. Of the other four countries for which results are reported in this chapter (and which are all included in Geary & Kennan's sample) only the UK shows any relation, and that is not at a high level of statistical significance. The other three countries all demonstrate independence between the non-trend wage and non-trend employment series which is what is also reported in Geary & Kennan.

It has already been argued, above, that Symons & Layard's (1984) demand for labour approach, which yields negative real wage effects, is not comparable with the direct testing of the actual pattern of cyclical wages over the business cycle. With that proviso the remainder of this section compares the numbers reported by Symons & Layard with those reported in this chapter.

Without the introduction of material costs, Symons & Layard actually find a more positive correlation between wages and employment than that reported in this chapter. In addition to their wage–

employment correlations being generally more positive, the order of the six countries (ranked from the most positive correlation to the most negative) is slightly different: a relatively minor difference is the case of West Germany (which in the tests reported in this chapter showed no significant correlation) which in the order switches places with the United States; the major difference in country order, which survives comparisons of the two sets of results with the addition of materials, is Canada which in the tests reported above showed no significant correlation, while in the results reported by Symons & Layard Canada shows a more negative correlation than any of the other countries.

This extreme result for Canada from Symons & Layard's tests is surprising, particularly as it puts the American and Canadian economies at polar opposites of the international comparisons. The pattern of coefficients reported for Canada which go to make up their result does appear strange. On contemporaneous and four lagged values of wages they have the following pattern of coefficients using either of their regression techniques: −ve, +ve, −ve, +ve, −ve; the latter two being precisely opposite and equal in both cases. The only other possible clue given in their paper for the Canadian results is that a different price series is used from the other five countries.

The major difference between the numbers reported by Symons & Layard and those reported in this chapter results from the different effects of the introduction of materials. Symons & Layard's materials measure is negatively related to employment, and its introduction also makes the wage–employment correlation more negative than previously. In contrast to this, the materials index tested in this chapter has no effect on the wage–employment correlation, although the materials index itself is positively correlated to employment (although not as positively correlated as it is with output). Thus the total direct cost index is less negatively related to employment than is the wage index alone.

Two more general points can be made concerning the relation which the Symons & Layard-type labour demand schedule literature bears to the cyclical wage literature. The first has been referred to in Chapter 3: namely, that the negative coefficient on wages in a labour demand schedule cannot necessarily be interpreted to mean that wages are counter-cyclical. Just as a negative coefficient on real material prices or strike behaviour cannot necessarily be interpreted to mean that material prices and strike behaviour are counter-cyclical. A related point concerns the different materials index constructed in the work reported in this book (the cost of materials used per hour's labour) from that used by Symons & Layard. The relevant statistic for deciding whether to employ the marginal worker in the boom would be the total direct costs of employing the marginal (hour of) labour. That turns out to be pro-cyclical due to the pro-cyclical movement of materials used per hour of labour. This directly pro-cyclical influence was actually purged from the series used in this work by simply using the trend of inputs per hour; (see Appendix 2). That such a purging of the pro-cyclical influence was necessary is in itself a contradiction of the counter-cyclical marginal productivity assumptions which underlie the neoclassical requirement for counter-cyclical wages.

4. Conclusion

In Chapter 3 it was argued that the appropriate correlation to test for an inquiry into the cyclical behaviour of wages is the output–wage correlation. The results of such tests were reported in Chapter 4. To test instead for possible wage–employment correlations would be likely to produce generally more negative coefficients because of the presumed negative correlation between non-trend fluctuations in employment not associated with the output cycle and non-trend wages. Such a negative (counter-cyclical) 'bias' was indeed found in the tests, the results of which are reported in this chapter.

The actual *pattern* of results is similar in Chapters 4 and 5. Relative changes in that pattern between countries do not appear directly related to the closeness or otherwise of the output–employment correlation.

Taken together the results do give a more comprehensive picture with which to compare the empirical literature on the cyclical behaviour of wages, as summarized in Chapter 3. The basic conclusion of Chapter 4—that no common pattern emerges— is fully vindicated by the results of this chapter.

6
Phases of the Cycle

Geary & Kennan (1982b) state that 'a serious concern is the stability of the results over alternative sample periods (in particular, preliminary tests show instability of the UK results)'. Such stability, and lack of it, has been tested for in the preceding two chapters (as reported in Chapter 4, Section 8 and, for the Chapter 5 data, Appendix 3) finding, like Geary & Kennan, the UK results to be particularly unstable; and is considered further in this chapter with reference to British quarterly data.

Chapter 2 outlined the theory behind the neoclassical belief that wages are (counter-)cyclical. It is this belief which has been tested, empirically, in the studies surveyed in Chapter 3. The results reported above suggest that the idea that there are economic forces necessitating a fixed cyclical pattern of product wages, is not supported by the evidence.

In addition to outlining the neoclassical model, Chapter 2 also incorporated those neoclassical assumptions within a wider framework incorporating Kaleckian assumptions. This wider model implied that while there may be no necessary cyclical pattern to wages, the influence which the output cycle has on wages (and vice versa) may in any case vary over the cycle, between different cycle phases. These implications of the theory as outlined in Chapter 2 are investigated in this chapter. The output cycles are divided into their different phases, with reference to the cycle turning points. It is thus possible to test for the existence of any hypothesized correlation within any given cycle phase alone taking data from across all cycles.

1. Methods

1.1 *Phase average trend*

The Phase Average Trend (PAT) method was used for picking the cyclical turning points required in order to separate the series out according to different cycle phases. This is a sophisticated method of both taking the trend of a series (and thus calculating the ratio to trend) and picking the turning points in that trend. See Appendix 5 for a discussion of the technique.

1.2 Dependent and independent variables

Changes in the ratio of actual output to trend output are taken as indicators of the cycle. The cyclical variable with which earnings are compared is, then, output rather than employment. The cycle is then divided into peaks, 'slumps', troughs and 'booms', where the 'slump' quarter is midway between the preceding peak and subsequent trough, and the 'boom' quarter is midway between the trough and the following peak. The cyclical turning points are summarized in Table 6.1. These are as selected by the PAT programme, with the exception of the final trough and peak, as explained in Appendix 5.

Table 6.1 Final turning points of the ratio to final trend

Troughs	Peaks
1948 II	
1952 III	1951 II
1958 IV	1955 I
1963 I	1960 I
1967 III	1965 I
1972 I	1969 IV
1975 II	1973 III
	1979 II

Table 6.2 shows the corresponding ratios to trend for output (Q), earnings (W), cost of non-labour direct costs ('materials') used per hour (MC), and the composite index of total (labour and non-labour) direct costs (DC). Tables 6.3–6.5 summarize the cyclical earnings information given in Table 6.2.

Earnings tend to be above trend earnings at the cycle peak, particularly if the first cycle, during which earnings fluctuate wildly, is ignored. Over the rest of the cycle, however, earnings seem to show no clear patterns.

Regression tests were performed not simply as in Chapter 4, but also against data falling only within each cycle phase. The results are reported in the following section.

2. Results

In order to include the cyclical behaviour of series in 1948, and 1979, all series constructed in this chapter were extended backwards and

Table 6.2 Ratios to trend of Q, W, MC and DC.

Cycle Phase	Quarter(s)	Q	W	MC	DC
Trough	1948 II	91.4	108.8	94.7	98.6
Boom	1949 IV	98.0	106.8−	91.0−	99.6+
Peak	1951 II	106.2	87.0−	123.0+	104.2+
Slump	1951 IV– 1952 I	101.3	88.5+	105.5−	98.6−
Trough	1952 III	92.0	94.7+	99.2−	98.5−
Boom	1953 IV	100.6	97.0+	94.6−	97.4−
Peak	1955 I	106.7	101.6+	101.0+	101.6+
Slump	1956 IV	100.7	101.1−	105.4+	102.4+
Trough	1958 III	94.4	99.99−	98.7−	99.2−
Boom	1959 II	99.6	99.5−	99.6+	99.5+
Peak	1960 I	104.8	100.03+	101.5+	100.3+
Slump	1961 III	100.6	101.6+	99.3−	101.0+
Trough	1963 I	94.5	99.6−	98.4−	99.4−
Boom	1964 I	100.2	100.8+	101.4+	101.0+
Peak	1965 I	103.3	101.0+	100.8−	101.0
Slump	1966 II	101.1	102.6+	102.4+	102.3+
Trough	1967 III	97.0	100.6−	97.0−	99.5−
Boom	1968 III– 1968 IV	101.9	98.7−	101.6+	99.9+
Peak	1969 IV	102.6	98.3−	106.8+	101.6+
Slump	1970 IV– 1971 I	99.2	99.4+	100.2−	99.5−
Trough	1972 I	93.3	103.5+	90.3−	99.4−
Boom	1972 IV	101.2	101.7−	89.1−	97.3−
Peak	1973 III	105.2	101.2−	100.7+	101.2+
Slump	1974 II– 1974 III	102.8	95.5−	106.7+	99.6−
Trough	1975 II	94.1	99.0+	94.5−	97.4−
Boom	1977 II	96.3	92.9−	103.4+	97.5+
Peak	1979 II	103.7	107.8+	101.0−	104.0+

Notes
1. +/− beside each ratio indicates whether it is greater or less than the previous value. A strictly pro-cyclical movement would begin, with these series, with '++' followed by '−−', '++' and so on.
2. Where there are an even number of quarters between peaks and troughs the boom or slump is taken as the average of the middle two quarters.
3. Figures are given to one decimal place except where two are necessary to indicate above or below trend (simply for convenience of tables 6.4 and 6.5).

Table 6.3 Direction of movement.

	Product Earnings: W					
	--	++	-+	+-	+	-
Trough to Peak	3	2	2	0 :	4	3
Trough to Boom					2	5
Boom to Peak					4	3
Peak to Trough	1	2	1	2 :	2	4
Peak to Slump					4	2
Slump to Trough					3	3

Table 6.4 Total Sample.

	Relation to trend		average value	normalized*
	above	below		
Troughs	3	4	100.9	101.4
Booms	3	4	99.6	100.1
Peaks	5	2	99.6	100.1
Slumps	3	3	98.1	98.5

* 'normalized' to average 100.0

Table 6.5 Sample minus first cycle.

	Relation to trend		average value
	above	below	
Troughs	2	4	99.6
Booms	2	4	98.4
Peaks	5	1	101.7
Slumps	3	2	100.0

forwards by extrapolating the trend movements to allow deviations from trend to be calculated. Unlike previous chapters, therefore, no observations are lost through detrending. The series were seasonally adjusted by either seasonal dummies or by a common seasonal adjustment procedure; the results being not significantly altered. When raw data were used the seasonal variations were clearly affecting the coefficients on lagged variables.

The regression tests on these data series produced similar results to those reported for the UK in Chapter 4: over the whole sample period taken together neither earnings nor material costs (nor the composite direct cost index) were significantly correlated with output.

The negative correlation between wage costs and material costs (both in product terms) reported in Chapter 4, which there proved not to be statistically significant, now is so at the 5% level of both the t-statistic and F-tests:

$$W = 0.11.MC$$
$$(2.53)*$$

$\bar{R}^2 = 0.041$; DW $= 1.84$ (indicates no autocorrelation); SER $= 1.76$; F-stat $= 6.39$†
Cochrane–Orcutt iterative technique (CORC) 1948 I–1979 IV; Constant term not statistically significant.

It was, in fact, these quarterly data (which were taken back to the first quarter of 1948, including the deviation from trend series, by extrapolating the trend series) which first suggested that non-labour costs might help explain the behaviour of labour costs over the cycle; that the behaviour of labour costs over the cycle might depend, first, on the relation of total direct costs over the cycle, and, second, on the relative movements of the two component parts of the direct cost series—labour costs and non-labour (materials) costs. This hypothesis was suggested by the fact that the huge fall in earnings between the 1948 II trough and 1951 II peak was not due to the fact that it was a cyclical expansion but, rather, to the behaviour of world material prices over this period. The implication is that the boom in material prices forced a corresponding fall in labour costs (wages).

2.1 Cycle phases

Having determined the cyclical turning points, the data series were divided into cycle phases so that all data from, say, a peak to a trough phase, could be pooled. The data series were divided up in two different ways, and each time all regression tests were repeated on the resulting data series. First the series were divided into two composite series corresponding to, first, all trough to peak years and, second, all peak to trough years. Next the series were divided between four more specific cycle phases: trough to boom, boom to peak, peak to slump, and slump to trough.

The above results held across all cycles within each of the six cycle phase divisions: pooling the data from all cycles but corresponding to only one cycle phase in turn, neither earnings nor material costs nor the composite direct cost index were significantly correlated with output. As discussed in the previous chapter, however, the British results are heavily influenced by the negative wage–output (and wage–employment) correlation in later years. All regression tests were therefore repeated for data from the trough of 1952 III to the trough of 1967 III.

2.2 *1952 III to 1967 III*

The results from regressing wages on output for the data from 1952 III to 1967 III are reported in Table 6.6. The Cochrane–Orcutt (CORC) procedure was used. The overall correlation remains not statistically significant. Splitting the cycle into two phases—from trough to peak, and peak to trough—this lack of statistical significance applies to the upswing but not to the downswing. The latter demonstrates a statistically significant pro-cyclical relation. Thus, depending on the hypothesized direction of causation, reduced output tends to reduce wages, or reduced wages tend to reduce output, while increased wages appears to have no statistically significant relation to output (and vice versa). Splitting each of such phases into two, of the resulting four cycle phases, three demonstrate similarly non-significant correlations, while the fourth phase, of trough to boom (that is the first half of the upswing) demonstrates a statistically significant positive correlation.

This tendency for product wages to accompany, or be accompanied by, increased output in the beginning of the upturn, but not during the second half (leading up to the downturn) does not seem consistent with assumptions of profits squeezed by wages choking off the boom; although such a profit squeeze might result from slower productivity growth as the boom continues. The increased wages, whether or not they *cause* the increased output, at least do not appear to choke off such output growth. And whatever leads to the cyclical upturn being choked off, it does not appear to be increased wages.

3. Conclusion

While the tests reported in this chapter required a large number of regression equation estimations (over different sample periods), the

Table 6.6 Wages regressed on output over different cycle phases

Phase $N; F$	Coefficient (t-stat.)	$\bar{R}^2$ DW	SER F-stat.
All 60; $F(1,58)$	0.11 (1.86)	0.040 1.83	0.91 3.46
Trough to Peak 22; $F(1,20)$	0.02 (0.14)	−ve 1.96	0.88 0.02
Peak to Trough 38; $F(1,36)$	0.17* (2.29)	0.103 1.49	0.93 5.26†
Trough to Boom 11; $F(1,9)$	0.35* (2.38)	0.386 1.55	0.80 5.65†
Boom to Peak 11; $F(1,9)$	−0.09 (0.45)	−ve 0.92	0.98 0.20
Peak to Slump 19; $F(1,17)$	−0.08 (0.40)	−ve 0.93	1.17 0.16
Slump to Trough 19; $F(1,17)$	0.12 (1.40)	0.051 1.88	0.55 1.97

* Significant at the 5% level.
† Significant at the 5% level.
CORC 1952 III–1967 III; DW statistics are indeterminate for 'peak to trough' but indicate autocorrelation for 'boom to peak' and for 'peak to slump'; constant term insignificant.

different patterns which emerged did so within the statistically non-cyclical wage–output (and direct-cost–output) correlation indicated by the data series as a whole. These statistically non-significant results have not, therefore, been reproduced in tables of results. Instead the following patterns are described.

With respect to the post-Second World War British data the earnings series is clearly subject to very different influences over time. The period for which we might predict the influence of the output cycle to be significant is for the trough of 1952 III to the trough of 1967 III. Prior to this, the overriding influence appears to be the explosion in world commodity prices. Since 1967 III there has been a succession of 'non-cyclical' influences on earnings including devaluation, deflation, incomes policies and material price shocks (particularly oil).

Thus if there are reasons for us to expect the output cycle to have an effect on the behaviour of earnings we would expect this effect to be more significant in periods when other influences are less significant. Regression results did not, however, indicate a clear increase in significance of the cyclical wage–output correlation. Within this 1952 III to 1967 III sample, though, different correlations were found between different phases of the cycle. The only such statistically significant correlations proved to be positive.

7
Individual Industries and the Aggregate Economy

Geary & Kennan (1982a, p. 865) refer to unpublished work on disaggregated data as follows:

> In related work (Kennan 1979), the Haugh technique has been applied to monthly data, using the WPI deflator, for the US (1947–77) and Canada (1961–77). For both countries, strong contemporaneous correlations were found between the innovations in real wages and employment, and independence was therefore rejected. Only three of nine two-digit Canadian industries studied showed this positive contemporaneous relationship, however, and independence was accepted in five of the nine industries. These disaggregated results provide strong evidence against Sargent's hypothesis of a stable dynamic labour demand curve, since Sargent's model of profit maximisation by an individual firm should work better with disaggregated data.

While Geary & Kennan find no neoclassical counter-cyclical relation at the disaggregated level, nevertheless, given the pro-cyclical relation they report at the aggregate level the non-cyclical results at the disaggregated level are in the right empirical direction for neoclassical theory, albeit not strong enough.

The neoclassical prediction of counter-cyclical wages would be expected to apply with greater certainty to individual industries than to the aggregate of manufacturing industry, being derived from a diminishing marginal product of labour at the individual (firm and industry) level. The aim of this chapter is to test whether wages are more counter-cyclical (less pro-cyclical) at the industry level as compared with the aggregate level of manufacturing industry.

Quite aside from testing this hypothesis there is another reason why aggregate studies should test their results against industry data and that is to investigate the possibility of aggregation effects. For example a cyclical behaviour of wages established at an aggregate level may obscure quite different wage patterns between industries. Further, if there were such different wage patterns across industries, the aggregate result may be affected by changing percentages of total output being accounted for by each industry over the cycle. Again, shifts in aggregate cyclical behaviour over time may be due to shifts at industry level or,

100 INDIVIDUAL INDUSTRIES AND THE AGGREGATE ECONOMY

instead, to relative changes in total output (and employment) shares between industries over time.

Two further hypotheses are developed and tested later in the chapter. The first concerns the relative correlation of, on the one hand, *industry* output with industry wages; and, on the other, *aggregate* output with industry wages. The second concerns the industry output–wage correlation in aggregate booms versus aggregate slumps.

1. Methods

Annual data from 1948 to 1974 inclusive were taken on output, money wages per hour, and a price index for the price of value added, for seven British manufacturing industries: chemicals (including petrol) (C); textiles, leather and clothing (T); stone, etc. (S); paper, print and publishing (P); engineering and shipbuilding (E); vehicles (V) and metal manufacture (M). The data series are discussed further in Appendix 4, but the following points should be made before discussing the methods used. No attempt was made to construct series for the price of non-labour inputs used per hour for any of the industries, as had been done for the manufacturing sector as a whole. This had two implications for the data series used. First, the appropriate index for prices was the price of value added rather than the price of total output. Second, the series were not tested for after the oil shock of the early 1970s: without being able to take account (as had been done above when testing for the aggregate manufacturing sector) of changes in non-labour input prices, it would not be sensible to have included the later values—particularly for industries such as 'chemicals including petrol'.

The statistical and econometric methods used were as described in previous chapters. All tests in this chapter were rerun against employment in place of output, but the pattern of results was similar; and the sign and significance of the coefficients were in line with the relation between the Chapter 4 and Chapter 5 results. In this case the correlation of wages with output was significantly positive, while the correlation with employment was not statistically significant.

2. Results

For each of the seven industries in turn, and for aggregate manufacturing, the percentage deviation of both output and product wages were plotted together over time. The two series were also graphed against each other, again for each of the seven industries in turn. These plots and graphs tended to suggest a positive correlation between the two series.

The percentage deviation from trend of product wages were then regressed on the percentage deviation of output from trend, for each of the seven industries in turn, as well as for the corresponding series for aggregate manufacturing (A). The results, which are reported in Table 7.1 indicate that product wages at the industry level are positively correlated with that industry's output.

Table 7.1 Wages regressed on (industry) output

Industry	Coefficient (t-stat.)	$\bar{R}^2$ DW	SER $F(1,20)$
C	0.78* (2.59)	0.213 2.15	3.87 6.69†
T	0.40* (2.25)	0.161 2.41	3.42 5.04†
S	0.45* (2.30)	0.170 1.72	3.08 5.30†
P	0.21* (2.54)	0.206 1.01	1.96 6.46†
E	0.90*** (4.07)	0.426 2.28	3.23 16.6‡
V	0.63** (3.78)	0.331 1.81	3.67 11.4‡
M	0.25 (1.78)	0.093 2.08	3.47 3.16
A	0.31** (3.37)	0.330 2.08	1.12 11.3‡

* Significant at the 5% level; ** 1% level; *** 0.1% level.
† Significant at the 5% level; ‡ 1% level.
HILU 1950–72; DW statistics indicate non-autocorrelation except Print which (unlike Textiles, and Vehicles) had shown non-autocorrelation when originally estimated with OLSQ:

                        0.26*   0.231   2.28
                        (2.76)   2.18   7.62†;

constant term insignificant.

The regression equations were re-estimated with the inclusion of leads and lags on output (both with and without contemporaneous output) but the general pattern of results was not significantly altered.

102 INDIVIDUAL INDUSTRIES AND THE AGGREGATE ECONOMY

This pro-cyclical behaviour of product wages contrasts with the previously reported lack of a statistically significant correlation at the aggregate level of British manufacturing. The regression tests were therefore re-estimated on the Chapter 4, 6 and 7 data over the same years. The seemingly different results turn out to be due to the previously discussed question of the role of non-labour direct ('materials') costs. Since in this chapter only labour costs are being considered, the appropriate price deflator is an index of the price of value added, rather than total output. Starting with similar nominal wage behaviour in each case, it is the different cyclical patterns of the two price series (although themselves very positively correlated) which result in the more procyclical pattern of product wages in value added terms.

It is not the sign of the estimated correlation coefficient with which the tests in this chapter are concerned, however: that having already been established in Chapter 4 (the non-cyclical results for the United Kingdom from Chapter 4 being compatible with the pro-cyclical results reported in this chapter with different time periods and price deflators). Rather, what has been shown is that the failure of the UK data in Chapter 4 to have shown a statistically significant counter-cyclical pattern was *not* due to some fallacy of composition: the correlations at industry level were similar to those at the aggregate level.

3. Aggregate output and industry wage

The industry-level wage series were now regressed on *both* the respective industry-level output series *and* total manufacturing output. While the neoclassical prediction of counter-cyclical product wages should apply more directly at the industry level, there is no necessary reason why this should not be directly reflected in the aggregate behaviour. Thus the idea, cited above from Geary & Kennan, that the neoclassical negative correlation 'should work better with disaggregated data' should, to be totally fair to the neoclassical case, read 'at least as well, if not better'.

What should be true for the neoclassical view that a diminishing marginal product of labour (mpl) necessitates (or causes or is caused by) reduced product wages, is that the negative correlation between industry-level wages and aggregate output should be merely the result of such a relation at the industry level.

Alternative models of cyclical wage behaviour (including in this term models of non-cyclical wage behaviour) such as discussed in Chapter 2 may imply this pattern of causation (with the causal mechanism being the spreading of overhead costs at the disaggregate level), but do not necessarily. Aggregate output fluctuations could, according to such assumptions, have a direct effect on industry-level wages, and, consequently, a part at least of any correlation between industry wages and industry output could be simply capturing this other correlation

The general (Kaleckian-type) model posed in Chapter 2 as a broad alternative to the neoclassical one would predict positive correlations to be generated independently by, on the one hand, aggregate output and industry wages, and, on the other hand, industry output and industry wages. Aggregate output would enter the industry wage picture from both the supply and demand sides. The higher is aggregate output (in the cycle), the lower is unemployment (and the threat of unemployment). Hence the higher will be union wage demands. On the supply side, the greater will be labour shortage and hence companies' (and industries') willingness to agree to the wage demands in order to keep their work-force from being attracted elsewhere. Both these effects will be reflected at the industry level with an expansion of that industry's output. The former effect, operating via unemployment, will apply specifically to the industry to the extent that employment is industry-specific (for skill, regional, or other reasons). The latter effect, of labour shortages, will apply to industries in relation to how full their order books are. In general terms this will influence the extent to which they are prepared to 'bid up' wages to maintain, or expand, their workforce. It may also influence their willingness to meet any wage claims rather that risk industrial action.

None of these (aggregate or industry) influences on money wages necessarily affect product wages, but various mechanisms will influence this. At the aggregate level these would tend to include factors such as international competition. At the disaggregate level the ability to pay increased (labour or non-labour) costs without passing them on in the form of increased prices may vary with output. If over the expansion the industry faces constant marginal costs and is able to spread overheads over an increased output, then the ability to absorb increased money wages in the form of increased product wages would tend to produce a positive correlation between industry product wage and industry output.

To consider the (possibility of this) joint influence of industry output and aggregate output on industry product wages, both output terms were included as regressors. The results are reported in Table 7.2. The pattern of results was similar with regression equations including leading and lagged terms. The latter results are not, therefore, reported.

The obvious problem in attempting to estimate the above regression equations is the high correlation to be expected between the two regressors—the deviation of an industry's output from trend and the deviation of total manufacturing output from trend. This expectation was confirmed by plots of the two series. Thus the results reported in

Table 7.2 Wages regressed on industry and aggregate output

	Coefficient and t-stat.		$\bar{R}^2$ DW	SER $F(2,19)$
	Ind. Q (t-stat.)	Aggreg. Q (t-stat.)		
C	1.02	−0.27	0.177	3.96
	(1.36)	(0.35)	2.12	3.09
T	0.53	−0.22	0.125	3.50
	(1.45)	(0.42)	2.43	2.37
S	0.78**	−0.61	0.247	2.94
	(2.94)	(1.74)	1.72	4.20†
P	0.09	0.23	0.144	1.99
	(0.54)	(0.72)	0.95	2.61
E	0.83**	0.19	0.408	3.28
	(3.30)	(0.63)	2.22	7.79‡
V	0.26	0.83	0.404	3.46
	(0.97)	(1.85)	1.53	7.68‡
M	0.20	0.14	0.049	3.55
	(0.80)	(0.27)	2.06	1.46

** Significant at the 1% level.
† Significant at the 5% level; ‡ 1% level.
HILU 1950–72; DW statistics indicate non-autocorrelation except for P, indicating serial correlation, & V which is indeterminate; constant term insignificant.

Table 7.2 would be expected to suffer from multicollinearity. That this is the case can be seen both from the regression statistics reported in Table 7.2 and by comparing the results reported in Table 7.2 with those reported in Table 7.1 when wages were regressed on industry output alone.

'Vehicles' is the most glaring example of an equation with a high explanatory power (according to the equation's F-statistic, and $\bar{R}^2$) and yet no statistically significant coefficients. Thus the explanatory variables do jointly determine the behaviour of the dependent variable (or at least are correlated with the latter). The problem is in isolating the individual effects (correlations).

In addition, with the two explanatory variables having a high positive correlation, the estimators would be subject to opposing biases. That this effect is operating can be seen by comparing the results from Table 7.2 with not only the results from Table 7.1, of wages regressed on industry output alone, but also with the results of regressing wages on total manufacturing industry output alone which are reported in Table 7.3. The coefficients on manufacturing output now all become

Table 7.3 Wages regressed on aggregate output

	Coefficient (t-stat.)	$\bar{R}^2$ DW	SER $F(1,20)$
C	0.69* (2.11)	0.142 2.23	4.04 4.46†
T	0.44 (1.66)	0.077 2.33	3.59 2.74
S	0.12 (0.41)	−ve 1.82	3.45 0.16
P	0.38* (2.33)	0.174 0.91	1.95 5.43†
E	0.64 (1.93)	0.115 2.15	4.01 3.73
V	1.15*** (3.92)	0.406 1.46	3.46 15.3‡
M	0.46 (1.58)	0.066 2.03	3.52 2.49
A	0.31** (3.37)	0.330 2.08	1.12 11.3‡

* Significant at the 5% level; ** 1% level; *** 0.1% level.
† Significant at the 5% level; ‡ 1% level.
HILU 1950–72; DW statistics indicate non-autocorrelation except P; constant term insignificant.

positive, and statistically significant (as are the regression equations) in three of the seven cases.

However, since we know that the explanatory variables are not orthogonal it is not satisfactory to rely on such simple regressions of the dependent variable on each of the explanatory variables in turn. It could be that the seeming relation of industry wages with aggregate output in such a simple regression is nothing other than a reflection of the industry-level effect, given the correlation between industry output and aggregate output. In other words the apparent correlation of aggregate output with industry wages may be simply picking up the correlation of the wage series with that element of aggregate output which is correlated with (though not necessarily totally accounted for by) output fluctuations of the industry concerned.

This problem is a special case of collinearity between two explanatory variables: a collinearity due to composition effects, one series being a composite of a number of others one of which is the other explanatory variable. Assuming the collinear output movement is correlated with earnings, adjusting one or other of the output series to remove the multicollinearity will simply remove that part of the explanatory power of the series being adjusted. Such an adjustment was made to the aggregate output series. This is simply to tackle the multicollinearity. The resulting loss of explanatory power of the aggregate output series is not being presented as representing a more 'genuine' relation but, rather, is the price paid for having no entirely satisfactory method of removing the statistical effects of what is a real (multicollinear) economic correlation.

For each industry, the series for aggregate manufacturing was regressed on the series for that industry's output in order to establish the correlation between the industry output and aggregate output, thus:

$$Q = bq_i + v_i \qquad (7.1)$$

where Q is aggregate manufacturing output; q_i is industry output; and v_i is that component of Q orthogonal to q_i. The resulting coefficients indicated the proportion of the industry level output series correlated with the aggregate series: 0.86, 0.55, 0.57, 0.46, 0.34, 0.48, and 0.40 for the seven industries respectively. By subtracting the estimated aggregate output from the actual a series was derived (v_i in equation (7.1) above) for that portion of aggregate output fluctuations uncorrelated with output fluctuations at the industry level.

For each industry, then, the industry-level wage series was regressed on both the corresponding industry-level output and the series for the component of output fluctuations uncorrelated with the fluctuations in industry output:

$$w_i = fq_i + gv_i \qquad (7.2)$$

The latter two regressands are, of course, now totally uncorrelated so that the problem of multicollinearity has been eliminated in the sense that individual simple regressions will now give the same information as will the multiple regression. The problem now reappears in the form of the reduced significance of the series from which the information has been lost in the adjustment process. The results are given in Table 7.4. Comparing the results reported here with those in Tables 7.1–7.3, it can be seen that orthogonalizing the explanatory variables simply results in a reparameterization, whereby the coefficient on industry output reflects not only the effect of industry output itself (as in Table 7.2), but also the effect of industry output proxying for that part of aggregate manufacturing output with which the industry output is correlated (as in Table 7.1) while the coefficient on manufacturing output reflects (as in Table 7.2) only that part of the manufacturing

INDIVIDUAL INDUSTRIES AND THE AGGREGATE ECONOMY 107

Table 7.4 W regressed on industry, and adjusted aggregate, output

	Coefficient on		$\bar{R}^2$	SER
			DW	$F(2,19)$
	industry (t-stat)	adj. man (t-stat.)		
C	0.78*	−0.27	0.177	3.96
	(2.51)	(0.35)	2.12	3.09
T	0.41*	−0.22	0.125	3.50
	(2.23)	(0.42)	2.43	2.37
S	0.45*	−0.61	0.247	2.94
	(2.42)	(1.74)	1.72	4.20†
P	0.19*	0.23	0.144	1.99
	(2.23)	(0.72)	0.95	2.61
E	0.89***	0.19	0.408	3.28
	(3.98)	(0.63)	2.22	7.79‡
V	0.63**	0.83	0.404	3.46
	(3.57)	(1.85)	1.53	7.68‡
M	0.25	0.14	0.049	3.55
	(1.73)	(0.27)	2.06	1.46

* Significant at the 5% level; ** 1% level; *** 0.1% level.
† Significant at the 5% level; ‡ 1% level.
HILU 1950–72; DW statistics indicate non-autocorrelation except for P, indicating serial correlation, & V which is indeterminate; constant term insignificant.

output series which is orthogonal to the individual industry series (v_i in equation (7.1)). Thus:

$$w_i = hq_i + gQ \tag{7.3}$$
$$= h(cQ + u_i) + g(bq_i + v_i) \tag{7.4}$$
where $q_i = cQ + u_i$ \hfill (7.5)

and the parameters h and g are those reported in Table 7.2, while the reparameterization involved in Table 7.4 is as follows:

$$w_i = hq_i + g(bq_i + v_i) \tag{7.6}$$
$$= (h + gb)q_i + gv_i \tag{7.7}$$

where the coefficient f in equation (7.2) consists of $(h + gb)$. Similarly, then, were the orthogonalization achieved by adjusting the individual industry output series (by running the regression of equation (7.5), the reparameterization would result in the coefficients on q_i (now u_i) and Q being h and $(g + fc)$ respectively.

To conclude on the results reported this far (and in Tables 7.1–7.4, specifically): the significant positive correlation between industry-level wages and aggregate output fluctuations appears to be (statistically rather than causally) a correlation between the industry-level wage series and the collinear movement of the respective industry-level output series and the aggregate output series. This makes regression analysis limited to that which has so far been stated: any adjustments for multicollinearity tend to remove that from which any additional information would be, in theory, forthcoming. The problem which regression tests have in allocating the variation in the regressand among the (collinear) regressors is replaced with the problem of arbitrarily adjusting one or other of the regressors in order to orthogonalize them. In order to consider further the effect of aggregate output fluctuations on disaggregate wage series (and on the correlations, over the cycle, between industry-level output and industry-level wages) a different approach was adopted, as reported in the following section.

4. Wage–output correlation and the aggregate cycle

As discussed above, different theoretical assumptions lead to different expectations of whether or not cyclical output fluctuations will be associated with cyclical wage fluctuations, and, if so, the nature of any such association. Different such assumptions also imply different foundations of a wage–output correlation, whether micro or macro.

The neoclassical marginal product of labour (mpl) foundation of cyclical wage behaviour operates at a micro level. As the firm (industry) cyclically expands output the mpl, and therefore the product wage, will be cyclically reduced. This relation should hold regardless of aggregate, macro, behaviour. The macro is simply the aggregate of the micro foundations.

The general alternative view of the economy outlined previously would expect not only different micro foundations of macro relations but would also expect the micro relations to be affected by the macro. Thus the behaviour of an industry's product wages during a cyclical expansion of the industry's output could not be predicted without knowing the corresponding behaviour of the cycle in aggregate output. The latter may, for example, affect the relative bargaining power of the employers and employees in the industry concerned (as would the industry's cyclical predicament).

This alternative formulation of the hypothesis of whether the cyclical wage–output correlation at the industry level will be independent of the aggregate cycle allows an additional comparison to be made of the two models of the economy. Thus while previous studies have tested the neoclassical (non-neoclassical) hypothesis according to whether aggregate cyclical wage behaviour is counter-cyclical (non-counter-cyclical), whatever the results of the literature to date are taken to be, they have been rationalized by neoclassicals within a neoclassical model. Thus Tatom (1980, p. 385) 'accepts' that 'One of the more settled facts about the cyclical behaviour of the US economy is that real wages are pro-cyclical, rising during expansions and falling during recessions'. But he goes on to reconcile pro-cyclical wages with the neoclassical diminishing returns to labour hypothesis. Tatom's cyclical wage theory would, as with the standard neoclassical theory, apply whether aggregate output was in a cyclical boom or a cyclical slump. Therefore aggregate output should add nothing to the cyclical wage–output relation at the industry level. But also the same disaggregate relation should be found whether tested against all data, or only data from one or other of the upswing and downswing. Thus this section tests for the independence of the cyclical wage–output correlation from the aggregate output cycle.

Setting out whether the time series for output and earnings are above or below their own trend for each of the seven industries as well as for aggregate manufacturing indicates, as would be expected, that the industry output series are broadly in line with each other and with aggregate manufacturing output. This restricts the ability to compare contrasting industry and total manufacturing output behaviour. For each industry in turn, the output expansions were divided between those occurring during aggregate expansions and those occurring during aggregate contractions, and similarly for all industry downturns. Pooling the results over the seven industries over the 22 years gives 154 observations. The correspondence between industry booms and slumps, and aggregate booms and slumps, is given in Table 7.5. The four numbers in the top left hand corner of the table indicate, starting with the '59' and moving clockwise, the number of industry expansions

Table 7.5 Booms/slumps in aggregate/disaggregate output

Aggregate level	Industry level			
	Booms	Slumps		
Booms	59	11	:	70
Slumps	13	71	:	84
	72	82	:	154

occurring during aggregate booms, the number of industry contractions occurring during aggregate booms, the number of industry contractions occurring during industry contractions, and the number of industry expansions occurring during aggregate contractions. The proportion of these observations for which product wages were above trend are given in Table 7.6. These conditional probabilities give the percentage probability of wages being above trend in each of the four possible states. It can be seen, for example, that the likelihood of wages being above trend in an industry contraction depends heavily on the state of the aggregate economy.

Table 7.6 Conditional probabilities (per cent)

Aggregate level	Industry level	
	Booms	Slumps
Booms	71	64
Slumps	62	34

5. Conclusion

One possible explanation for the failure of the international data to indicate statistically significant negative correlations between cyclical output and cyclical earnings for all countries (for example the United Kingdom) would be the presence of aggregation effects blurring what might be a statistically significant negative correlation at the industry level. The results reported in Section 2 above do not support such a hypothesis. The failure of the British data in Chapter 4 to have shown a statistically significant counter-cyclical pattern was *not* due to some fallacy of composition: the correlations at industry level were similar to those at the aggregate level.

Section 3 attempted to identify whether any correlation of industry-level earnings with cyclical output is with aggregate or industry-level output fluctuations, and found both to be the case, the two series (disaggregate and aggregate output) being correlated and it being this collinear component (at least of the aggregate series) with which wages move (in a pro-cyclical direction—at least for British 1948–1974 data of nominal wages deflated by the value added price).

Finally, the industry output cycle's correlation with cyclical earnings was tested for consistency over the aggregate cycle and appeared not to be totally independent of the latter.

8
The History of the Cyclical Wage Debate

It has been demonstrated in previous chapters that, to the extent that product wages *are* correlated with the output cycle (and it has been shown that there is *no* such consistent correlation across countries), there is no reason to expect that correlation to be stable over time. Either such correlations are simply contingent rather than necessary, or else the economic assumptions underlying any particular necessary correlation are time-specific (as well as country-specific) and therefore such assumptions cannot be taken as necessarily of any relevance to the future behaviour of economic variables.

Thus the British data, for example, indicated a counter-cyclical correlation of the output and product wage series during the period around the Korean War, a correlation clearly caused by sharp fluctuations in the price of non-labour manufacturing inputs (in a pro-cyclical direction, causing a sharp pro-cyclical movement in the price of manufacturing output, causing a counter-cyclical movement in the product wage). This pattern (clearly the result of factors other than the output and product wage series themselves) was superceded by several business cycles relatively free from such exogenous influences, during which product wages moved pro-cyclically. Since then this correlation, too, has broken down.

Comparing such post-war results on British data with pre-war results, the well-known counter-cyclical pattern of product wages over the 1929–37 cycle was clearly not the result of any requirement of the British economy such as would operate over the twentieth century taken as a whole. The 1929–37 pattern has clearly not held consistently since.

Bernanke & Powell (1984) find a similar failure of the output and product wage series to display a historically consistent pattern with American data, finding (lagged and weak) counter-cyclical product wage behaviour before the war and (in line with the American results reported in Chapter 4) pro-cyclical product wages after the war.

The studies which have tested historical data fall largely into two categories. First are those which are interested in how wages actually behaved in some particular cycle: most notably the 1929–37 cycle in the United Kingdom—see Worswick (1984c) and the papers by him and others in Bank of England (1984a) and National Institute (1984). Second are those such as Bernanke & Powell which are interested in how the cyclical pattern of wages has altered over time—see Sachs

(1980), Taylor (1984), Gordon, Weisskopf & Bowles (1983), and Schor (1985).

The results from testing the British data compiled for this chapter showed little correlation for the inter-war period, although the counter-cyclical pattern between 1929 and 1937 was evident. The hypothesis of Gordon *et al.* of pro-cyclical wages in 'normal' cycles (during prosperous long-swings), and counter-cyclical wages in long-swing recessions, was tested and, while the results certainly did not contradict the hypothesis, the results were not considered sufficient to establish a long-swing mechanism to be at work, and hence are not reported here.

The bulk of studies reporting results from testing historical data are heavily criticized by Solow (1985, p. 330):

> As I inspect current work in economic history, I have the sinking feeling that a lot of it looks exactly like the kind of economic analysis I have just finished caricaturing: the same integrals, the same regressions, the same substitution of t-ratios for thought. Apart from anything else, it is no fun reading the stuff any more. Far from offering the economic theorist a widened range of perceptions, this sort of economic history gives back to the theorist the same routine gruel that the economic theorist gives to the historian. Why should I believe, when it is applied to thin eighteenth-century data, something that carries no conviction when it is done with more ample twentieth-century data?

He argues that because of the path down which economics has gone, economic theory learns nothing from economic history.

Rather than report the results of repeating the previous tests on this chapter's data, then, the issue of inference, and how theory relates to empirical observations, is considered by looking, historically, at the role played by inference, and how observations did relate to theory. The following section, then, uses historical British data to retrace, following Keynes (1939), the historiography of the neoclassical assumptions.

1. Historiography

Commenting on criticisms from Dunlop (1938) and Tarshis (1939), Keynes (1939) stated that his 1936 view—'this common belief'— needed to be reconsidered, and that he had, in the *General Theory*, accepted, without taking care to check the facts for himself, a belief which had been widely held by British economists. He traced this belief to a generalization made by Marshall from the 1880–6 data[1]. Extending the data to 1914, Keynes reported the pro-cyclical pattern shown in Table 8.1, save for the initial 1880–6 cycle. From this, Keynes concludes (1939, p. 38) that 'we have been living all these years on a generalisation which held good, by exception, in the years 1880–86, which was the formative period in Marshall's thought in this matter, but has never once held good in the fifty years since he crystallised it!' This chapter tests for the pre-1914 changes in the cyclical pattern of real wages, setting out the 1855–1913 data, and the 1880–6 cycle within that.

Table 8.1 Keynes's description of cyclical wage behaviour

	Cyclical Phase	Real Wages
1880–1884	Recovery	Falling
1884–1886	Depression	Rising
1886–1890	Recovery	Rising
1890–1896	Depression	Falling
1896–1899	Recovery	Rising
1899–1905	Depression	Falling
1905–1907	Recovery	Rising
1907–1910	Depression	Falling
1910–1914	Recovery	Rising

The money wage series was deflated by an index for the price of the principal industrial products. Table 8.2 shows the percentage deviation of this product wage series from trend at each cyclical peak and trough. The direction of movement of the wage deviation is also recorded. The product wage (W) can be seen to move in a strong counter-cyclical fashion from the peak of 1877 through to the trough of 1886 (roughly the years looked at by Marshall). This is confirmed by the appropriate regression equation:

$$W = -0.25 - 0.68Q \qquad (8.1)$$
$$(0.36) \quad (3.16)$$
$$1876–1886\ (N = 11);\ \bar{R}^2 = 0.474;\ DW = 2.63$$

[1] Keynes (1939) refers to Marshall's data as being from the 1880–6 cycle. The output data used in this chapter suggest, however, that this cycle began in 1879, and this also agrees with other standard references, from Rostow (1947) to Matthews, Feinstein and Odling-Smee (1982).

Table 8.2 Deviation of product wages from trend

Cycle Phase	Year	Q	W	Change
Peak	1860	2.7	−0.1	
Trough	1863	−3.8	−6.3	Decrease
Peak	1866	5.3	1.7	Increase
Trough	1869	−6.9	7.0	Increase
Peak	1871	3.8	1.2	Decrease
Trough	1873	−0.1	−5.7	Decrease
Peak	1877	1.1	−2.8	Increase
Trough	1879	−6.6	5.1	Increase
Peak	1883	3.8	−2.7	Decrease
Trough	1886	−5.9	4.4	Increase
Peak	1891	3.1	3.0	Decrease
Trough	1893	−4.8	−4.2	Decrease
Peak	1896	1.5	−1.8	Increase
Trough	1897	−0.4	5.0	Increase
Peak	1899	2.5	−5.4	Decrease
Trough	1904	−3.0	4.1	Increase
Peak	1907	4.8	−8.1	Decrease
Trough	1908	−3.5	11.4	Increase
Peak	1913	0.9	0.4	Decrease

In contrast, the pre-1887 data show no cyclical relation (the value of the $\bar{R}^2$ statistic for the appropriate regression showing that the output deviation fails to explain any of the movement in the wage deviation).

While Keynes, and Dunlop, contrast the counter-cyclical behaviour of the Marshall data with the subsequent pro-cyclical relation, it can be seen from Table 8.2 that the W series does not appear to conform to this, and is in marked contrast to Table 8.1 from Keynes. The appropriate regression confirms the post-1886 counter-cyclical relation suggested by the pattern of the wage series in Table 8.2:

$$W = 0.19 - 0.95Q \qquad (8.2)$$
$$(0.25) \quad (2.91)$$
$$1887-1914 \ (N = 28); \ \bar{R}^2 = 0.157; \ \text{DW} = 1.79$$

Thus, in contrast to the argument of Keynes and Dunlop, the counter-cyclical behaviour of wages in the cycle considered by Marshall appears not to have been the freak result suggested. Instead, the counter-cyclical relation, while strongest for the 1879–86 cycle, nevertheless holds for the entire pre-1914 sample:

$$W = 0.02 - 0.53Q \qquad (8.3)$$
$$(0.05) \quad (2.84)$$
$$1859-1914 \ (N = 56); \ \bar{R}^2 = 0.114; \ \text{DW} = 1.93$$

These tests illustrate a point which Keynes drew attention to in 1939: namely that the data which Marshall had available to him when formulating his ideas on the cyclical behaviour of wages were not typical of the pre-1914 data as a whole. However, the post-1886 pro-cyclical pattern reported by Keynes (Table 8.1) is contradicted by the series here tested. The opposite relation from that suggested by Keynes and Dunlop is found for the post-1886 sample. This counter-cyclical relation is only absent in the pre-1880 data (not referred to by Keynes); and when these are pooled with the post-1880 data, the counter-cyclical relation is shown to be robust.

1.1 Comparison with Dunlop and Keynes

How can Keynes's results be explained in the light of the evidence reported above? The series so far tested were constructed to correspond as closely as possible to the economic variable appropriate to marginal productivity theory. Alternative series are now constructed in order to see to what extent the different results can thereby be explained. First, though, a bit more can be said about the results which are to be explained.

In his evidence to the Indian Currency Committee, Marshall (1899) states that he accumulated a great number of facts, but that nearly everything he accumulated is implied in a table taken from Bowley (1898) which does not, however, report annual data which would allow the cyclical behaviour of wages to be subjected to the above tests; and the same is true of the other four tables contained in Bowley (1898). Marshall did submit a number of diagrams and statistical tables to the Committee on Indian Currency which are not reproduced in Marshall (1899), but are deposited in the Marshall Library in the University of Cambridge. However, these largely relate to India and include no annual wage series. It is not, therefore, possible to submit Marshall's own results to regression analysis.

Keynes does not report his annual data, nor his data sources, but implies that they correspond to Dunlop's. Dunlop gives annual figures for the change in money wages and for the deviation from trend of real wages, between 1860–1 and 1912–13; (no trend adjustment was, in fact, performed for the period 1900–1 to 1912–13). He also corrected for changes in the terms of trade, although this did not materially alter his results. Based on these data, the behaviour he reported is shown in Table 8.3. Real wages (trend eliminated up to the 1893–1900 upswing) are shown to move pro-cyclically in every cycle save for the one from which Marshall took his data. Thus Dunlop's results appear to show strongly pro-cyclical real wages.

Table 8.3 Dunlop's description of cyclical wage behaviour

Years	Phase	Money Wage Rates	Real Wage Rates	Real Wage Rates: Trend Eliminated
1860–62	Downswing	+1.8	+1.9	−2.6
1862–66	Upswing	+13.8	+10.5	+6.2
1866–68	Downswing	−1.6	−5.2	−9.2
1868–73	Upswing	+19.2	+16.4	+7.2
1873–79	Downswing	−5.8	+7.0	−0.6
1879–83	Upswing	+2.1	+1.5	−3.0
1883–86	Downswing	−0.8	+8.6	+2.7
1886–90	Upswing	+10.0	+9.9	+5.1
1890–93	Downswing	−0.6	+0.6	−5.0
1893–1900	Upswing	+10.5	+9.6	+7.8
1900–4	Downswing	−3.3	−7.0	
1904–7	Upswing	+5.2	+3.7	
1907–9	Downswing	−1.5	−3.4	
1909–13	Upswing	+5.2	+1.2	

However, regressing Dunlop's annual series against the previously used output series (Dunlop does not give any output figures) shows that this pro-cyclical relation for real wages is not statistically significant. The only sub-period in which cyclical output explains any of the change in the real wage variable is post-1887, and even in this case the coefficient on output is not significant:

$$\text{DUNLOP'S REAL WAGE} = 0.20 + 0.19Q \qquad (8.4)$$
$$(0.57) \quad (1.25)$$
$$1887-1913 (N = 27); \bar{R}^2 = 0.021; \text{DW} = 1.50$$

To conclude the description of Dunlop's (and Keynes's) results: the findings reported here—of counter-cyclical wages—appear to be diammetrically opposed to the results of both Keynes (Table 8.1) and Dunlop (Table 8.3); but when the real wage data being described by Dunlop are analysed more closely they turn out not, after all, to follow any statistically significant pro-cyclical pattern.

There remains, however, a difference between the statistically significant counter-cyclical results, and the statistically insignificant, but seemingly pro-cyclical, pattern of real wages described by Keynes and Dunlop. It turns out that this can largely be accounted for by the fact that, while recognizing the relevant variable to be the product wage, both Keynes and Dunlop considered, instead, the real wage.

Wage series The wage series used above was measuring wage rates, which will tend to be less pro-cyclical than actual hourly earnings. The problem is that there are no accurate statistics available for actual hourly earnings. The alternative measure, of weekly earnings, will be biased in the opposite direction, being *more* pro-cyclical than hourly earnings because of the pro-cyclical patterns of hours worked. Denoting the previous series—wage rates in product terms— by W, a series of weekly earnings in product terms, denoted by W_e, was then constructed. The effect on the cyclical behaviour of the series is reported below along with the effect on both these series of altering the price deflator.

Price series The above two wage series were deflated by a consumer price index in order to test whether this explains any of the difference between Keynes's and Dunlop's results, and those reported above. There are now, therefore, four alternative wage indices as shown in Table 8.4. Table 8.5 now reproduces Table 8.2 with the W series replaced by the RW series. Table 8.5 demonstrates the irony of Marshall's data sample for a consideration of the cyclical behaviour of real wages. Looking at the movement of real wages between the cyclical

Table 8.4 Alternative wage measures

Wage Series	Price Index	
	Price of Principal Industrial Products	CPI
Wage Rates:	Product Wage Rates (W)	Real Wage Rates (RW)
Weekly Earnings:	Product Wage Earnings (W_e)	Real Wage Earnings (RW_e)

peak of 1877 and the trough of 1886, the counter-cyclical pattern is clear. Altering the price deflator has also accounted for the remaining puzzle over Keynes's and Dunlop's results. The direction of movement of the real wage is now pro-cyclical in every cycle outside the 'Marshall sample' other than the 1904–7 boom and subsequent slump to 1908. Dunlop and Keynes report pro-cyclical movements for this cycle also (although both date it slightly differently from here, and from each other). The RW_e series actually reproduces such pro-cyclical results for this cycle also, although in general the choice of wage series does not significantly alter the cyclical result.

Having generated results at odds with those implied in Keynes (1939) and Dunlop (1938), it was first demonstrated that their results are not statistically significant, and, second, it was shown how the counter-cyclical wage series tested in Section 1 could, with a different price deflator, exhibit the type of pro-cyclical pattern contained in the tables from Keynes's and Dunlop's articles. It now remains to test the statistical significance of the pro-cyclical relation so generated.

As would be expected the RW and RW_e series which reproduce the Keynes–Dunlop cyclical pattern are, like Dunlop's data, not significantly pro-cyclical. The regressions over the whole sample cannot account for any of the movement in RW nor RW_e and the following regression is the closest the RW_e series got to being significantly pro-cyclical over the whole sample:

$$RW_e = \underset{(0.20)}{0.04} + \underset{(1.06)}{0.08Q} \qquad (8.5)$$

1859–1914 ($N = 56$); $\bar{R}^2 = 0.003$; DW = 1.66

Table 8.5 Deviation of real wages from trend

Cycle Phase	Year	Q	W	Change
Peak	1860	2.7	−2.1	
				Decrease
Trough	1863	−3.8	−2.6	
				Increase
Peak	1866	5.3	2.2	
				Decrease
Trough	1869	−6.9	−1.0	
				Increase
Peak	1871	3.8	0.6	
				Decrease
Trough	1873	−0.1	−2.1	
				Increase
Peak	1877	1.1	−2.0	
				Increase
Trough	1879	−6.6	2.1	
				Decrease
Peak	1883	3.8	−2.5	
				Increase
Trough	1886	−5.9	1.5	
				Increase
Peak	1891	3.1	1.8	
				Decrease
Trough	1893	−4.8	−2.6	
				Increase
Peak	1896	1.5	1.5	
				Decrease
Trough	1897	−0.4	−0.7	
				Increase
Peak	1899	2.5	2.4	
				Decrease
Trough	1904	−3.0	−0.7	
				Decrease
Peak	1907	4.8	−1.3	
				Increase
Trough	1908	−3.5	1.3	
				Increase
Peak	1913	0.9	2.2	

1.2 Materials and total direct costs

The importance of the cost of material inputs in explaining real wage behaviour has been discussed and tested in previous chapters. Such a total direct cost series can be constructed using either of the two product wage series (combined with the appropriately deflated materials series), as indicated in Table 8.6. Of course, the two corresponding real wage series could be used, but the resulting real direct costs (as opposed to product direct costs) is not an economically meaningful variable.

Table 8.6 Alternative direct cost measures

Wage Series	Price Index
	Price of Principal Industrial Products
Wage Rates	DC
Wage Earnings	DC_e

Table 8.7 repeats the analysis of Tables 8.2 and 8.5, showing the relation to trend of both the materials and the direct cost indices over cyclical peaks and troughs, where the two alternative direct cost measures are indicated in the table. The results reported in Table 8.7 suggest a counter-cyclical pattern for material costs in product terms (MC). The basic pattern of cyclical fluctuations of total direct costs appears similar whether the labour component was calculated using the 'rates' or 'earnings' series: in product terms both DC indices appear to move counter-cyclically between 1877 and 1886, and post-1897. These observations are confirmed by regression analysis.

A summary of regression results are shown in Table 8.8. The following pattern emerges. There is no cyclical relation during the early part of the time series being considered. For the middle portion direct costs behaved counter-cyclically. The final (post-1887) years see direct costs moving counter-cyclically in product terms. Taking the sample as a whole, then, the total direct cost series moved counter-cyclically, with statistical significance for the series compiled from wage-rate data, but not for the series compiled from earnings data.

On the basis of previous discussion, the most relevant indices for wages and direct costs from the point of view of the theory being considered, would be constituted from the producer price index and an earnings index somewhere between the two indices available, for rates and earnings. That is, for direct costs, somewhere between the DC_e and DC series (Table 8.9).

Table 8.7 Deviation of materials and direct costs from trend

Cycle Phase	Year	Q	MC	Wage Index	
				Rates DC	Earnings DC_e
Peak	1860	2.7	0.4	0.1	0.5
Trough	1863	−3.8	0.0	−3.7	−2.3
Peak	1866	5.3	−0.2	0.9	1.6
Trough	1869	−6.9	9.7	8.1	7.8
Peak	1871	3.8	−2.1	−0.2	−1.3
Trough	1873	−0.1	0.3	−3.3	−1.1
Peak	1877	1.1	0.4	−1.6	−1.1
Trough	1879	−6.6	1.2	3.7	3.3
Peak	1883	3.8	−1.9	−2.4	−2.0
Trough	1886	−5.9	1.8	3.5	2.2
Peak	1891	3.1	1.4	2.4	1.8
Trough	1893	−4.8	−1.5	−3.3	−3.0
Peak	1896	1.5	−0.9	−1.5	−1.8
Trough	1897	−0.4	1.4	3.8	3.3
Peak	1899	2.5	−2.4	−4.4	−4.5
Trough	1904	−3.0	1.2	3.0	2.3
Peak	1907	4.8	0.7	−4.7	−3.0
Trough	1908	−3.5	3.9	8.5	8.7
Peak	1913	0.9	0.4	0.4	−0.7

To conclude: the data for the two components of total direct costs in product terms (labour and materials costs) tended to move in a similar cyclical pattern. This is also true for Marshall's data sample, and hence the counter-cyclical pattern of wages over that cycle was not due to the product wage being 'squeezed' by movements in non-labour direct costs.

2. 1920–1939

Broadberry (1983) argues that 'wages and prices in interwar Britain have received surprisingly little attention', and attempts to describe the wage–price process. His paper does not, however, attempt to look at the cyclical real wage process. First, it is not explicitly testing for *real wages*, and, second, it does not attempt to isolate trend and cycle processes. The paper concludes that *in the long run* the real wage was a function of the terms of trade and labour productivity, and that unemployment had little, if any, impact on wage settlements. He does

Table 8.8 DC regressed on Q

Sample Years (number of years in sample)	Wage Index			
	Rates DC		Earnings DC_e	
1859–1875 (17)	no relation			
1876–1886 (11)	−0.52 3.40	0.513 2.42	−0.39 2.88	0.422 2.19
1887–1914 (28)	−0.60 2.61	0.177 2.01	−0.53 2.35	0.144 1.96
1859–1914 (56)	−0.42 3.15	0.140 2.05	no relation	

Note: The only explanatory variable other than Q in the regression equations was a constant term. This was insignificant in all cases.

Table 8.9 Cyclical behaviour of DC indices

Level of significance	Cyclical pattern
	Counter-cyclical
Insignificant	DC_e
Significant	DC

not test for the effect of an output variable, although presumably such a variable would have been positively related to productivity or negatively to unemployment. His paper concludes that aggregate demand could have been raised without leading directly to pressure on nominal wages and prices. It could be argued, however, that the productivity variable in his wage equation was (at least partly) proxying for demand fluctuations within cyclical output (deviation from trend) and the positive coefficient thus indicates that an increase in demand would have led to higher wages and/or prices.

With reference to the lack of any significant coefficient on the unemployment term, Phillips (1958) did not test for the inter-war period. His paper used pre-First World War data to construct the curve which was then superimposed on the inter-war data which fitted, although in a clustered fashion with the data for the 1920s generally above the curve and the data for the 1930s generally below. Lipsey (1960) did test for inter-war data, but without significant results for unemployment.

Regression tests on this chapter's British inter-war data indicated no statistically significant correlation between cyclical wages and output, although a statistically significant negative correlation was found over the 1929–37 cycle.

Beenstock, Capie & Griffiths (1984) argue that such counter-cyclical wage movements were responsible for the cyclical fluctuations in output, a view disputed by Worswick (1984a; 1984b; 1984c) and Dimsdale (1984) who argue, first, that the causes of the output fluctuations lay elsewhere, and, second, that the timing of the wage fluctuations do not fit the Beenstock *et al.* (neoclassical) story.

This debate (in Bank of England 1984a; and National Institute 1984) relates more to the interpretation of an established counter-cyclical pattern than to determining whether such a counter-cyclical pattern was present. Worswick's point is that counter-cyclical wage behaviour does not necessarily imply the operation of neoclassical causation nor the applicability of neoclassical policy prescriptions.

The point being made in this book is that such counter-cyclical wage behaviour (as occurred over 1929–37) is not, in any case, a general economic 'law' (or valid assumption). It was shown, in Chapter 2, that there are valid theoretical reasons for predicting that such neoclassical assumptions are not necessarily universally valid (if at all). The contradictory results of the literature to date were shown to be partly due to different studies using data taken from different countries and time periods which, were the textbook assumptions valid, would not upset the results; and partly also due to different studies employing different methods and therefore picking up to different degrees the 'ultimately' reduced form of the cyclical wage–cyclical output correlation.

The regression results reported in Chapters 4 and 5 confirmed that no such universal 'cyclical pattern of wages' operates internationally, so that either there are different 'data generating processes' or else the data generating process common to advanced capitalist countries refers to economic variables other than the product wage, the behaviour of the latter being contingent to the common data generating process. Even within the data series of one country (the United Kingdom) the cyclical wage pattern appeared, from the results reported in Chapter 6, to conform to no necessary pattern across the entire output cycle; and appeared at industry level, according to the tests reported in Chapter 7, to vary according to aggregate output effects. This argument, that assumptions involving necessarily counter-cyclical product wages prove empirically not universally valid, is confirmed by the British data from 1859.

3. Conclusion

While not claiming that results from pre-Second World War data would be the appropriate ones to inform current economic policy, nevertheless the historical data exhibit the same lack of consistent patterns as do post-war data. Any correlation between cyclical output and wage fluctuations is of limited statistical significance, if any. And the sign of any such correlation itself alters: both between cycles and, possibly, within a pattern of long swings.

Whether product wages do decline (in cyclical terms) in the upswing depends on relative nominal wage and price movements. The data show that the outcome of the cyclical behaviour of these two series varies, resulting in different patterns of output-product wage correlations between cycles over time: sometimes pro-cyclical, sometimes counter-cyclical and sometimes non-cyclical. The fact that the pattern is in some cases *not* counter-cyclical thereby suggests that any such counter-cyclical pattern is not a necesary condition for the upswing. And the fact that there are cyclical reductions in product wages during come cyclical output downturns in turn suggests that such cyclical reductions in product wages are not a sufficient condition for an output expansion.

Thus the historical data suggest that reductions in product wages are neither a sufficient nor a necessary condition for an output expansion. This is in contradiction to what has been referred to in this book as the 'standard' ('1930s', 'Treasury') neoclassical theory of counter-cyclical product wages. That theory, Keynes showed, derived from an inference by Marshall from historical observations. A closer look at that inference reveals the following:

1. Marshall's conclusion that wages move counter-cyclically is seen to be supported by the data for the years from which Marshall took his evidence.
2. The seemingly pro-cyclical pattern of wages in the years not considered by Marshall, drawn attention to by Keynes and Dunlop, turns out not to be statistically significant, even when Dunlop's data are used.
3. The years following those considered by Marshall actually suggest the opposite, of counter-cyclical wages, when the money wage is deflated by the product price.
4. Total (wage and material) direct costs are more pro-cyclical/less counter-cyclical than wage costs alone. The shifts in the cyclical behaviour of this direct cost index are broadly in line with the corresponding shifts in the cyclical behaviour of wages.

It was shown in Chapter 3 that the 'cyclical wage' literature originated in the 1930s with Keynes's statement of an a priori belief as to the implications of economic theory for the empirical behaviour of wages. While Keynes (1939) admitted to not having taken care to check his theoretical statement with the facts, that same theoretical belief had originated from Marshall allowing the 'facts to speak for themselves', and inferring from them a more general theory than was, methodologically, appropriate.

The contrast between the way these two authors reported the cyclical wage behaviour is perhaps symptomatic of their methodological differences. Pheby (1985, p. 100) reports that Marshall's view of himself as representing a 'dull mean' between the two methods of induction and deduction is not shared by Coase (1975), who argues that Marshall was more inclined towards induction, nor by Keynes who made a similar observation (Keynes 1973, p. 296).

9
Conclusion

In times of prolonged recession—when the 'normal' cyclical expansion of output (and employment) fails to materialize—the topic of the 'cyclical behaviour of wages' tends to emerge as an area of debate. This was the case in the 1930s, and is the case again today.

The situation of prolonged recession and accompanying unemployment raises the theoretical question of why the economy is not returning to full employment equilibrium: why the 'normal' cyclical upturn in output (and employment) has not worked itself through. Similarly the cyclical recovery in the United States up to 1985 raised the question of what lay behind the different output behaviour there. The corresponding debate over what did cause expansion of the British economy during the period 1931–7, and the role (if any) played by the behaviour of wages, has been referred to in Chapter 8.

These questions of economic theory and empirical evidence should then inform the political debate over economic policy proposals for overcoming the obstacles to cyclical output expansion. It might, of course, be suspected that it is, rather, the debates over policy proposals which determine the corresponding debates in economic theory: but certainly the two areas of debate—over economic theory and government policy—are inextricably linked.

The 1930s slump sparked such a debate: both at the level of government policy prescriptions and in the economic literature. The former lasted only as long as the slump. The latter had got no further than establishing that further empirical work was required when the attention of the economics profession was diverted to other matters, such as *How to Pay for the War?*

Following the Second World War and the post-war reconstruction, sustained economic growth developed and the attention of economists turned to growth theory. Worswick recalls the prevailing belief amongst economists that they had solved the economic problems of slumps and the cycle, and that the task before them was simply to publicize their solutions beyond the economics profession (Worswick 1985, p. 1).

From the 1950s, theories of economic fluctuations were gradually replaced in economic publications by growth theory, the neoclassical model, at least, stressing the equilibrating tendencies of the system. Conditions for convergence to steady-state growth were investigated in detail, with the rate of growth of output equalling the rate of growth of the capital stock, the rate of growth of the profit rate being zero, and the rate of growth of real wages being equal to the rate of growth of productivity, with a constancy of income distribution between capital and labour. Thus the behaviour of wages was investigated, but in terms of equilibrium growth rates rather than cyclical fluctuations.

The failure to have settled the cyclical wage debate allowed the question to slip back into its textbook context where the neoclassical synthesis allowed the neoclassical belief in counter-cyclical real wages to reappear within the micro marginal product of labour (mpl) context. At the same time the emphasis of the Keynesian macro part of the synthesis on macro pro-cyclical aggregate demand, far from challenging the micro side of the neoclassical synthesis, allowed that micro assertion of counter-cyclical real wages to appear relatively unimportant. It was with the breakdown of that apparently equilibrium growth and the intensification of cyclical behaviour, that attention returned to cycles, and to the cyclical behaviour of wages.

1. The cyclical wage debate

The debate over the cyclical movement of wages centres on whether or not wages have a necessary correlation with the output cycle; and if so, whether they are pro-cyclical or counter-cyclical. This might appear a strange object of economic controversy. Whether or not the output cycle would have any necessary implications for wages would depend on the causes of the output cycle. Different 'shocks' to output would have different implications for wages. Hence different cyclical wage implications. Further, the concept of decomposing time series into 'cyclical' and trend components is itself theoretically—and practically—problematic; and whether or not the cyclical wage series was thought correlated to the cyclical output series would clearly be influenced by what was understood by 'cyclical'; and whether the predicted correlation was detected would depend on the statistical method of detrending.

Nevertheless, the publication of Keynes's *General Theory* (1936) did lead to just such a debate over the cyclical behaviour of wages. Not only was that debate of some importance in the 1930s, but the cyclical wage debate has re-emerged in the literature with Bodkin (1969), and a number of studies since the mid-1970s. From a methodological standpoint the literature can be divided into two: first, the debate in the 1930s; and second, the current studies. The doubts expressed above—as to the point of searching for a 'stylized fact' of cyclical wage behaviour—relate differently to these two categories of work.

128   CONCLUSION

Considering first the debate in the 1930s: it was sparked by Keynes's (1936) assertion of just such a necessary relation. And as Keynes (1939) was at pains to point out, his 1936 statement had not been intended as a bold prediction but, on the contrary, as a passing reference to what all knew to be true (that wages moved counter-cyclically). It is true that the 1930s debate did not satisfactorily resolve the empirical question; and that the 1970s cyclical wage literature has continued the search for the 'stylized fact'. It was argued in Chapter 1, however, that to understand the cyclical wage debate—in the sense of an economic controversy which deserves serious study as an episode in the history of economic thought—requires some analysis of the meaning and significance of the debate; and that this could be examined at a number of levels.

The explanation for the re-emergence of the cyclical wage debate in face of the above objections to such an object of inquiry goes deeper, then, than simply a desire to fill in a 'descriptive statistic' gap in the literature. That re-emergence is described in the following terms in one of the recent additions to the literature:

> The approach stands or falls by the establishment of a negative correlation between employment and the wage. That such a correlation did not exist was, until a few years ago, thought to be an established fact in macroeconomics, but since Sargent's [1978] paper, the negative correlation and thus the labour demand equation have made something of a comeback (Newell & Symons 1985, p. 1).

It is argued in the following section that this comeback was not due to a change in the 'facts', nor even because a more accurate observation of the facts was achieved, but rather because fashions in inference changed.

2. The three levels of the debate

2.1 *The search for a stylized fact*

At one level, the aim of the work reported in this book has been to contribute to the understanding of the cyclical behaviour of product wages, the 'stylized fact' of cyclical wage behaviour. The importance of this question is due to its implications for the debate as to whether a cyclical reduction in product wages is a necessary condition for a cyclical expansion of output.

Whether or not a cyclical decline in product wages is viewed as being a necessary condition depends on the theoretical assumptions made about the economy; and specifically the assumptions about the marginal product of labour (mpl). The competing views of the economy were discussed in Chapter 2. The declining marginal product view is that of the 1920s Treasury, of neoclassical textbooks, and of modern New Classicals.

Firms facing a declining mpl, and being price-takers, make a reduced product wage *necessary* for increased output. Whether or not such a reduction in product wages would be *sufficient* for increased output depends on additional assumptions as to how the economy operates. It was on this last point that Keynes departed from the Treasury view in 1936 (as well as over whether or not money wage cuts would in any case reduce real wages).

The alternative view that firms are not necessarily price-takers, and can be demand-constrained, was put well by Sraffa (1926, p. 543):

> The chief obstacle against which they have to contend when they want gradually to increase their production does not lie in the cost of production—which, indeed, generally favours them in that direction—but in the difficulty of selling the larger output of goods without reducing the price, or without having to face increased marketing expenses. This necessity of reducing prices in order to sell a larger quantity of one's own product is only an aspect of the usual descending demand curve, with the difference that instead of concerning the whole of a commodity, whatever its origin, it relates only to the goods produced by a particular firm...
> This method of regarding the matter appears the most natural and that which adheres to the reality of things.

Reduced product wages are, from this view, not necessary, and may even worsen a cyclical decline in output by reducing aggregate demand. A typical example of this demand-generating role of wages being cited is from a commentary on the British economy: 'economic growth should be maintained through 1985. A key factor will be a resumption in *consumer spending growth*: *earnings growth* should comfortably outstrip inflation' (Barclays Bank 1984; emphasis added).

Modern empirical studies, following from those sparked off by these policy debates in the 1930s, were reviewed in Chapter 3. It was seen that no consistent results have, to date, emerged. The results of the empirical work reported in this book aim to fill that gap, and are as follows:

1. The cyclical output–wage correlation varies significantly: (i) across countries; (ii) within the cycle; and (iii) over time.
2. The variation is from significantly pro-cyclical (United States) to significantly counter-cyclical (Japan).

3. Cyclical wages tend to be negatively related to lagged cyclical output and positively related to future cyclical output.
4. Cyclical labour costs tend to be negatively related to cyclical non-labour costs.
5. This negative correlation between the two series—labour costs and non-labour ('materials') costs—is, however, accompanied by no consistent cyclical pattern for total direct costs.

The relation between employment and wages will depend partly on output, and hence will reflect the above patterns, and partly on non-cyclical factors, which, given output, imply a negative correlation. This description of the two sources of possible wage–output correlations turned out to be consistent with the results of the Chapter 4 tests, thus demonstrating that there is, similarly, no 'stylized fact' or a correlation between wages and cyclical employment to be found.

What, then, of the recent comeback made by the labour demand equation and related negative correlation between employment and wages?

2.2 Theory, facts and falsification

It was argued in Chapter 1, Section 2, that the response of Keynes (1939) to the apparent falsification of the theory held by Keynes (1936) was particularly striking in terms of the methods used to immunize theories against such falsification. Thus Ward (1972, pp. 174–5) argues that

> the notable thing about both the *General Theory* and the massive discussion in the leading economic journals that followed its publication, is the dearth of empirical studies ...
>
> Given the importance which nearly all economists attached to ending depressions, one would expect that at least in the area of policy solid empirical work would play a central role in the development of Keynesianism. But this does not seem to be the case. To take just one example, consider the magnitude of the impact multipliers ... The standard textbook version (and early discussion) of Keynes did not attempt to isolate this change by estimating impact multipliers empirically ... and the first public presentation of estimates of impact multipliers of policy relevance does not occur until 1958, twenty-two years from the publication date of the *General Theory*.

The irony was noted in Chapter 3 of the empirical debate in the 1930s having been provoked by a statement from Keynes presented very much as a prior belief. The more general irony of Keynes, who was opposed to attempts to fill in real values for the variable functions in a model, nevertheless giving rise to the mass of Keynesian empirical work after the war, has been noted by others (notwithstanding Ward's rather different assessment). The point, however, is that that empirical work has been largely devoted to policy implementation rather than the attempted falsification, or verification, of theories. Indeed, the 1970s macro models (including the Treasury's), assumed the Kaleckian rather than neoclassical version of cyclical behaviour outlined in Chapter 2; (see Wren-Lewis 1985, p. 68). The recent comeback by the labour demand function has not been the result of a shift in favour of empirical work, but rather is an attempt to overthrow the Keynesian (/Kaleckian) theoretical assumptions implicit in the bulk of applied macro econometric work up to the late 1970s.

Just as the economic crisis in the 1930s provoked a crisis in economics when the policy prescriptions (of wage cutting) were found not to work, so the economic crisis in the 1970s provoked a crisis in economics when the policy prescriptions (of fiscal reflation) were found not to work. Keynes (1936) was the clearest exponent of the futility of attempting to escape a recession via wage cutting; and Keynes (1939) argued that no cyclical reduction in the real wage was, in any case, required. Perhaps the 1970s counterpart to Keynes—the most famous conversion to the futility of attempting to escape a recession via fiscal reflation—was the Labour Prime Minister in Britain:

> We used to think that you could spend your way out of a recession, and increase employment by cutting taxes and boosting Government spending. I tell you in all candour that that option no longer exists, and that in so far as it ever did exist, it only worked on each occasion since the war by injecting a bigger dose of inflation into the economy, followed by a higher level of unemployment as the next step (Callaghan 1976).

In the 1930s, then, the neoclassical marginal product of labour assumption, and corresponding wage cutting policy proposals, were replaced by Keynesian (Kaleckian) theories of demand-determined output levels with mark-up pricing, implying no necessary requirement for any particular cyclical pattern to real wages. The cyclical wage debate, and literature, played some part in this process.

Now, in the 1970s and 1980s, the neoclassical marginal product of labour theory, and corresponding policy implication that an increase in employment requires a reduction in real wages (below the alternative, unemployment-causing, level), is making a comeback. And it is therefore considered important to verify (e.g. Sargent 1978; Neftci 1978) or falsify (e.g. Geary & Kennan, 1982a; 1982b) the neoclassical diminishing marginal product of labour theory, by subjecting its supposed corollary—of counter-cyclical real wages—to empirical testing. That is the methodological background to the reappearance of the cyclical wage debate. This takes us to the third of the three levels of the debate identified in Chapter 1: the question of how observations relate to theories.

2.3 *Inference*

The argument from Ward, cited in the previous section, continues as follows:

> statistical tests are of very little help in resolving controversies until there is general agreement on the properties of the surrounding theory. Without that general agreement, even tests that are accepted as decisive, as was the case with Tarshis, do not change anyone's mind (Ward 1972, p. 176).

The controversies in economics in the 1930s, and again in the 1970s and 1980s, had more to do, then, with the economic climate, the lack of success of government policies in dealing with them, and a subsequent battle of ideas, than they had to do with the statistical tests reported in the respective cyclical wage literatures. (As shown in Chapter 3, Ward's description of Tarshis (1939) as being 'accepted as decisive' is not actually accurate; but the point remains, and would no doubt have had validity even had Tarshis's tests been accepted as technically beyond criticism.)

The results reported in the empirical chapters of this book would claim to show decisively that there is no cyclical pattern to wages (as have Geary & Kennan), but such a demonstration, even were it to be accepted as decisive, would not stop the attempted comeback of the diminishing marginal product of labour theory. Thus Tatom (1980) (and Canzoneri 1978) claim to show empirical support for the diminishing marginal product of labour theory while accepting that the resulting counter-cyclical pattern of product wages does not in fact occur, due to the pro-cyclical pattern of capital utilization. While Tatom clearly sees his results as aiding the neoclassical comeback, the theoretical, as well as empirical, results are perfectly compatible with the Kaleckian model outlined in Chapter 2, and underlying the macro econometric models of the 1970s; namely, that in the cycle capacity utilization increases with constant marginal costs (and product) and no requirement for any particular pattern of cyclical wage movements (although with spreading overheads profits will be pro-cyclical, allowing the possibility of pro-cyclical wages), until full capacity utilization is reached when marginal costs not only rise, but, for Kalecki, rise so steeply as to prevent further expansion. Thus Tatom infers a neoclassical marginal product of labour theory from the same (non-cyclical, or even pro-cyclical) wage data as is compatible with, indeed predicted by, the Keynesian (Kaleckian) theory he wishes to challenge.

Tatom is not typical of supporters of the comeback. Others, as has been shown, hang the *theoretical* challenge on an *empirical* one; inferring a marginal product of labour theory from a negative wage–employment correlation. But being an exception, Tatom proves the rule: that theories inferred from observations change not only with changes in empirical observations, but also with changes in fashions of inference.

3. Government economic policy

The different methodological motives behind the different contributions to the current cyclical wage literature also underlie the different theoretical and empirical methods adopted between studies. Thus Bernanke & Powell (1984, p. 1) acknowledge that while a descriptive analysis of the cyclical data may be useful in restricting the class of structural models or hypotheses which may subsequently be considered, it allows no direct structural inferences. This is the (unstated) view underlying Keynes's response to Dunlop and to Tarshis. On the other hand, the rather different literature which does formulate and test a specific structural model of labour markets during the cycle necessarily requires implicit identifying assumptions. Any resulting statistical correlation necessarily reflects those assumptions. The data alone can tell us nothing about the underlying theoretical structure.

Returning to the irony that the mass of empirical work after the war was undertaken by Keynesians—despite Keynes's view that 'it is of the essence of a model that one does not fill in real values for the variable functions'—even were Keynes right in being dubious as to the value of empirical work for testing theory, nevertheless descriptive statistical work could still be of use in informing policy analysis. Thus if Dunlop and Tarshis were correct in concluding that there is no counter-cyclical pattern to real wages, then the argument that to overcome a cyclical recession (and the accompanying unemployment) government expansionary policy should be accompanied by wage cuts is shown not to be valid, and the corresponding policy prescriptions should be rejected: 'If we can advance farther on the road towards full employment than I had previously supposed without seriously affecting real hourly wages or the rate of profits per unit of output, the warnings of the anti-expansionists need cause us less anxiety' (Keynes 1939, p. 41). Keynes continues the above passage with a call for further statistical work before discarding 'our former conclusions'—that a cyclical expansion in employment requires a cyclical reduction in real wages—which 'have a priori support and have survived for many years the scrutiny of experience and common sense'. As reported in Chapter 3, Keynes's call was ignored for 30 years. The subsequent study (Bodkin 1969) has been criticized and challenged in the post-1978 literature. It was argued above, however, that that literature was initiated not so much as an answer to Keynes's call, but rather as an attempt at verification of the 'former conclusions' referred to by Keynes. The statistical work reported in this book suggests, however, that there is indeed no requirement for real wages to move counter-cyclically.

Thus, to repeat Keynes's conclusion: we can advance farther on the road towards full employment than would otherwise be the case—the warnings of the anti-expansionists need cause us less anxiety.

Appendix 1 Using Alternative Price Deflators

This appendix considers the implications of using one or other of the two possible price deflators for constructing a *product* wage series. Sachs (1983), for example, criticizes Geary & Kennan's (1982a) study for using the WPI rather than the price of value added (Pv). These two 'product' wages are denoted by W_{wpi} and W_{Pv} respectively. This is only a serious issue when we have (relatively) large movements in material costs, thus allowing the different series to indicate precisely *opposite* movements for the product wage series. The example Sachs gives (taken from recent experience) is an increase in material costs leading to a fall in the W_{wpi} while the W_{Pv} is actually rising. For Sachs, this behaviour suggests that the W_{Pv} index is the more appropriate.

If the real price of non-labour inputs increases, then this will tend to increase the real price of total direct costs. It is this which will hit profits, and may lead to reduced employment and output. These results do *not* stem from an increase in product wages, although even if workers are unsuccessful in protecting themselves against a fall in the wage deflated by the WPI, their (unsuccessful) attempts at doing so may well result in the wage deflated by the Pv rising. Table A1.1 gives such an example, where the doubling of the money value of materials results in the real cost of materials (deflated by either price index) rising.

Deflating by the WPI, both profits and wages suffer. The fall in the profits mark-up over direct costs combined with the unsuccessful attempt at preventing the fall in W_{wpi} via the money wage being increased by 50 per cent, does, however, result in the W_{Pv} rising. It can be seen that the W_{wpi} and W_{Pv} move in opposite directions and hence focusing on one or other may lead to different conclusions. It is not, however, a case of one misleading while the other leads to a correct understanding. Both (opposite) movements are caused by changes in non-labour costs, and the fall in profits is not due to the increased W_{Pv} but, rather, to the increased direct costs. Hence the importance of considering movements in the cost of non-labour inputs. If this is done, however, the more appropriate deflator is certainly the price index for total output (WPI) rather that the price index for value added alone (Pv).

Table A1.1 Pre- and post-price of raw materials shock

	State	
	Pre-shock	Post-shock
mat	1	2
W	1	1.5
dc	2	3.5
m	0.25	0.2
PR	0.5	0.7
VA	1.5	2.2
p	2.5	4.2
PR_{Pv}	1/3 = 0.33	0.32
PR_{wpi}	1/5 = 0.20	0.17
W_{Pv}	2/3 = 0.67	0.68
W_{wpi}	2/5 = 0.40	0.36
mat_{Pv}	2/3 = 0.67	0.91
mat_{wpi}	2/5 = 0.40	0.48
dc_{Pv}	4/3 = 1.33	1.59
dc_{wpi}	4/5 = 0.80	0.83

where *mat* is non-labour direct costs ('materials')
       W is labour costs ('wages')
       dc is total direct costs (= *mat* + *W*)
       m is the mark-up over direct costs
       PR is profits (= *dc.m*)
       VA is value added (= *W* + *PR*): the $_{Pv}$ price deflator
       p is price (= *dc* + *PR*): the $_{wpi}$ price deflator; and non-subscripted variables are in money terms.

Appendix 2 Construction of Total Direct Cost Index

Coutts, Godley & Nordhaus (1978, p. 40), report the share of materials in sales for total manufacturing less food, drink and tobacco as being 17.8 per cent. For the same year (1963), Cowling (1982, p. 170) reports the ratio of the materials bill to the wages bill as being 4.25. Since he also reports the ratio of salaries to wages as 0.431, this gives a ratio of materials to total earnings (wages plus salaries) of 2.97. Combining this figure with the above percentage share of materials in output would give a share of earnings in sales of 6 per cent, which is clearly incorrect. Turvey (1980, pp. 105–6) reports that the gross output of manufacturing industry in 1977 consisted of 57 per cent cost of goods and work purchased from other firms, and 43 per cent payment for certain services and value added to materials by the process of production, about half of this being wages and salaries, which thus constitute 22 per cent of total output. Maynard (1978) takes the gross profits component of final product price as 20 per cent, the remaining 80 per cent representing direct costs. Within this, he derives a 60:40 weighting for labour costs to raw material and fuel costs.

Cowling calculates ratios over time, while the other three studies analyse the picture for a single year. Coutts *et al.* take 1963, Maynard takes 1971 and Turvey takes 1977. The different dates could not possibly explain the different figures which they arrive at for share of material costs. These are, again, 17.8, 32 and 57 per cent respectively. This appendix attempts to reconstruct the data presented in these three studies in order to compare the measures, and hence decide on appropriate weightings for constructing a total direct cost index.

The Coutts *et al.* data are shown in Table A2.1. This shows the value of total stocks and work in progress, of total sales, and of purchases of materials. The fourth column then shows the share of materials in sales. These values are shown for various industry groupings as well as for total manufacturing less food, drink and tobacco. A striking feature of the table is that the figures for share of materials in sales for the various industry groupings are all between 32.3 and 49.8 per cent. An average of the seven industries would be 37.9 per cent. This is well above the figure for manufacturing industry as a whole, 17.8 per cent. It is much closer to Maynard's figure of 32 per cent. This divergence gives a hint at the source of the divergence between the studies.

Unfortunately, Coutts *et al.*'s only reference to how their data were constructed is to cite one source: 'derived from Department of Industry'. The Department of Industry does not appear in their Bibliography. The 1963 input–output tables were therefore used to reconstruct the Coutts *et al.* data. For each of the industry groups within total manufacturing industry (minus food, drink and tobacco), their purchases from all other manufacturing industrial groups was then calculated. By subtracting all purchases from other manufacturers, as

Table A2.1 Production period by industry, 1963

Industry	Total stocks and work in progress £m (end year)	Total sales £m (per year)	Purchases of materials £m (per year)	Share of materials in sales α %	Production period θ (in months)		
					Only progressively-added input $\beta = 0$	$\beta = \frac{2}{3}$	Only initial-entry inputs $\alpha = \beta = 1$
Chemicals and allied industries	362.7	1699.7	548.7	32.3	5.1	4.2	2.6
Mechanical engineering	967.5	2186.3	727.0	33.3	10.6	8.7	5.3
Electrical engineering	760.1	1629.3	607.4	37.3	11.2	9.0	5.6
Textiles	506.2	1405.3	485.5	34.6	8.6	7.0	4.3
Clothing and footwear	152.7	807.9	402.0	49.8	4.5	3.4	2.3
Timber and furniture	112.7	596.6	245.7	41.2	4.5	3.6	2.3
Paper industries	173.9	656.3	242.5	37.0	6.4	5.1	3.2
Total manufacturing less food, drink and tobacco	5426.7	13446.1	2390.1	17.8	9.7	8.7	4.8

α is the share of materials in total sales.
β is the share of materials entering at the beginning of the production period.

Source: derived from Department of Industry, cited in Coutts *et al.* (1978).

well as subtracting value added, we get a figure for total non-labour inputs for the manufacturing sector. Note that by including all possible inputs this is a broader category than what would normally be thought of as 'materials'. For the manufacturing sector, then, this broad input figure is £5,781.1 million, which is 42 per cent of 'total sales', defined by Coutts *et al.* as total gross output less purchases from other manufacturing industries. This is, however, to include categories such as taxes and imports of services under the aggregate of 'materials'. Defining materials as simply imports of goods plus purchases from non-manufacturing industries 1–11, plus gas, electricity and water, a figure of 19.1 per cent was derived as the share of materials in final sales. It is this figure of 19.1 per cent which was taken to calculate the weighting for the price index of materials in order to construct an index of total direct costs. The corresponding figure for earnings is 41.2 per cent. This gives direct costs a 60.3 per cent share of total sales—the remaining 39.7 per cent being made up of gross profits (16.7 per cent) and non-direct costs (23 per cent). The materials:earnings weighting is, then, 19.1:41.2 (= 31.7:68.3).

The following should be noted with regard to the series being constructed. First, the weighting is taken as constant (at the 1963 value) throughout the period, in the sense of the coefficient by which each of the two component series (of total direct costs) is multiplied (as in the formula for deriving the combined series, given below). Differential movements in the two component series themselves will still result, then, in a corresponding change in the share of total direct costs attributable to either labour or non-labour costs. Second, the price index is not yet directly comparable with the earnings index, as it is the price of a given bundle of materials, not of materials used per hour.

What is of interest here is the cost of an hour's labour, including the materials used by that labourer. The starting point is the price indexes for materials and labour. The cost of the extra hour's labour in terms of the labour is simply the hourly earnings index. The cost of the extra hour's labour in terms of the extra materials which will be consumed in that hour is more complex. It is measured by the price index of materials, multiplied by the quantity of materials used per hour. Following Coutts *et al.* (1978, p. 9), it can be assumed 'that the "productivity" of materials, fuel and services does not vary either cyclically or secularly'. This allows output to proxy for total materials used. Thus materials consumed per hour is proxied by output per hour.

This index of the cost of materials per hour was then combined with the previous data on the cost of labour per hour using the previously calculated weightings for materials and labour:

$$DC = L[(WE/h)/WPI] + m[(Q/h.E).(P/WPI)]$$

Where DC is total hourly direct costs, in product terms, L is the weighting for labour costs to correspond with their share in the 1963 input–output tables; m is the equivalent weighting for material and fuel costs bought from the non-manufacturing industry sector; WE is weekly earnings; h is average hours worked per week; WPI is the wholesale price index; Q is output; P is price index of materials; E is employment, $= F(FE.fh) + M(ME.mh)$, where FE is female employment, ME is male employment, fh is average hours worked per week by females, mh is average hours worked per week by males, F is the share of female employment in total, and M is the share of male employment in total.

Appendix 3 Statistical Tests

Chapter 4

Heteroscedasticity

The three basic regression equations from Chapter 4 which test for the three possible correlations, of output with wages, materials costs, and total direct costs, respectively, were tested for the null hypothesis of the error terms being homoscedastic, against the alternative hypothesis of their being heteroscedastic. The percentage deviations of output from trend were ordered according to absolute size for each of the six countries. The seven central observations in each case were omitted from the analysis, and the remaining 22 observations were divided into two subsamples of eleven observations each, one including the eleven smallest deviations from trend, the other the eleven largest. Separate regressions were then fitted to each subsample (the three regression equations being W on Q, MC on Q, and DC on Q) and the sum of squared residuals was obtained from each of them. The two subsamples were similar for all six countries, but none were identical, so each of the regression equations was run against data from 12 separate time periods—two per country. The regressions were fitted by OLS.

Obtaining the sum of squared residuals from each of the two regressions (for each of the six countries), the ratio of the two variances was calculated, F^*, which has an F distribution with $[(n - c - 2k)/2]$ degrees of freedom, where n is the total number of observations, c stands for the central observations omitted, and k represents the total number of parameters estimated from each regression. This test is due to Goldfeld & Quandt (1965). If the calculated value of F^* is greater than the theoretical value of F (at whatever level of significance has been chosen) with $(n - c - 2k)/2$ degrees of freedom, then we accept that there is heteroscedasticity.

The calculated values of F^* for each of the three regression equations, for each of the six countries, are shown in Table A3.1. The four values in brackets are calculated by dividing the sum of squared residuals from the regression run with the smaller values of the percentage deviation of output from trend by the sum of squared residuals from the other regression, rather than the other way round as was the case for all other values. Of the 18 calculated values of F^*, only two indicated heteroscedasticity: the regressions of total direct costs on output for the United States and France. In both cases, heteroscedasticity is demonstrated at the 1% level. The other 16 regression equations all demonstrate homoscedasticity.

Table A3.1 Test for heteroscedasticity: $F^*(9,9)$

	Regressand (on Q)		
	W	MC	DC
US	(1.94)*	1.88	13.06†
Canada	2.12	1.16	1.11
Japan	(1.19)*	1.03	1.84
France	3.08	1.48	5.85†
Germany	(1.73)*	(2.45)*	1.04
UK	2.18	1.80	1.42

* Those calculations represented by results in parenthesis gave values less than one when the sum of squared residuals from the regression on larger Q was divided by the sum of squared residuals from the regression on smaller Q. The inverse was, therefore, taken.
† Significant at the 1% level.

Higher-order serial correlation

The second test is a Lagrange multiplier test (Breusch & Pagan 1980) for up to fifth-order residual serial correlation. It has a chi-squared distribution with five degrees of freedom, and is calculated as NR^2 from the regression of the estimated residuals on five lagged values and the regressors which were in the original equation. The test regression was estimated over 1958–80, so $N = 23$. Table A.3.2 gives the calculated test statistics for each of the equations estimated against the data from each country. The original forms of the seven regression equations were:

1. MC on Q
2. W on MC
3. W on MC and Q
4. W on Q
5. DC on Q
6. MC on W and Q
7. MC on W.

Of the various statistical tests reported in Chapter 4 and in this appendix, this last comes closest to suggesting that the original equations should be respecified. However, the degree of higher-order serial correlation indicated may be preferable to any such respecification: first, not all the equations are affected. Equation 5 in Table A3.2 shows no higher-order serial correlation in

Table A3.2 Test for higher-order serial correlation

Equ.	US	Canada	Japan	France	Germany	UK
1.	8.85	11.34*	14.57*	11.11*	9.01	13.93*
2.	7.27	16.59**	6.50	9.01	2.08	10.40
3.	4.74	16.56**	1.69	8.67	3.16	10.18
4.	6.06	15.23**	2.91	7.92	6.86	9.91
5.	4.61	7.71	1.46	7.10	4.67	10.82
6.	6.43	9.93	7.01	11.60*	8.60	15.69**
7.	10.99	13.09*	2.75	14.40*	7.33	12.90*

For 5 degrees of freedom,
$P(x^2 > 11.07) = 0.05$ —denoted by *
$P(x^2 > 15.09) = 0.01$ —denoted by **
$P(x^2 > 16.75) = 0.005$ —not achieved.

the data of any of the six countries. Second, not all countries data are affected. The data from the United States and Germany show no higher-order serial correlation for any of the equations. Third, none of the 42 values of the test statistic indicate higher-order serial correlation at the 99.5% significance level.

Chapter 5

The same econometric tests were performed on various regression equations from Chapter 5 as were used, and discussed, in Chapter 4 and in this appendix, above:

1. parameter stability: Chow test;
2. heteroscedasticity: Goldfeld–Quandt;
3. higher-order serial correlation.

In view of the previous discussion, further comments are kept to a minimum. The regression results reported in Table 5.1, for the basic regression equation of W on E, are discussed.

Parameter stability

Rather surprisingly, the cyclical wage–output relation investigated in Chapter 4 turned out to be stable in terms of the parameter on the cyclical output variable when the wage series was regressed on it. Plotting the deviations from trend of both the employment and earnings series over time, the United Kingdom is the only country for which the relative behaviour of the wage and employment series clearly alters, despite the relatively large fluctuations in both series in all countries over the 1970s as compared with the 1950s and 1960s.

APENDIX 3

To test for such parameter stability (or lack of it in the case of the United Kingdom) the sample was broken at the same point as with the Chapter 4 tests: 1952–70, and 1971–80. The regression equations were then re-estimated and an F ratio was constructed in order to perform the Chow test, as before:

$$F^* = \frac{(\text{RRSS} - \text{URSS})/(k+1)}{\text{URSS}/(n_1 + n_2 - 2k - 2)}$$

Table A3.3 reports the calculated value of this F^* for the regression of W on L, as previously reported in Table 5.1. As expected all countries except the United Kingdom show parameter stability and in the United Kingdom the evidence for separate wage–employment correlations before and after 1970 is strong.

Table A3.3 Chow test for parameter stability: W on L

	Calculated $F^*(2,23)$
US	0.77
Canada	2.23
Japan	1.79
France	2.25
Germany	1.26
UK	5.79‡

‡ Signifies rejection at the 1% level of significance: to reject the null hypothesis is to accept that the two samples give different relationships.
HILU; Restricted sample: 1952–80; Unrestricted samples: 1952–70; 1971–80.

To give a more detailed picture, the separate regression results for 1952–70 and 1971–80 are reported for each country in Table A3.4. These separate results should be considered in relation to the restricted/whole sample results reported in Table 5.1. The United States, Canada and West Germany have non-significant coefficients in both subsamples and the whole sample. The size of the coefficient does increase quite considerably in absolute terms in the case of France, although in both sub-periods the coefficient remains statistically (very) significant. In the case of Japan a very stable coefficient has a very different standard error (hence t-statistic) between the two samples. Only in the case of the United Kingdom does the sign of the coefficient vary between the two sub-periods, from being non-significant (and positive) to being significantly negative. That the relative changes in the size of the coefficient between countries is not reflected exactly in the relative size of the calculated F^* values is due to the additional factor of changed standard errors between the two samples.

To conclude on the question of parameter stability, the change in the correlation for British data is in line with that suggested by the original graphing

APENDIX 3

Table A3.4 Post- and pre-break regression results

	Sample 1: 1952-70			Sample 2: 1971-80		
	L (t-stat.)	$\bar{R}^2$ DW	SER $F(1,16)$	L (t-stat.)	$\bar{R}^2$ DW	SER $F(1,7)$
US	0.06 (1.10)	0.012 1.25	0.74 1.21	0.26 (0.99)	−ve 1.82	2.84 0.98
Canada	−0.13 (1.23)	0.029 2.12	0.99 1.50	−1.11 (1.91)	0.249 1.77	2.96 3.65
Japan	−0.80*** (5.10)	0.596 1.81	1.40 26.0‡	−0.72 (1.66)	0.180 1.53	3.25 2.76
France	−1.76*** (4.49)	0.530 1.21	2.74 20.2‡	−3.57** (3.63)	0.604 1.55	3.98 3.19
Germany	−0.09 (0.99)	−ve 1.50	1.14 0.98	−0.19 (0.72)	−ve 1.79	1.86 0.52
UK	0.13 (0.85)	−ve 1.49	1.03 0.72	−0.98* (2.76)	0.452 2.81	3.03 7.61†

* Significant at the 5% level.
** Significant at the 1% level; *** 0.1% level.
† Significant at the 5% level; ‡ 1% level.
DW statistics indicate non-autocorrelation for 1952-70 sample except for United States and France which are both indeterminate. For the 1971-80 regressions, the DW statistic is appropriate to the sample size. The sign patterns of the residuals from each regression were therefore examined through contingency tables. The appropriate x^2 test could not reject the hypothesis of zero correlation even at the 10% level. While autocorrelation is clearly rejected in all cases, this rejection is least emphatic in the case of the UK, which is what the DW statistics would have indicated.

and plotting of the data series. That suggested that the resulting negative coefficient on the whole sample was due to the presence of a few outliers within the latter part of the wage data series. If so, this would suggest heteroscedasticity, as tested for in the following section.

Heteroscedasticity

Several of the regression equations were tested for the null hypothesis of the error terms being homoscedastic, against the alternative hypothesis of their being heteroscedastic. This section reports the results for the regression of the non-trend wage series on the non-trend employment series, reported in Table 5.1, and tested for parameter stability in the previous section. Again, the

Table A3.5 Test for heteroscedasticity

	$F^*(10,10)$
US	3.49†
Canada	1.04
Japan	1.03
France	2.45
Germany	(2.08)*
UK	5.08‡

* The calculated value of F^* for Germany, in brackets, was calculated by dividing the sum of squared residuals from the regression run with the *smaller* values of the percentage deviation of employment from trend by the sum of squared residuals from the other regression, rather than the other way round as was the case for all other values.

† Significant at the 5% level; ‡ 1% level.

procedure is as described above for tests on the Chapter 4 data. The results are reported in Table A3.5

Of the six countries' equations, only the United States and the United Kingdom indicate heteroscedasticity at the 5% level, and only the United Kingdom at the 1% level. The heteroscedasticity indicated by the UK results appears to be a result of the same parameter instability which was demonstrated in the previous section. Of the 11 years with the largest absolute size of employment deviation from trend the majority (seven) are 1970 and after.

Higher-order serial correlation

The final test is the Lagrange multiplier test (Breusch & Pagan 1980) for up to fifth-order residual serial correlation. The procedure is as set out above. The results for the calculated test statistics for the basic regression, of non-trend earnings on non-trend employment, are reported for each country in Table A3.6. There appears slightly more evidence of higher-order serial correlation in these results than in the previously reported results for the regression equation of non-trend wages on cyclical output reported in Table A3.2 above, for the Chapter 4 data (equation 4). Again, Canada is the only country exhibiting such correlation with 99% or greater probability, and again in no cases are the results significant at the 99.5% level. In the results reported here, however, the United States and United Kingdom now demonstrate such correlation at the 95% probability level. Again, then, of the three statistical tests, this last comes closest to suggesting that testing for possible correlation between the two series in the fashion reported here is invalid. On the other hand, the alternatives (taken to overcome this problem of

Table A3.6 Higher order serial correlation

	NR^2
US	11.75*
Canada	16.43**
Japan	4.62
France	8.24
Germany	8.68
UK	12.09*

For 5 degrees of freedom,
$P(x^2 > 11.07) = 0.05$ *
$P(x^2 > 15.09) = 0.01$ **
$P(x^2 > 16.75) = 0.005$ not achieved.

higher-order serial correlation) may get no closer to measuring the possibility of such a correlation.

First, if the correlation test were treated as an equation estimation exercise which was susceptible to equation respecification, then any additional variable introduced alongside cyclical output would immediately obscure the actual behaviour of wages in relation to cyclical output. The relation between non-trend wages and the additional explanatory variable might itself be responsible for changes in wages. When this is combined with the apparent behaviour of wages over the output cycle as indicated by the coefficient on the cyclical output variable, the resulting pattern of wage fluctuations over time ('pattern' not being meant necessarily to imply a non-random walk pattern) might differ in relation to the output cycle from that implied by the coefficient on the output cycle term alone. Thus, for example, the coefficient on output might imply a definite cyclical behaviour of wages, but when the additional behaviour of wages related to the additional variable is added, the composite behaviour of non-trend wages might no longer bear any significant relation to the output cycle.

Second, it may be the cyclical form the series are in which needs correcting: but then that is the data form with which a test for cyclical patterns is interested. This is not to say that if serial correlation is present it should not be tackled. Only that the cure might be as bad as the original problem in terms of the correlation being described.

Lastly, however, three of the six countries show no such higher order serial correlation. These include the two with the most 'definite' (non random walk) correlation coefficients. For this latter reason, at least, the results are left as reported above.

Appendix 4 Data

Chapter 4

The major problem in choosing data series for individual countries for use in an international study is to use series which are as comparable as possible. In all cases, therefore, data were taken from sources which were reporting data for all the countries here covered. The sources appearing to make the greatest effort at such comparability are the unpublished US Department of Labor (1983a; 1983b) which were, therefore, the sources used in all appropriate cases. Where these were not suitable, or not adequate, data were taken from OECD and UN sources. Abbreviations used in the notes to data tables for data sources are as follows:

OECD: *Main economic indicators*   (1984)   (April)
                                            (1984a) (March)
                                            (1982)   (March)
                                            (1982a) (April)
                                            (1981)   (March)
                                            (1981a) (December)
                                            (1979)   (March)
                                            (1962)   (February)

OECD *HS*: OECD Main Economic Indicators Historical Statistics 1960–1979
     HSa: 1955–1964
     HSb: 1955–1971

OEEC: Organisation for European Economic Co-operation, *Statistical Bulletin*, November 1960

Japan-SY: *Japan Statistical Yearbook*, various issues

UN-SY: United Nations Statistical Yearbook, various issues

MBS: United Nations Monthly Bulletin of Statistics, various issues.

Tables A4.1–A4.4 give the original series for output, nominal wages, output prices and material prices. A five-year moving average of output per hour (source: US Department of Labour 1983a, Table 2), relating for the United States and Canada to all employed persons (wage and salary earners, the self-employed, and unpaid family workers) and for all other countries to all employees (wage and salary earners), was used to proxy trend inputs per hour for use as a weight for cost of materials used per hour so that the price of materials becomes comparable with the price of labour used per hour (which even in real terms has a strong upward trend). This then allows the two indices (cost of labour used per hour, and cost of non-labour direct costs used per hour)

APPENDIX 4

Table A4.1 Output (Q) in manufacturing, indexes, 1977 = 100

	QUS	QC	QJ	QF	QG	QUK
1950	38.6	27.5	3.7	22.5	18.0	52.3
1951	43.0	29.9	5.2	24.6	20.7	53.8
1952	44.5	31.0	5.6	25.0	23.5	51.1
1953	47.5	33.2	6.9	25.7	26.2	54.8
1954	44.1	32.5	7.6	26.9	29.1	57.7
1955	48.9	35.6	8.2	28.5	33.9	61.4
1956	49.2	39.0	10.1	31.2	36.4	61.2
1957	49.5	38.9	12.0	33.0	38.7	62.7
1958	45.2	38.2	11.8	34.1	40.3	62.2
1959	50.5	40.9	14.3	35.5	43.9	65.7
1960	50.7	41.7	17.9	38.5	49.2	71.0
1961	50.7	43.3	21.5	41.0	52.6	71.1
1962	55.1	47.3	23.3	43.8	55.0	71.3
1963	59.6	50.5	26.0	47.2	56.4	73.8
1964	63.9	55.4	30.2	50.7	61.5	80.6
1965	69.8	60.4	31.4	52.8	66.4	82.9
1966	75.1	64.9	35.6	57.3	67.4	84.3
1967	75.0	66.8	42.7	59.7	66.0	84.9
1968	79.1	71.0	49.3	63.6	73.1	90.9
1969	81.7	76.3	57.3	69.4	81.9	94.3
1970	77.0	75.3	65.3	73.9	86.0	94.7
1971	78.7	79.7	69.4	78.6	86.9	93.6
1972	86.2	85.8	76.7	83.5	89.7	95.9
1973	95.9	94.9	87.4	89.3	95.2	104.7
1974	91.9	98.3	85.1	92.1	95.0	103.5
1975	85.4	92.6	82.2	90.2	90.4	96.2
1976	93.6	98.0	93.2	96.5	97.6	98.2
1977	100.0	100.0	100.0	100.0	100.0	100.0
1978	105.3	105.2	107.3	103.2	101.3	100.6
1979	108.2	111.4	118.0	105.9	106.1	100.7
1980	103.5	108.1	129.1	105.8	106.7	91.5
1981	106.5	110.4	130.4	103.0	105.1	85.7
1982	99.1	96.8	130.8	102.9	102.3	85.0

Series labels take the same form in each of the following tables, the first letter or letters denoting the economic variable (in this case output, denoted by 'Q'), the remaining letters denoting the country, namely:

- US: USA
- C: Canada
- J: Japan
- F: France
- G: Germany
- UK: United Kingdom

Source: US Department of Labor (1983a).

Table A4.2 Nominal wages(W)

	WUS	WC	WJ	WF	WG	WUK
1950	21.5	14.9	3.7	6.2	8.4	8.0
1951	23.6	16.8	4.7	8.0	9.6	8.7
1952	25.2	18.5	5.4	9.2	10.3	9.6
1953	26.5	19.4	5.7	9.5	10.8	10.1
1954	27.7	20.5	6.2	10.1	11.1	10.6
1955	28.8	21.1	6.5	10.8	11.9	11.4
1956	30.6	22.3	6.8	11.8	12.9	12.4
1957	32.5	23.8	7.1	12.7	14.4	13.2
1958	33.9	25.0	7.3	14.1	15.6	14.1
1959	35.2	26.0	8.1	14.9	16.9	14.5
1960	36.7	27.3	8.9	16.1	18.9	15.5
1961	37.7	28.0	10.4	17.8	21.2	16.7
1962	39.1	28.8	11.8	19.6	24.0	17.6
1963	40.3	29.9	13.2	21.5	25.6	18.4
1964	42.0	31.0	14.9	23.2	27.5	19.7
1965	42.8	32.6	16.7	25.0	30.3	21.6
1966	44.8	35.1	18.5	26.7	32.8	23.5
1967	47.0	37.8	20.7	28.9	34.6	24.2
1968	50.4	40.6	24.1	32.8	36.7	26.0
1969	53.9	43.6	28.5	34.0	39.9	28.4
1970	57.6	46.9	33.9	38.0	46.3	32.3
1971	61.1	50.5	39.3	42.5	52.0	37.0
1972	64.4	54.1	45.4	47.5	57.6	41.9
1973	69.0	59.6	55.7	54.1	65.0	46.7
1974	76.3	69.1	73.0	64.7	74.7	58.3
1975	85.4	78.9	85.4	77.0	84.0	75.8
1976	92.3	90.1	91.1	87.9	90.5	88.8
1977	100.0	100.0	100.0	100.0	100.0	100.0
1978	108.3	106.7	105.9	112.8	108.5	116.5
1979	118.8	117.5	112.8	128.1	116.4	138.7
1980	132.7	129.3	120.2	146.6	126.7	172.5
1981	145.8	143.7	128.5	168.6	136.1	200.2
1982	158.2	159.5	132.9	199.7	143.4	218.3

'Hourly compensation in manufacturing, national currency basis': compensation adjusted to include changes in employment taxes that are not compensation to employees, but are labor cost to employers. The data relate to all employed persons (wage and salary earners, the self-employed, and unpaid family workers) in the US and Canada, and all employees (wage and salary earners) in other countries.

Source: US Department of Labor (1983a).

Table A4.3 Output prices (*P*)

	PUS	PC	PJ	PF	PG	PUK
1950	41.5	44.2	36.1	27.5	49.0	21.2
1951	46.2	50.2	50.1	36.9	57.6	24.9
1952	45.0	47.3	51.1	36.2	59.3	25.4
1953	44.3	46.2	51.3	36.2	57.6	24.9
1954	44.4	45.4	50.9	36.2	56.4	24.9
1955	44.6	42.6	50.0	34.1	58.1	25.9
1956	45.9	43.9	52.2	36.6	59.3	27.1
1957	47.5	45.1	53.8	41.3	60.4	28.0
1958	48.6	45.2	50.3	45.3	61.0	28.4
1959	48.5	45.8	50.7	43.4	60.4	28.6
1960	48.9	45.9	51.8	44.9	61.6	29.1
1961	48.6	46.4	56.0	46.4	62.5	29.9
1962	48.6	46.9	55.1	46.8	63.3	30.2
1963	48.5	47.5	56.1	48.2	63.6	30.4
1964	48.8	47.9	56.2	49.7	64.3	31.0
1965	49.4	48.6	56.7	49.7	65.9	31.8
1966	50.4	49.9	57.9	51.2	67.0	32.7
1967	51.2	50.9	59.1	50.6	66.4	32.9
1968	52.5	52.0	59.1	49.7	65.7	34.2
1969	54.3	53.9	60.1	55.0	67.1	35.3
1970	56.3	55.2	62.2	59.1	70.5	37.9
1971	58.4	56.4	61.5	60.3	73.5	41.8
1972	60.5	58.9	62.1	63.3	75.2	44.3
1973	64.5	65.5	71.4	72.2	80.4	47.8
1974	78.8	79.6	89.9	93.4	91.1	63.9
1975	87.9	88.4	92.4	88.1	94.0	72.5
1976	93.5	92.9	97.3	94.7	97.3	84.7
1977	100.0	100.0	100.0	100.0	100.0	100.0
1978	107.3	108.4	99.2	100.8	100.9	109.3
1979	120.9	124.1	104.2	105.9	106.3	124.3
1980	137.1	140.7	119.5	115.1	114.3	146.6
1981	149.9	155.1	120.9	130.5	121.4	157.6
1982	156.0	164.4	121.4	142.0	127.3	168.4

Source:

US	1982	OECD (1984, p. 22)		1950–51	*Japan-SY* (1953, p. 307)
	1980–81	OECD (1982, p. 20)	F	1981–82	OECD (1984, p. 22)
	1960–79	OECD *HS*, p. 72		1979–80	OECD (1982)
	1955–59	OECD *HSa*, p. 77		1977–78	OECD (1981, p. 110)
	1950–54	*OEEC* (1960, p. 50)		1968–76	*UN-SY* (1979/80, p. 714)
C	1982	OECD (1984, p. 22)		1959–67	*UN-SY* (1969, p. 518)
	1980–81	OECD (1982, p. 20)		1950–58	*UN-SY* (1959, p. 435)
	1979	OECD (1981, p. 166)	G	1982	OECD (1984, p. 22)
	1976–78	OECD (1979, p. 64)		1980–81	OECD (1982a, p. 112)
	1960–75	OECD *HS*, p. 32		1960–79	OECD *HS*, p. 338
	1955–60	OECD *HSa*, p. 32		1956–59	OECD (1962, p. 11)
	1950–54	*OEEC* (1960)		1950–55	*OEEC* (1960, p. 50)
J	1982	OECD (1984, p. 22)	UK	1981–82	OECD (1984a, p. 166)
	1980–81	OECD (1982, p. 20)		1980	OECD (1981a)
	1967–79	*HS* p. 118		1960–79	OECD *HS*, p. 604
	1960–67	*Japan-SY* (1968, p. 369)		1955–59	OECD *HSb*, p. 460
	1954–59	*Japan-SY* (1962, p. 333)		1950–54	*UN-SY* (1959, p. 472)
	1952–53	*Japan-SY* (1955/6, p. 321)			

Table A4.4 Input prices for Materials (M)

	MUS	MC	MJ	MF	MG	MUK
1950	48.9	40.8	21.2	26.0	45.8	19.1
1951	56.0	45.5	25.4	39.2	57.8	26.7
1952	51.3	42.0	32.1	36.8	62.9	22.3
1953	47.5	39.6	31.9	34.6	59.9	20.1
1954	47.0	39.2	30.8	33.3	57.6	19.7
1955	45.1	40.0	32.3	34.0	61.7	21.1
1956	45.3	41.2	33.7	35.5	62.4	21.6
1957	46.4	39.9	36.2	37.1	62.9	22.3
1958	47.4	39.9	32.7	37.8	62.9	20.4
1959	46.2	40.2	33.2	41.0	62.4	20.5
1960	45.1	40.0	33.8	42.1	62.9	20.7
1961	44.9	40.5	35.7	43.3	62.9	20.7
1962	45.3	42.7	34.6	43.2	62.9	20.5
1963	44.3	43.3	36.1	44.6	62.9	20.7
1964	43.9	43.1	36.6	48.0	64.1	21.6
1965	65.6	44.1	36.8	48.4	65.5	22.1
1966	49.1	46.3	39.1	50.1	66.3	22.8
1967	46.5	46.9	40.3	48.8	64.0	22.5
1968	47.2	47.5	40.8	47.7	63.7	25.0
1969	50.4	49.6	42.1	54.6	65.6	26.0
1970	52.2	50.5	43.3	59.9	68.7	26.7
1971	53.4	48.7	41.9	58.0	70.3	27.6
1972	59.7	52.3	43.3	59.3	72.1	28.7
1973	81.2	70.5	53.7	74.8	79.0	37.7
1974	91.6	89.8	89.6	98.7	93.7	61.2
1975	92.2	89.8	94.4	81.9	94.5	70.5
1976	95.8	91.3	102.2	92.5	99.6	89.4
1977	100.0	100.0	100.0	100.0	100.0	100.0
1978	112.1	107.1	86.6	101.6	100.2	98.0
1979	131.2	126.1	106.6	114.7	106.5	118.2
1980	145.6	144.4	149.7	122.2	116.9	151.6
1981	157.3	172.0	155.4	136.4	126.7	164.9
1982	152.7	186.3	165.4	143.8	133.8	176.2

Source:

US	1979–82	*MBS* (1984, p. 180)		1960–79	OECD *HS*, p. 296
	1972–78	*UN-SY* (1979/80, p. 718)		1955–59	OECD *HSb*, p. 234
	1955–71	OECD *HSb*, p. 77		1950–54	*UN-SY* (1957, p. 469)
	1950–54	*UN-SY* (1957, p. 472)	G	1981–82	OECD (1984a, p. 124)
C	1979–82	*MBS* (1984, p. 170)		1980	OECD (1981a, p. 122)
	1972–78	*UN-SY* (1979/80, p. 713)		1960–79	OECD *HS*, p. 340
	1955–71	OECD *HSb*, p. 30		1952–59	*UN-SY* (1961, p. 476)
	1950–54	*UN-SY* (1957, p. 463)		1950–51	*UN-SY* (1953, p. 406)
J	1979–82	*MBS* (1984, p. 176)	UK	1981–82	OECD (1984a, p. 166)
	1972–78	*UN-SY* (1979/80, p. 176)		1980	OECD (1981a, p. 164)
	1955–71	OECD *HSb*, p. 169		1960–79	OECD *HS*, p. 605
	1950–54	*Japan-SY* (1957, p. 317)		1955–59	OECD *HSb*, p. 461
F	1981–82	OECD (1984a, p. 118)		1950–54	*UN-SY* (1957, p. 472)
	1980	OECD (1981, p. 116)			

APPENDIX 4

to be combined in a total direct costs index. The resulting series for the cost of materials used per hour is given in Table A4.5. The combined index for the cost of labour and non-labour direct costs used per hour in product terms, is given in Table A4.6.

Table A4.5 Cost of materials used per hour, nominal

	MUS	MC	MJ	MF	MG	MUK
1950	24.6	14.0	2.2	6.5	10.2	8.2
1951	28.8	16.4	2.8	10.3	13.6	11.7
1952	27.0	15.8	3.8	10.2	15.7	10.0
1953	25.7	15.6	4.2	10.0	15.8	9.1
1954	25.8	16.1	4.3	10.1	16.1	9.0
1955	25.3	17.0	4.9	10.7	18.3	10.0
1956	25.8	18.1	5.3	11.6	19.4	10.4
1957	26.9	18.3	6.0	12.8	20.9	11.0
1958	27.8	18.9	5.9	13.7	22.2	10.4
1959	27.6	19.8	6.6	15.5	23.5	10.8
1960	27.6	20.6	7.3	16.7	25.3	11.2
1961	28.6	21.9	8.5	18.1	26.8	11.6
1962	30.1	24.0	9.1	18.9	28.5	12.0
1963	30.7	25.5	10.3	20.6	30.2	12.6
1964	31.6	26.4	11.3	23.4	32.5	13.7
1965	34.3	28.0	12.5	25.0	35.2	14.7
1966	37.4	30.7	14.8	27.8	37.8	16.0
1967	36.0	32.6	17.0	28.9	38.6	16.4
1968	37.0	34.4	19.6	29.9	40.3	18.9
1969	40.4	37.6	22.6	36.4	43.6	20.4
1970	43.2	40.3	25.9	42.3	47.9	21.9
1971	45.9	40.8	27.8	43.1	51.4	23.6
1972	52.7	45.6	31.1	46.2	55.2	25.5
1973	73.9	63.6	41.1	61.0	63.8	34.5
1974	86.0	83.5	73.5	85.4	80.3	57.8
1975	88.7	86.0	82.6	73.9	85.6	68.0
1976	93.8	89.3	95.0	87.8	94.9	87.6
1977	100.0	100.0	100.0	100.0	100.0	100.0
1978	114.0	109.5	93.5	106.6	104.4	100.6
1979	135.5	130.7	122.1	124.8	114.8	125.1
1980	152.3	149.8	179.6	138.4	129.5	165.8
1981	166.7	180.5	194.1	159.7	144.5	182.8
1982	163.8	197.5	214.7	173.9	157.1	197.9

Table A4.6 Total direct costs used per hour, in product terms (DC)

	DCUS	DCC	DCJ	DCF	DCG	DCUK
1950	54.3	33.1	9.0	22.9	18.1	38.1
1951	54.7	33.2	8.2	23.7	18.5	39.2
1952	57.3	37.4	9.6	26.2	19.7	38.3
1953	59.2	39.4	10.2	26.7	21.0	39.2
1954	61.1	42.1	11.1	27.9	22.0	40.5
1955	62.0	46.5	12.0	31.3	23.3	42.2
1956	63.3	47.9	12.2	32.1	24.7	43.2
1957	64.7	48.9	12.5	30.8	26.6	44.4
1958	65.7	51.2	13.7	30.8	28.4	45.1
1959	67.5	52.5	15.1	34.8	30.8	46.1
1960	69.1	54.8	16.3	36.3	33.4	48.2
1961	71.5	56.2	17.5	38.6	36.2	50.1
1962	74.4	58.3	19.9	41.8	39.7	51.8
1963	76.7	59.9	22.0	44.0	42.1	53.8
1964	79.3	61.8	24.6	46.8	44.8	56.8
1965	81.1	64.2	27.3	50.3	47.9	60.4
1966	84.1	67.5	27.3	52.8	50.9	63.9
1967	84.7	71.0	33.2	57.0	53.7	65.3
1968	87.7	74.4	38.4	64.1	57.3	68.9
1969	91.2	77.4	44.5	63.2	60.9	72.6
1970	94.0	81.2	50.6	66.6	66.3	75.7
1971	96.1	84.2	58.3	70.8	70.5	77.4
1972	100.2	87.0	66.2	74.4	75.8	81.7
1973	109.5	93.0	71.8	78.0	80.5	88.8
1974	100.8	92.5	81.4	76.3	83.6	91.0
1975	98.4	91.8	91.5	86.2	89.9	100.9
1976	99.3	96.7	94.8	92.8	94.2	104.3
1977	100.0	100.0	100.0	100.0	100.0	100.0
1978	102.6	99.2	103.0	109.9	106.4	101.5
1979	102.7	98.1	111.0	120.0	109.1	107.7
1980	101.5	96.5	115.6	125.1	111.5	116.1
1981	101.8	100.2	122.7	127.0	113.9	123.2
1982	102.6	104.3	129.7	134.8	115.5	125.4

Chapter 5

The data sources are as reported for Chapter 4, with the exception of total hours worked in manufacturing, and total employment in manufacturing, both of which were introduced in Chapter 5 and which are reported in Tables A4.7 and A 4.8 respectively.

Table A4.7 Total hours in manufacturing (L)

	LUS	LC	LJ	LF	LG	LUK
1950	78.2	79.3	40.8	89.0	81.9	116.0
1951	84.2	82.8	46.1	92.3	91.2	119.8
1952	85.4	83.7	47.3	90.9	94.5	118.6
1953	89.8	86.7	51.5	88.7	98.5	121.2
1954	82.1	81.3	52.7	90.1	105.3	123.6
1955	86.6	83.6	54.4	91.3	115.1	127.1
1956	87.9	87.8	62.9	92.4	120.3	126.8
1957	86.5	87.0	68.4	96.4	117.8	126.6
1958	79.4	82.6	71.9	96.4	116.8	123.2
1959	84.7	84.1	74.8	94.2	117.5	125.2
1960	84.4	82.6	81.5	96.9	123.1	127.7
1961	82.3	81.5	86.4	98.7	124.9	126.8
1962	85.6	84.6	89.8	100.7	122.8	124.0
1963	86.5	87.0	92.7	102.9	120.3	121.9
1964	88.4	91.3	95.0	104.7	121.7	124.2
1965	93.6	96.0	94.7	103.2	123.4	123.7
1966	99.8	99.8	97.5	104.5	120.9	121.3
1967	99.6	99.6	101.9	103.5	111.2	116.7
1968	101.4	99.0	104.5	98.7	115.2	116.6
1969	103.1	100.5	105.3	104.0	121.9	118.1
1970	97.3	97.7	106.4	105.4	126.0	117.6
1971	93.7	96.6	106.3	106.4	122.3	111.9
1972	97.8	99.6	105.5	106.7	118.6	106.3
1973	103.2	103.6	109.0	108.3	118.8	109.3
1974	101.2	105.0	104.3	108.1	112.4	107.2
1975	91.4	101.4	96.4	102.6	101.6	101.7
1976	95.9	102.0	99.9	101.5	102.4	99.8
1977	100.0	100.0	100.0	100.0	100.0	100.0
1978	104.5	103.4	99.5	97.7	98.1	97.4
1979	106.6	106.4	100.5	95.7	98.0	94.3
1980	101.8	105.7	103.0	94.0	97.1	84.7
1981	101.2	107.0	103.2	90.0	93.2	75.0
1982	93.0	96.6	102.5	84.2	89.2	71.9

Source: US Department of Labor (1983a, Table 4).

Chapter 6

Pre-1963 earnings data were taken from the *British Labour Statistics Historical Abstract, 1886–1968* (Department of Employment and Productivity, London, HMSO, 1971) which gives an index of average hourly earnings for full time manual workers in UK manufacturing industry (p. 161, Table 85). These data are reproduced in Table A4.9. Apart from not being quarterly, the immediate

Table A4.8 Employment in manufacturing

	US	C	J	F	G	UK
1950	78.0	73.1	37.8	79.5	62.7	101.2
1951	83.7	77.6	41.9	81.9	70.3	103.7
1952	84.9	79.4	42.6	81.8	72.7	103.4
1953	89.5	81.8	45.9	80.0	75.8	104.8
1954	83.3	78.2	47.1	80.3	80.4	106.2
1955	86.1	80.1	48.1	81.2	88.0	108.8
1956	87.8	83.4	53.9	82.7	94.0	109.5
1957	87.5	83.8	59.0	85.6	97.2	109.5
1958	81.3	79.5	62.5	86.7	98.2	107.7
1959	85.0	80.4	64.0	85.2	99.2	108.6
1960	85.6	79.6	69.0	86.5	104.4	111.8
1961	83.2	79.0	74.4	87.7	108.2	112.6
1962	85.8	81.1	79.3	89.3	109.0	111.3
1963	86.4	83.1	82.5	91.7	108.4	109.5
1964	87.7	86.9	85.2	93.9	109.2	110.7
1965	91.8	91.4	86.5	93.4	111.7	112.0
1966	97.4	95.7	88.6	94.3	111.2	111.9
1967	98.6	96.1	92.4	94.1	104.4	108.6
1968	100.3	95.4	95.1	92.8	105.8	107.6
1969	102.2	97.3	97.3	95.2	111.8	109.0
1970	98.2	95.0	99.5	97.6	116.0	110.3
1971	94.4	94.5	101.1	99.2	115.2	107.6
1972	97.1	97.5	100.9	100.6	112.9	103.3
1973	102.2	101.9	104.9	103.0	113.7	104.7
1974	101.8	103.9	105.2	104.4	110.7	106.7
1975	93.0	101.6	99.8	101.5	103.3	102.6
1976	96.5	102.0	100.2	100.5	100.8	100.4
1977	100.0	100.0	100.0	100.0	100.0	100.0
1978	104.2	103.2	98.9	98.4	99.4	97.6
1979	107.0	106.9	98.8	96.6	99.8	95.1
1980	103.3	106.6	101.3	95.3	100.4	89.5
1981	102.7	108.6	102.2	91.8	97.9	80.6
1982	96.1	98.6	101.7	90.0	94.3	75.9

Source: US Department of Labor (1983a, Table 5)

Table A4.9 Average hourly earnings

Date	Male	Female	Date	Male	Female
1948	59.1	60.1	1959	112.9	113.0
	61.0	61.2		115.3	115.9
1949	61.6	63.2	1960	122.2	121.2
	62.8	64.6		125.1	124.3
1950	63.9	66.0	1961	130.3	130.0
	65.2	67.4		132.7	132.0
1951	68.5	71.4	1962	135.8	135.1
	71.5	74.2		138.3	138.5
1952	75.3	77.3	1963	140.9	140.7
	76.8	78.8		144.5	144.1
1953	79.7	81.9	1964	151.2	150.3
	81.1	83.6		155.6	154.3
1954	84.2	85.8	1965	162.7	160.5
	86.5	88.4		171.0	168.7
1955	91.4	92.1	1966	178.2	176.6
	93.7	94.6		180.5	179.7
1956	99.3	98.6	1967	182.8	182.3
	100.7	101.4		188.9	188.2
1957	102.3	103.7	1968	195.6	194.1
	107.6	107.6		20.16	200.9
1958	108.6	109.1			
	110.9	111.3			

drawback is that the data are given separately for males and for females. The two indices reported in Table A4.9 had, therefore, to be weighted to construct a single index for employees earnings. The *Historical Abstract* gives figures for number of employees in employment by industrial order, 1948–68 (Table 133 for Males, Table 134 for Females), as shown in Table A4.10. An index was then constructed for average hourly earnings (E), for all employees (male plus female), as $[(ME * MN) + (FE * FN)]/N$, as shown in Table A4.11.

From 1963, weekly earnings figures for all employees in manufacturing, were taken from OECD (1980 p. 603). These are for Great Britain rather than the United Kingdom, so when linking with the above statistics these data were linked to the previous data, rather than linking backwards as is normal. Also, there is no reading for 1972 I, which is, therefore, taken to be (1971 IV + 1972 II)/2.

These data refer to weekly earnings. As has been seen, however, weekly earnings may have a cyclical movement caused by fluctuations in hours worked, and so the weekly earnings data were divided by the weekly hours of work figure (from OECD 1980, p. 602) to obtain earnings per hour. Note that 1971 I is calculated as above. E/H is, then, E divided by H, all multiplied by 100.

Table A4.10 UK Manufacturing Industry: number of employees (N)

Year	Unlinked		MN	FN	N
	Males (MN)	Females (FN)			
1948	5433.1	2694.9	5092.1	2592.4	7684.5
1949	5543.3	2751.3	5195.4	2646.7	7842.1
1950	5657.1	2862.6	5302.1	2753.8	8055.9
1951	5761.5	2984.4	5399.9	2870.9	8270.8
1952	5794.6	2874.7	5430.9	2765.4	8196.3
1953	5829.8	2917.3	5463.9	2806.4	8270.3
1954	5956.5	3017.0	5582.7	2902.3	8485.0
1955	6119.1	3103.2	5735.1	2985.2	8720.3
1956	6199.0	3093.6	5810.0	2976.0	8786.0
1957	6224.0	3061.1	5833.4	2944.7	8778.1
1958	6218.5	2964.9	5828.2	2852.2	8680.4
1959	6196.8	2924.9			
59	5717.9	2776.0	5807.9	2813.7	8621.6
1960	5949.1	2901.4	6042.7	2940.8	8983.5
1961	6046.2	2926.0	6141.4	2965.7	9107.1
1962	6015.8	2877.5	6110.5	2916.6	9027.1
1963	5936.5	2816.7	6029.9	2854.9	8884.8
1964	6016.0	2864.9			
64	6025.2	2882.9	6110.7	2903.8	9014.5
1965	6133.1	2895.2	6220.1	2916.2	9136.3
1966	6139.9	2915.0			
66	6227.0	2936.1	6227.0	2936.1	9163.1
1967	6082.0	2796.4	6082.0	2796.4	8878.4
1968	6018.1	2772.1	6018.1	2772.1	8790.2

These data refer to 'number of employees' while the earnings data referred to 'full-time manual workers'. Also, these data were only available annually, so the annual data were used to proxy for both the April and October earnings data for that year. The data had to be taken from numerous editions of the *Monthly Digest of Statistics*, as there is no long-run historical table.

The original data (unlinked) are shown, as well as the linked data, calculated by multiplying the 1965 and 1964 Males figures by 6227/6139.9; the 1963, 1962, 1961, 1960 and 1959 figures by 6110.7/6016 (where 6110.7 = 6025.2* [6227/6139.9]) and the pre-1959 figures by 5807.9/6196.8; and similarly for Female workers. The two linked series were then summed.

Table A4.11 UK index for average hourly earnings (E)

Year		E	Year	E
1948	April	59.4	1959	113.9
	October	61.1		115.5
1949		62.1	1960	121.9
		63.4		124.8
1950		64.6	1961	130.2
		66.0		132.5
1951		69.5	1962	135.6
		72.4		138.4
1952		76.0	1963	140.8
		77.5		144.4
1953		80.4	1964	150.9
		81.9		155.2
1954		84.7	1965	162.0
		87.1		170.3
1955		91.6	1966	177.7
		94.0		180.2
1956		99.1	1967	182.6
		100.9		188.7
1957		102.8	1968	195.1
		107.6		201.4
1958		108.8		
		111.0		

The pre-1963 quarterly earnings data had to be derived by interpolating the half-yearly data. The earnings data were adjusted to include employers' national insurance contributions.

Prices

The above data are, of course, still in money terms. This series was then deflated by the price index of the output of all manufactured products. From April 1948 to October 1961 these data were collected from various issues of the Central Statistical Office's *Monthly Digest of Statistics*, the various series then being linked. This series was then linked to the OECD's (1980, p. 604) data from 1960. The OECD series is excluding food, beverages and tobacco, although this is unlikely to affect the cyclical findings aggregated over manufacturing industry as a whole.

Output

All data were collected in seasonally unadjusted form, for reasons discussed below (Appendix 6). Unfortunately, however, the CSO's *Economic Trends* does not give seasonally unadjusted data. The OECD, which does give these data, does not give them to sufficient significant places to allow cyclical analysis. An index was therefore compiled from various issues of the CSO's *Monthly Digest of Statistics*, calculated from monthly data (quarterly not being given). In fact even this has now ceased to show unadjusted data, although they remain available by writing directly to the CSO. The resulting data series used (prior to detrending) are reproduced in Tables A4.12–A.4.16.

Table A4.12 Output

	I	II	III	IV
1948	45.8	44.4	43.5	47.1
1949	48.3	49.1	46.4	51.0
1950	53.0	53.5	51.1	56.6
1951	56.0	57.8	53.3	56.6
1952	57.1	53.3	48.7	55.3
1953	56.7	56.7	53.8	60.9
1954	61.4	61.8	58.1	65.4
1955	67.1	66.5	60.9	69.0
1956	67.1	65.9	60.1	67.1
1957	67.9	66.7	62.8	68.3
1958	67.9	65.7	60.8	67.9
1959	66.9	70.9	65.6	75.5
1960	76.6	76.4	70.9	77.7
1961	76.8	77.7	71.3	76.6
1962	76.4	77.5	72.4	77.7
1963	76.6	79.2	75.9	83.8
1964	84.3	87.3	80.1	88.9
1965	89.8	89.1	82.5	91.3
1966	92.4	90.6	84.3	89.5
1967	88.4	90.9	82.5	92.0
1968	93.3	93.9	88.0	98.0
1969	96.2	97.5	90.9	100.1
1970	97.2	98.6	91.4	101.7
1971	98.2	98.3	91.7	100.0
1972	96.7	101.1	95.2	107.8
1973	111.1	110.8	103.8	113.0
1974	106.5	108.7	103.2	108.4
1975	105.3	100.7	93.9	102.6
1976	102.8	102.2	97.1	106.2
1977	106.7	101.7	97.0	104.8
1978	104.3	105.5	99.6	105.4
1979	104.5	107.3	98.0	106.3

Table A4.13 Nominal earnings

	I	II	III	IV
1948	58.4	59.4	60.2	61.1
1949	61.6	62.1	62.8	63.4
1950	64.0	64.6	65.3	66.0
1951	67.8	69.5	71.0	72.4
1952	74.2	76.0	76.8	77.5
1953	79.0	80.4	81.2	81.9
1954	83.3	84.7	85.9	87.1
1955	89.4	91.6	92.8	94.0
1956	96.6	99.1	100.0	100.9
1957	101.8	102.8	105.2	107.6
1958	108.2	108.8	109.9	111.0
1959	112.4	113.9	114.7	115.5
1960	118.7	121.9	123.4	124.8
1961	127.5	130.2	131.4	132.5
1962	134.0	135.6	137.0	138.4
1963	139.6	141.2	141.7	143.3
1964	149.2	150.2	150.7	153.9
1965	161.4	162.4	163.5	166.7
1966	174.1	177.8	175.7	177.8
1967	179.4	182.6	184.7	187.9
1968	196.4	197.5	197.5	201.2
1969	208.6	211.3	212.9	220.8
1970	231.4	238.9	245.2	255.8
1971	265.4	275.5	276.5	284.5
1972	305.2	304.7	311.6	323.8
1973	330.7	339.7	346.6	363.6
1974	388.5	391.2	422.5	460.2
1975	491.5	512.8	546.2	572.2
1976	596.1	614.1	620.0	639.1
1977	653.9	668.8	667.2	707.6
1978	730.4	772.3	780.8	813.7
1979	846.6	891.7	889.1	961.3

Table A4.14 Wholesale Price Index

	I	II	III	IV
1948	22.7	23.2	23.3	23.2
1949	23.3	24.2	24.2	25.2
1950	25.8	26.8	28.0	30.2
1951	32.2	33.7	34.0	34.7
1952	35.0	34.6	34.2	34.3
1953	34.4	34.9	34.5	34.4
1954	34.3	34.5	34.7	34.8
1955	35.1	35.5	35.9	36.3
1956	36.9	37.3	37.5	37.7
1957	38.8	38.8	38.8	39.0
1958	39.0	39.1	39.1	39.2
1959	39.3	39.2	39.2	39.3
1960	39.4	39.7	39.9	40.0
1961	40.4	40.6	41.1	41.3
1962	41.6	41.7	41.8	41.9
1963	42.0	42.2	42.2	42.5
1964	42.8	43.4	43.7	43.9
1965	44.4	45.1	45.3	45.5
1966	45.9	46.2	46.5	46.5
1967	46.6	46.6	46.9	47.1
1968	48.0	48.6	48.9	49.2
1969	49.9	50.3	50.7	51.2
1970	52.3	53.5	54.6	56.0
1971	57.5	58.8	59.7	60.0
1972	60.6	61.4	62.5	63.9
1973	64.7	65.0	67.2	69.9
1974	75.2	80.5	83.7	88.0
1975	93.7	98.5	101.2	105.7
1976	110.3	114.5	119.2	125.2
1977	133.0	139.6	143.8	145.8
1978	149.2	151.8	154.8	157.3
1979	161.6	168.0	176.4	181.8

Table A4.15 Price index for materials inputs

	I	II	III	IV
1948	20.9	22.1	22.3	22.6
1949	22.8	22.6	21.4	23.9
1950	25.3	26.7	30.7	36.8
1951	45.0	43.4	39.0	39.1
1952	37.9	35.0	33.8	32.9
1953	32.5	31.7	30.8	30.6
1954	30.4	31.1	30.9	31.8
1955	32.5	32.2	33.5	33.1
1956	33.4	33.4	33.5	34.2
1957	34.5	33.8	32.8	31.5
1958	30.9	31.2	31.2	31.2
1959	31.3	31.2	31.4	31.7
1960	31.8	31.7	31.2	31.2
1961	31.1	31.2	31.0	30.8
1962	31.4	31.1	30.7	31.0
1963	31.5	31.6	31.4	32.8
1964	32.9	32.8	33.1	33.7
1965	33.6	33.6	33.3	33.6
1966	34.3	34.9	34.3	34.1
1967	33.8	33.6	33.7	35.8
1968	37.6	36.9	37.0	37.3
1969	37.9	38.4	38.7	39.7
1970	40.4	40.6	40.6	41.3
1971	41.9	42.7	43.0	42.6
1972	43.0	43.2	44.5	47.0
1973	51.3	54.2	61.3	68.2
1974	85.5	85.3	85.6	90.6
1975	92.2	95.5	101.8	110.5
1976	115.4	124.6	128.9	138.9
1977	144.8	148.8	146.5	142.2
1978	140.2	146.3	144.9	147.1
1979	153.4	163.3	169.9	183.9

Table A4.16 Output per hour

	I	II	III	IV
1948	65.3	63.4	67.0	66.5
1949	67.5	68.9	70.4	70.6
1950	70.8	71.8	74.0	74.9
1951	73.3	75.7	75.4	73.3
1952	75.2	70.4	69.2	72.0
1953	73.7	74.0	75.7	78.6
1954	76.9	77.6	78.6	81.2
1955	81.9	81.4	80.5	83.4
1956	81.9	80.7	79.3	81.2
1957	83.4	81.9	83.4	83.1
1958	85.1	82.4	82.4	84.3
1959	82.9	88.0	88.0	92.8
1960	93.0	93.0	93.0	93.5
1961	93.7	94.9	94.2	92.5
1962	94.7	96.1	97.1	95.4
1963	95.4	99.0	102.2	103.4
1964	103.9	108.0	106.7	108.7
1965	110.6	110.1	110.1	111.6
1966	116.1	114.2	114.9	115.6
1967	114.2	117.8	115.4	117.8
1968	120.7	121.7	123.1	125.5
1969	123.1	125.1	125.8	126.7
1970	127.2	129.2	129.2	131.6
1971	136.6	137.1	138.1	137.8
1972	137.8	144.6	147.0	152.3
1973	155.7	155.7	157.3	156.6
1974	150.1	153.7	157.3	151.3
1975	160.7	154.2	155.2	155.2
1976	158.8	158.6	162.7	162.7
1977	164.1	156.9	161.2	159.5
1978	161.2	163.6	166.7	161.4
1979	164.8	169.9	167.2	166.0

Chapter 7

The annual UK data series from 1948 to 1974 inclusive for the seven industries and for aggregate manufacturing on output, earnings, employment and price of value added were supplied to me in their present form, already prepared (linked and so on), and are reproduced in Tables A4.17–A4.20 below. The earnings data were, however, for earnings per head rather than per hour, so indices of hours actually worked had to be constructed (Table A4.21).

Table A4.17 Output

	CHEM.	TEXT.	STO.	PR.	ENG.	VEH.	M.M.	MAN.
1948	297.3	1085.5	321.4	529.0	1649.8	608.5	682.9	6721.1
1949	307.5	1170.4	351.0	577.4	1771.6	653.5	686.1	7144.7
1950	348.3	1253.8	389.5	640.6	1775.3	698.6	721.5	7780.1
1951	371.0	1237.7	411.9	664.8	1863.9	714.1	749.4	8020.2
1952	350.6	1063.6	399.7	545.1	1860.2	716.9	767.6	7624.8
1953	396.0	1218.7	405.5	610.7	1886.0	814.1	761.2	8161.4
1954	433.4	1255.3	411.9	715.4	2000.5	924.0	820.2	8613.2
1955	455.0	1240.6	427.3	771.7	2151.8	1062.0	888.8	9149.8
1956	484.5	1228.9	421.5	761.4	2181.3	995.8	902.7	9135.6
1957	508.3	1220.1	408.1	777.5	2236.7	1069.1	914.5	9347.4
1958	525.3	1117.7	402.3	802.8	2221.9	1108.5	829.8	9248.6
1959	579.8	1192.3	427.3	840.7	2299.4	1200.0	866.3	9785.2
1960	639.9	1247.9	475.4	921.2	2421.2	1297.2	1004.6	10575.9
1961	651.3	1224.5	495.3	906.3	2816.2	1204.3	945.6	10590.0
1962	671.7	1188.0	504.3	905.1	2609.5	1226.8	893.1	10618.2
1963	719.3	1224.5	520.3	932.7	2631.6	1286.0	934.9	10999.5
1964	792.0	1296.2	600.5	1017.8	2853.1	1393.0	1061.4	12016.1
1965	846.4	1337.2	608.2	1039.7	2956.4	1370.5	1109.6	12369.1
1966	895.2	1335.7	603.7	1067.3	3148.3	1356.4	1047.4	12595.0
1967	938.3	1299.1	628.8	1063.9	3236.9	1331.0	986.3	12679.8
1968	1013.2	1446.9	665.3	1106.4	3377.2	1445.1	1050.7	13555.2
1969	1074.5	1468.9	667.9	1142.0	3576.5	1501.5	1075.3	14063.5
1970	1134.6	1463.0	641.6	1150.1	3690.9	1408.5	1072.1	14120.0
1971	1159.6	1495.2	693.6	1119.0	3709.4	1400.0	978.8	14063.5
1972	1219.7	1528.8	739.1	1180.0	3676.1	1460.6	979.9	14458.9
1973	1361.5	1612.2	815.5	1289.3	4056.3	1480.3	1072.1	15645.0
1974	1423.9	1508.4	748.1	1251.3	4019.4	1426.8	983.1	15263.7

The eight columns represent the following:

CHEM.—Chemicals
TEXT. —Textiles
STO. —Stone etc.
PR. —Print
ENG. —Engineering
VEH. —Vehicles
M.M. —Metal manufacturing
MAN. —Aggregate manufacturing.

Chapter 8

A widely accepted (and easily accessible) source of British data from 1855 is Feinstein (1972). To allow the results reported here to be easily repeated, wherever possible data were taken from Feinstein. An attempt was made to reproduce, and hence expand along the above lines, Marshall's results from his own data. However, the Marshall library, where the statistical tables compiled by Marshall for this aspect of his work were deposited, have no annual series on

Table A4.18 Nominal earnings per head

	CHEM.	TEXT.	STO.	PR.	ENG.	VEH.	M.M.	MAN.
1948	3.19	2.34	2.93	3.40	3.07	3.51	3.78	2.95
1949	3.41	2.46	3.28	3.57	3.02	3.77	3.99	3.08
1950	3.58	2.65	3.43	3.72	3.18	3.86	4.18	3.25
1951	4.02	2.86	3.77	4.15	3.55	4.16	4.49	3.54
1952	4.34	3.02	4.02	4.41	3.96	4.46	4.96	3.87
1953	4.58	3.29	4.45	4.83	4.19	4.89	5.16	4.13
1954	4.93	3.40	4.60	5.11	4.41	5.26	5.35	4.34
1955	5.30	3.59	4.86	5.51	4.69	5.76	5.84	4.66
1956	5.78	3.76	5.11	5.93	5.12	6.10	6.35	5.02
1957	6.12	3.97	5.50	6.35	5.42	6.49	6.81	5.34
1958	6.43	4.17	5.72	6.37	5.62	6.84	6.98	5.59
1959	6.80	4.34	5.86	6.66	5.96	7.37	7.44	5.94
1960	7.12	4.51	6.11	6.91	6.19	7.63	7.78	6.21
1961	7.52	4.74	6.45	7.25	6.58	8.11	8.01	6.56
1962	7.91	4.92	6.80	7.62	6.77	8.35	8.32	6.81
1963	8.29	5.17	7.19	7.95	6.98	8.82	8.63	7.12
1964	8.83	5.51	7.63	8.56	7.48	9.59	9.33	7.63
1965	9.64	6.50	8.16	9.11	8.07	10.41	10.01	8.23
1966	10.26	6.39	8.24	9.80	8.51	11.02	10.36	8.64
1967	10.57	6.72	8.75	10.19	8.73	11.40	10.59	9.01
1968	11.64	7.66	9.25	11.04	9.43	12.66	11.33	9.77
1969	12.72	7.89	9.63	11.92	11.13	13.63	12.59	10.61
1970	14.09	8.91	11.61	13.57	12.58	15.22	14.78	12.11
1971	14.06	10.06	13.29	15.44	13.83	17.03	16.17	13.58
1972	18.91	11.92	16.56	18.25	16.58	20.00	18.20	16.12
1973	21.66	14.08	18.38	21.65	19.38	23.42	21.20	18.80
1974	25.44	28.46	21.96	25.46	23.04	27.44	25.39	22.39

wages, prices or output. The data used by Keynes and Dunlop come largely from the many publications of Bowley (1937), although strangely Bowley (1898)[1] is not referred to. The major such references are Bowley (1895a; 1895b; 1898; 1899) and Wood (1909).

Wages

The money wage variable being considered is the amount actually paid per hour. Keynes stressed this in private correspondence with Dunlop (Keynes 1979, pp. 284–7), both then attempting to measure the value of one hours wages to the worker. As discussed below under 'Prices', the money-wage series was also used to approximate the cost of one hour's wages to the employer. The two wage series in Feinstein (1972, Table 65, pp. T140–1) measure average weekly wage rates and average weekly earnings (reproduced in Table A4.22 below). The wage rate series measures the average movement in the level of full-

---

[1] Bowley's (1898) article is actually listed in the *Economic Journal* Index under 'Dowley'.

Table A4.19 Employment

	CHEM.	TEXT.	STO.	PR.	ENG.	VEH.	M.M.	MAN.
1948	421.2	1644.0	314.5	459.4	1822.2	670.7	549.4	7568.5
1949	433.7	1717.3	319.5	479.3	1877.4	683.4	554.1	7723.7
1950	450.0	1787.5	330.7	504.7	1899.6	704.3	561.6	7933.2
1951	462.6	1818.8	337.8	514.6	1952.4	727.8	569.3	8144.0
1952	469.2	1639.2	340.6	510.0	2021.8	766.9	579.6	8072.5
1953	467.1	1725.9	336.2	500.2	2010.3	782.8	570.3	8145.1
1954	478.9	1752.2	340.8	524.5	2064.5	820.7	571.6	8356.8
1955	495.7	1704.1	347.2	545.8	2177.8	858.9	591.7	8587.6
1956	505.2	1679.3	346.9	557.6	2217.1	874.7	601.9	8652.9
1957	511.3	1677.9	337.4	568.6	2235.6	854.6	601.7	8646.1
1958	514.7	1575.4	326.5	599.8	2244.9	865.9	587.4	8551.4
1959	517.3	1535.2	327.2	574.5	2217.5	869.7	573.9	8493.9
1960	530.3	1557.0	339.3	603.0	2327.7	919.8	617.1	8850.5
1961	531.3	1550.8	347.5	618.7	2404.8	898.0	633.1	8972.3
1962	518.0	1499.7	351.7	627.2	2428.5	883.5	596.0	8893.3
1963	513.8	1458.7	341.0	626.6	2371.7	874.3	592.0	8753.2
1964	510.5	1462.5	355.3	629.6	2428.6	879.7	622.3	8908.1
1965	517.5	1319.9	358.3	639.7	2505.1	870.1	632.4	9028.3
1966	527.3	1425.0	364.9	650.9	2590.5	853.2	623.0	9163.1
1967	518.1	1331.7	352.5	640.3	2556.0	823.0	591.8	8878.5
1968	500.3	1311.2	355.1	641.7	2507.0	811.0	580.1	8790.2
1969	519.6	1331.1	353.8	649.0	2347.7	830.2	585.1	8910.6
1970	526.0	1273.3	344.9	654.9	2402.0	837.0	591.7	8898.4
1971	570.5	1211.6	333.7	624.3	2355.0	814.6	555.2	8599.9
1972	457.4	1094.1	304.3	579.2	2013.0	779.0	516.1	7767.1
1973	456.6	1081.0	308.6	574.2	2025.0	792.0	518.0	7817.4
1974	463.2	1056.0	304.4	588.7	2065.0	786.9	507.0	7860.5

time weekly rates of wages. It covers the main categories of manual workers. The weekly earnings series is for actual average weekly earnings for manual workers in the main industries and services.

Prices

The wage, materials and direct cost series were deflated by both a consumer price index to reconstruct and test the 'real wage' series being discussed by Keynes and Dunlop, and by a producer price index. The 'consumer price' series is from Feinstein (1972, Table 65, pp. T140-1), column 3 of Table A4.22. The series for the price of the principal industrial products up to 1913 was taken from Mitchell & Deane (1971, pp. 472-3), reproduced in Table A4.23 below. A wholesale price index from 1871 to 1938 is reported in Mitchell & Deane (1971, pp. 476-7) reproduced in Table A4.24 below.

The original index of the price of materials used was taken from Mitchell & Deane (1971, pp. 474-5, column 8) (reproduced in Table A4.25 below).

Table A4.20 Index for price of value added

	CHEM.	TEXT.	STO.	PR.	ENG.	VEH.	M.M.	MAN.
1948	74.28	58.95	42.22	46.29	44.56	49.14	45.04	51.29
1949	76.69	59.75	42.51	44.01	42.84	48.15	48.36	50.50
1950	72.66	62.46	40.24	44.54	41.93	45.23	48.45	49.29
1951	86.55	66.98	46.54	54.55	51.17	53.96	47.50	56.13
1952	100.54	68.20	50.44	59.56	64.87	60.66	51.13	63.73
1953	99.50	68.78	54.01	58.10	64.91	65.74	49.63	63.03
1954	104.70	68.62	57.10	57.33	65.29	64.34	49.92	64.53
1955	105.46	67.79	58.44	58.61	66.03	60.98	60.00	66.18
1956	108.74	68.47	60.23	62.20	72.19	67.83	63.58	70.77
1957	113.38	75.22	64.06	64.71	74.44	66.08	68.78	72.39
1958	132.68	81.28	66.79	66.40	77.89	70.55	82.78	75.93
1959	111.51	73.90	67.09	64.90	78.77	70.97	80.78	76.11
1960	110.67	79.06	66.59	65.54	80.31	70.26	81.07	77.31
1961	109.14	82.65	68.04	68.96	74.08	73.18	83.06	79.48
1962	108.12	83.99	68.87	73.07	83.03	73.89	81.32	80.41
1963	107.07	85.29	69.09	74.13	84.12	77.90	83.04	81.59
1964	109.24	86.14	70.40	75.06	85.86	76.88	76.32	82.01
1965	116.92	88.41	72.85	78.06	88.95	81.42	83.42	85.89
1966	109.63	94.59	74.00	80.47	122.85	82.57	82.23	87.36
1967	106.69	96.05	73.11	83.53	90.05	84.06	79.45	88.28
1968	108.70	90.96	73.90	87.48	92.15	84.77	79.40	88.55
1969	101.16	96.78	75.64	89.72	93.02	87.63	85.84	91.11
1970	100.00	100.00	100.00	100.00	100.00	100.00	100.00	100.00
1971	104.79	106.48	104.14	110.87	110.19	111.15	114.69	109.70
1972	116.71	108.93	115.58	121.03	116.95	124.62	119.87	117.39
1973	128.48	127.36	113.31	128.55	120.50	150.65	113.60	126.21
1974	107.89	242.18	131.08	149.24	130.05	166.41	159.59	142.58

Output

The index for industrial production was taken from Feinstein (1972, Table 8, pp. T24–5, column 2) reproduced in Table A4.26 below. An attempt has been made to choose series to be consistent, with as similar as possible industrial coverage. This has turned out to be, in general terms, 'industrial production'.

Direct Cost index

Deciding the appropriate weight for the two series (labour costs and materials costs) to be used to create the total direct cost series poses problems for such early data. The weighting was, therefore, initially calculated from the 1963 input–output tables. The resulting relative weights (wages 68 per cent, materials 32 per cent) were compared with the results of the same exercise performed on input output tables referring to 1948 (Stewart 1958) and 1935 (Barna 1952). These suggested a 67:33 ratio and a 64:36 ratio, respectively. In view of the lack of comparability between the tables and the need to assume that Stewart's wages–profits ratio held for 1935, this seems reasonably consistent, and certainly does not imply that this ratio shifts so as to affect any of the results.

Table A4.21 Hours worked per head per week

	CHEM.	TEXT.	STO.	PR.	ENG.	VEH.	M.M.	MAN.
1948	47.0	46.4	46.0	45.1	46.5	45.7	47.3	46.5
1949	47.3	46.6	45.8	46.3	46.4	45.5	47.3	46.6
1950	48.2	47.1	47.4	46.4	47.7	46.4	48.1	47.5
1951	48.0	46.4	48.1	46.7	48.2	46.9	48.2	47.6
1952	47.2	46.8	48.1	45.6	48.3	46.8	47.9	47.6
1953	48.3	47.4	47.9	47.4	48.1	47.2	47.9	47.9
1954	48.7	47.6	48.6	48.0	48.9	47.7	48.6	48.5
1955	49.1	47.6	49.7	48.1	49.2	47.8	48.9	48.7
1956	48.6	47.3	49.4	47.2	48.9	46.5	48.5	48.2
1957	48.6	47.0	48.5	47.0	48.4	47.1	48.0	48.0
1958	48.1	46.5	48.7	46.8	47.5	46.1	46.4	47.3
1959	48.5	47.6	50.5	47.7	48.2	47.5	47.9	48.2
1960	47.4	47.1	50.9	47.5	47.5	44.8	47.4	47.4
1961	46.9	45.9	49.6	46.7	47.2	44.9	46.1	46.8
1962	46.4	45.5	50.8	45.9	46.2	44.4	45.4	46.2
1963	46.8	46.2	51.1	46.4	46.7	45.4	46.6	46.8
1964	47.0	46.0	51.5	46.8	47.1	45.0	46.7	46.9
1965	46.1	45.7	50.3	46.5	46.0	43.6	46.1	46.1
1966	45.2	44.7	51.0	45.5	45.3	41.3	45.0	45.0
1967	45.5	44.5	50.5	45.8	45.0	43.4	45.0	45.3
1968	46.0	45.2	50.7	46.2	45.6	43.9	46.0	45.8
1969	45.9	44.8	51.5	46.1	45.5	43.6	45.8	45.7
1970	44.8	43.9	51.8	45.3	44.7	42.4	45.1	44.9
1971	44.0	43.4	49.3	44.4	43.2	41.2	43.3	43.6
1972	44.1	43.9	49.0	44.7	43.5	42.3	44.6	44.1
1973	44.4	44.2	48.8	45.1	44.3	43.0	45.1	44.7
1974	44.2	43.0	48.0	43.9	43.8	42.3	44.8	44.0

Different series relate to different editions of the Standard Industrial Classification and are not therefore fully comparable. All series linked backwards. For example, 'Chemicals and allied industries' (Order IV; Minimum List Headings [MLHs] 261–277) in the 1958 edition was replaced by two Orders in the 1968 edition: 'Coal and petroleum products' (Order IV; MLHs 261–263) and 'Chemicals and allied industries' (Order V; MLHs 271–279). To construct a single series after the split the two series were weighted according to relative employment (June 1971 = 39.3:311.8).

Source: Department of Employment, *British Labour Statistics: Yearbook*, 1975 (p. 56, Table 22); 1972 (p. 54, Table 22); and *Historical Abstract* (p. 108, Table 45).

Table A4.22 Earnings and prices

	Average weekly wage rates (1)	Average weekly wage earnings (2)	Retail prices (3)		Average weekly wage rates (1)	Average weekly wage earnings (2)	Retail prices (3)
1855	72	59	112	1896	88	84	81
1856	72	59	112	1897	89	85	83
1857	69	57	115	1898	91	88	86
1858	68	56	104	1899	93	90	84
1859	68	57	106				
				1900	97	95	89
1860	69	58	111	1901	95	94	88
1861	69	58	110	1902	94	92	88
1862	70	58	111	1903	93	92	89
1863	71	60	113	1904	93	90	90
1864	74	60	113	1905	92	90	90
1865	76	62	111	1906	94	92	91
1866	78	66	112	1907	94	97	93
1867	77	66	112	1908	94	95	91
1868	76	64	111	1909	94	95	92
1869	76	64	109				
				1910	94	95	94
1870	78	66	108	1911	95	96	95
1871	81	69	111	1912	98	99	98
1872	86	76	118	1913	100	100	100
1873	90	83	120	1914	101	101	101
1874	91	81	113	1915	108	117	121
1875	89	80	109	1916	118	133	143
1876	88	79	108	1917	139	170	173
1877	87	78	108	1918	179	211	199
1878	85	75	102	1919	215	241	211
1879	83	73	99				
				1920	257	278	244
1880	83	73	103	1921	256	260	222
1881	83	73	101	1922	198	209	179
1882	83	76	100	1923	176	193	171
1883	84	76	100	1924	178	196	172
1884	84	76	95	1925	181	198	173
1885	83	74	89	1926	181	193	169
1886	83	73	87	1927	179	197	164
1887	83	74	86	1928	177	194	163
1888	83	76	86	1929	176	195	161
1889	86	81	87				
				1930	175	193	155
1890	90	84	87	1931	173	189	145
1891	90	84	87	1932	170	185	141
1892	89	84	88	1933	168	184	137
1893	88	84	87	1934	168	186	138
1894	88	84	83	1935	170	189	140
1895	87	84	81	1936	173	194	144

APPENDIX 4

	Average weekly wage rates (1)	Average weekly wage earnings (2)	Retail prices (3)		Average weekly wage rates (1)	Average weekly wage earnings (2)	Retail prices (3)
1937	180	199	152	1951	373	538	311
1938	185	207	153	1952	403	582	338
1939	187	..	158	1953	422	617	349
				1954	441	657	355
1940	207	269	179	1955	470	713	371
1941	226	294	197	1956	507	771	389
1942	242	331	210	1957	533	813	404
1943	254	364	217	1958	552	841	416
1944	267	370	222	1959	567	864	418
1945	280	368	226				
1946	302	383	236	1960	581	914	422
1947	313	412	249	1961	606	978	437
1948	329	449	268	1962	628	1012	455
1949	337	468	275	1963	651	1055	465
				1964	681	1147	480
1950	344	490	283	1965	711	1240	503

Source: Feinstein (1972, pp. T140–1, Table 65)

Table A4.23 Producer prices

	Principal Industrial Products (c)		Principal Industrial Products (c)
1845	99	1880	95
1846	99	1881	92
1847	104	1882	95
1848	92	1883	94
1849	87	1884	89
1850	93	1885	85
1851	89	1886	79
1852	93	1887	79
1853	112	1888	82
1854	126	1889	84
1855	122	1890	83
1856	120	1891	79
1857	124	1892	77
1858	112	1893	78
1859	116	1894	71
1860	117	1895	71
1861	114	1896	73
1862	124	1897	71
1863	128	1898	75
1864	125	1899	87
1865	118	1900	95
1866	118	1901	87
1867	114	1902	85
1868	112	1903	86
1869	100	1904	86
1870	109	1905	91
1871	112	1906	103
1872	127	1907	104
1873	129	1908	87
1874	115	1909	93
1875	110	1910	100
1876	107	1911	103
1877	103	1912	108
1878	92	1913	114
1879	88		

(c) Viz. up to 1850—coal, pig iron, mercury, tin, lead, copper, hemp, cotton, wool, flax, tar, tobacco, hides, skins, tallow, hair, silk, and building wood; after 1850—coal, pig iron, tin, lead, copper, wool (two quotations), hemp, cotton, linseed oil, palm oil, flax, tar, jute, hides, skins, tobacco, silk, foreign tallow, native tallow, and building wood.

Source: Mitchell & Deane (1971, pp. 472–3)

Table A4.24 WPI

	Total Index		Total Index		Total Index (g)
1871	135.6	1906	100.8	1920	307.3
1872	145.2	1907	106.0	1921	197.2
1873	151.9	1908	103.0	1922	158.8
1874	146.9	1909	104.1	1923	158.9
1875	140.4	1910	108.8	1924	166.2
1876	137.1	1911	109.4	1925	159.1
1877	140.4	1912	114.9	1926	148.1
1878	131.1	1913	116.5	1927	141.6
1879	125.0	1914	117.2	1928	140.3
1880	129.0	1915	143.9	1929	136.5
1881	126.6	1916	186.5	1930	119.5
1882	127.7	1917	243.0	1931	104.2
1883	125.9	1918	268.1	1932	101.6
1884	114.1	1919	296.5	1933	100.9
1885	107.0	1920	368.8	1934	104.1
1886	101.0				
1887	98.8				
1888	101.8				
1889	103.4				
1890	103.3				
1891	106.9				
1892	101.1				
1893	99.4				
1894	93.5				
1885	90.7				
1896	88.2				
1897	90.1			1930	100.0
1898	93.2			1931	87.8
1899	92.2			1932	85.6
1900	100.0			1933	85.7
				1934	88.1
1901	96.7				
1902	96.4			1935	89.0
1903	96.9			1936	94.4
1904	98.2			1937	108.7
1905	97.6			1938	101.4

Note: The weights are as follows: total food—52; coal—10; iron and steel—24; other metals and minerals—10; cotton—16; wool—9; other textile materials—6; other articles—15.

Source: Mitchell & Deane (1971, pp. 476–7)

Table A4.25 Materials' price The Sauerbeck-*Statist* Price Indices, 1846–1938

(Average of 1867–77 = 100)

	Raw Materials Total		Raw Materials Total		Raw Materials Total
1846	85	1876	91	1906	83
1847	86	1877	89	1907	86
1848	73	1878	81	1908	74
1849	73	1879	78	1909	75
1850	78	1880	84	1910	81
1851	76	1881	80	1911	83
1852	81	1882	80	1912	88
1853	97	1883	77	1913	91
1854	104	1884	73	1914	88
1855	101	1885	70	1915	108
1856	102	1886	67	1916	140
1857	107	1887	67	1917	179
1958	94	1888	69	1918	206
1859	98	1889	70	1919	222
1860	100	1890	71	1920	264
1861	99	1891	68	1921	153
1862	107	1892	65	1922	132
1863	115	1893	65	1923	134
1864	119	1894	60	1924	146
1865	108	1895	60	1925	143
1866	107	1896	60	1926	131
1867	100	1897	59	1927	129
1868	99	1898	61	1928	124
1869	100	1899	70	1929	119
1870	99	1900	80	1930	97
1871	101	1901	72	1931	82
1872	115	1902	71	1932	81
1873	114	1903	72	1933	83
1874	100	1904	72	1934	85
1875	93	1905	75	1935	90
				1936	94
				1937	110
				1938	96

Note: These indices are based on wholesale prices and unit values of imports.

Source: Mitchell & Deane (1971, pp. 474–5), from A. Sauerbeck 'Price of Commodities and the Precious Metals', *J.S.S.* (1886), continued annually thereafter in the same source by Sauerbeck and subsequently by the editor of *The Statist*.

Table A4.26 Index numbers of output at constant factor cost, 1855–1965 (1913 = 100)

	Industrial production (2)		Industrial production (2)		Industrial production (2)
1855	26.3	1889	62.4	1927	122.8
1856	28.1			1928	119.5
1857	29.1	1890	63.3	1929	125.5
1858	28.5	1891	64.1		
1859	30.0	1892	61.0	1930	120.1
		1893	60.0	1931	112.3
1860	31.7	1894	63.5	1932	111.9
1861	31.7	1895	66.5	1933	119.3
1862	32.4	1896	71.4	1934	131.2
1863	32.5	1897	73.4	1935	141.2
1864	35.0	1898	77.0	1936	153.9
1865	37.3	1899	80.1	1937	163.1
1866	38.7			1938	158.7
1867	36.4	1900	80.1		
1868	36.4	1901	80.3	1946	162.6
1869	35.8	1902	81.7	1947	171.3
		1903	80.0	1948	186.0
1870	40.2	1904	81.0	1949	196.8
1871	43.5	1905	85.7	1950	208.0
1872	44.8	1906	89.3	1951	214.8
1873	45.3	1907	91.0	1952	210.0
1874	46.4	1908	83.7	1953	222.0
1875	46.7	1909	84.3	1954	235.6
1876	47.5			1955	247.6
1877	47.4	1910	85.5	1956	248.6
1878	47.3	1911	91.5	1957	253.1
1879	45.6	1912	93.9	1958	250.3
		1913	100.0	1959	263.1
1880	50.3				
1881	53.5	1920[d]	99.3	1960	281.6
1882	55.7		97.9	1961	285.1
1883	56.5	1921	79.7	1962	288.1
1884	54.4	1922	92.2	1963	297.9
1885	52.1	1923	97.6	1964	320.9
1886	51.0	1924	108.4	1965	330.2
1887	55.1	1925	112.7		
1888	58.3	1926	106.6		

Source: Feinstein (1972, pp. T24–5, Table 8)

Appendix 5 The Phase Average Trend Technique

The essentials of the method are described by Boschan & Ebanks (1978), and its application fully discussed in Friedman and Schwartz (1982) (and in Mintz 1969; and Bry & Boschan 1971).

Since cycle duration varies, constructing trends using moving averages may leave some residual cyclical movement in the moving average trend, an effect especially noticeable in the rate of growth in the trend line. The phase average trend (PAT) method was specifically designed to remove this bias without sacrificing fit or flexibility. The programme is designed: to select turning points (peaks and troughs) in data; to measure the long-term trend and its rate of change; and to produce trend-adjusted data. The trend is estimated in such a way as to cut through, and contain no significant elements of, the short-term cyclical movements in the series.

Specific turning points (determined by the programme) in the deviation (ratio or differences) from a centred 25-quarter (or 75-month) moving average trend (first trend) are used to break up the original series into segments (phases). The final trend is then interpolated (logarithmically or not) between the centred values of the averages of the data within these phases, and the programme selects turning points in the deviations of the raw data from the final trend.

The PAT programme was used for the quarterly data of Chapter 6. There were a few minor differences in turning points chosen as compared with my previous calculations prior to compiling and using the PAT programme. Most were very minor and the new choices were accepted (the PAT programme putting a greater weight on centring turning points in between the two opposite turns). The only major difference was at the series end when, running on data only to 1979 IV the programme could not specify 1979 II as a turning point (peak). In this case, then, the PAT turning points are not accepted.

The PAT programme requires data in seasonally adjusted form. The problems with using seasonally adjusted data are discussed in Appendix 6.

Appendix 6 Seasonal Adjustment

The question of seasonal adjustment only arose in relation to the Chapter 6 results, which were from quarterly data. The tests reported in that chapter were for the possible existence of *cyclical* relations between output and labour costs (as well as non-labour costs). Seasonally adjusted data might, therefore, seem more appropriate than unadjusted for these tests. Given that the series were already detrended, such seasonally adjusted series would reflect only the cycle (and irregular movements) rather than cycle plus seasonal. Certainly there may be a seasonal relation but, if so, this would, were we to use seasonally unadjusted data, prevent us from interpreting any results as giving any information on the *cyclical* relations.

Wallis (1974) and Sims (1974), however, question the use of seasonally adjusted data, at least of 'officially adjusted' data. Sims proposes a complex procedure which he suggests should only be attempted As a check in the final stages of research. Wallis concludes that applying the same filter to all series prevents distortions of the lagged relationships.

The Chapter 6 data were, therefore, all collected in unadjusted form, and then all adjusted by the same method. As a check, however, all tests were repeated using a simple moving average trend representation rather than the PAT programme. This allowed a comparison between the results using, on the one hand, the seasonally adjusted data and, on the other, the original, unadjusted data. The major difference between the results with adjusted, and those with unadjusted, data was the choosing of cyclical turning points. For this the adjusted data series is clearly the relevant one for cyclical testing. The peak or trough quarter must be selected because it is at the cycle peak or trough. Some other quarter close to these may, in the unadjusted data, be higher (or lower) for seasonal reasons, but such seasonal information is precisely what a cyclical analysis must abstract from.

Bibliography

Abramovitz, M. et al.. (1959). *The Allocation of Economic Resources: Essays in Honour of Bernard Francis Haley*. Stanford Studies in History, Economics and Political Science, 12. Stanford University Press, Stanford, CA.

Ackley, Gardner (1983). 'Commodities and Capital: Prices and Quantities', *American Economic Review*, vol. 73, no. 1, March, pp. 1–16.

Alogoskoufis, George S. (1982). 'Cyclical Innovations in Wages, Prices and Employment: Theory and Evidence'. LSE CLE Discussion Paper, no. 136, September.

Altonji, Joseph G. (1982). 'The Intertemporal Substitution Model of Labour Market Fluctuations: An Empirical Analysis', *Review of Economic Studies*, special issue, vol. 49, no. 5, pp. 783–824.

Altonji, Joseph G. and Orley Ashenfelter (1980). 'Wage Movements and the Labour Market Equilibrium Hypothesis', *Economica*, vol. 47, no. 187, August, pp. 217–45.

Andrews, Martyn (1983). 'The Aggregate Labour Market—an Empirical Investigation into Market-Clearing'. LSE CLE Discussion Paper, no. 154.

Azariadis, C. (1975). 'Implicit Contracts and Underemployment Equilibrium', *Journal of Political Economy*, vol. 83, pp. 1183–1202.

Bailey, M. N. (1974). 'Wages and Employment Under Uncertain Demand', *Review of Economic Studies*, vol. 41, pp. 37–50.

Bailey, M. N. (1981). 'The Productivity Slowdown and Capital Accumulation', *American Economic Review Papers and Proceedings*, vol. 71, no. 2, May, pp. 326–31.

Bank of England (1983). 'Monetary Trends in the United Kingdom'. Panel of Academic Consultants, Panel Paper no. 22, October (papers presented at the 22nd meeting of the Panel, on 28 October 1983).

Bank of England (1984a). 'The UK Economic Recovery in the 1930s'. Panel of Academic Consultants, Panel Paper no. 23, April.

Bank of England (1984b). 'Employment, Real Wages and Unemployment in the United Kingdom' Panel of Academic Consultants, Panel Paper no. 24, October.

Barclays Bank (1984). *UK Economic Survey*, 8 October.

Barna, T. (1952). 'The Interdependence of the British Economy', *Journal of the Royal Statistical Society*, vol. 115, part 1.

Barro, R. J. & Grossman, H. (1971). 'A General Disequilibrium Theory of Income and Employment', *American Economic Review*, vol. 61, March, pp. 82–93.

Barro, Robert J. & King, Robert G. (1984). 'Time-separable Preferences and Intertemporal-substitution Models of Models of Business Cycles', *Quarterly Journal of Economics*, vol. 99, no. 4, November, pp. 817–39.

Beach, Charles M. & James G. MacKinnon (1978). 'A Maximum Likelihood Procedure for Regression with Autocorrelated Errors', *Econometrica*, vol. 46, pp. 51–8.

Beenstock, Michael; Forrest Capie & Brian Griffiths (1984). 'Economic Recovery in the United Kingdom in the 1930s' in Bank of England (1984a), pp. 29–56.

Bernanke, Ben S. & James L. Powell (1984). 'The Cyclical Behaviour of Industrial Labour Markets: A Comparison of the pre-war and post-war eras'. National Bureau of Economic Research, Working Paper no. 1376, June.

Berndt, E. R. & Morrison, C. J. (1981). 'Capacity Utilisation Measures: Underlying Economic Theory and an Alternative Approach', *American Economic Review Papers and Proceedings*, vol. 71, no. 2, May, pp. 48–52.

Betancourt, Roger & Harry Kelejian (1981). 'Lagged Endogenous Variables and the Cochrane–Orcutt Procedure', *Econometrica*, vol. 49, no. 4, July, pp. 1073–8.

Blaug, Mark (1980). *The Methodology of Economics: Or How Economists Explain*. Cambridge University Press, Cambridge.

Boddy, Raford (1985). 'A Specious Solution to the "Problem" of Procyclical Productivity', *Journal of Political Economy*, vol. 93, no. 4, pp. 816–23.

Bodkin, R. G. (1969). 'Real Wages and Cyclical Variations in Employment: A Re-Examination of the Evidence', *Canadian Journal of Economics*, vol. 2, August, pp. 353–74.

Boland, Lawrence A. (1982). *The Foundations of Economic Method*. George Allen & Unwin, London.

Boschan, Charlotte and Walter Ebanks (1978). 'The Phase-Average-Trend: A New Way of Measuring Economic Growth', *Proceedings of the Business and Economic Section*, American Statistical Association, pp. 332–5.

Bowers, John; David Deaton & Jeremy Turk (1982). *Labour Hoarding in British Industry*. Basil Blackwell, Oxford.

Bowley, A. L. (1985a). 'Changes in Average Wages in the United Kingdom between 1880 and 1891', *Journal of the Royal Statistical Society*.

Bowley, A. L. (1985b). 'Wages in the United States and Great Britain', *Economic Journal*, vol. 5.

Bowley, A. L. (1898). 'Comparison of the Changes in Wages in France, the United States, and the United Kingdom, from 1840 to 1891, *Economic Journal*, vol. 8, December.

Bowley, A. L. (1899). 'Wages in the United States and Europe', *Economic Journal*, vol. 9.

Bowley, A. L. (1937). *Wages and Income since 1860*. Cambridge University Press, Cambridge.

Branson, W. H. (1972). *Macroeconomic Theory and Policy*. Harper & Row, New York.

Breusch, T. S. & A. R. Pagan (1980). 'The Lagrange Multiplier Test and its Applications to Model Specification in Econometrics', *Review of Economic Studies*, vol. 47, pp. 239–53.

Broadberry, Stephen N. (1983). 'Wages and Prices in Interwar Britain'. *Unpublished paper*, September.

Brothwell, John F. (1983). 'Wages and Employment: A reply to Maynard and Rose', *Journal of Post Keynesian Economics*, vol. 6, no. 1, pp. 101–4, Fall.

Bry, Gerhard & Charlotte Boschan (1971). *Cyclical Analysis of Time Series: Selected Procedures and Computer Programmes*. National Bureau of Economic Research, New York.
Burda, Michael C. (1985). 'New Evidence on Real Wage–Employment Correlations From U.S. Manufacturing Data', *Economics Letters*, vol. 18, nos 2–3, pp. 283–5.
Burns, Arthur F. & Wesley C. Mitchell (1946). *Measuring Business Cycles*. National Bureau of Economic Research, New York.
Caldwell, Bruce (1982). *Beyond Positivism: Economic Methodology in the Twentieth Century*. George Allen & Unwin, London.
Callaghan, James (1976). Speech to Labour Party Conference, *Report of the 75th Annual Conference of the Labour Party*, pp. 185–94.
Canzoneri, Matthew B. (1978). 'The Returns to Labour and the Cyclical Behaviour of Real Wages: The Canadian Case', *Review of Economics and Statistics*, vol. 60, pp. 19–24.
Carr, E. H. (1962). *What is History?* Penguin, London.
Central Statistical Office (1948). *Standard Industrial Classification*. London, HMSO.
Central Statistical Office (1982). *Annual Abstract of Statistics*. Edinburgh.
Central Statistical Office (1983a). *Monthly Digest of Statistics*, no. 455, November.
Central Statistics Office (1983b). *British Business*, 9–15 December.
Chiang, A. C. (1974). *Fundamental Methods of Mathematical Economics*, 2nd edn. McGraw-Hill, Kogakusha, Tokyo.
Chow, G. C. (1960). 'Tests of Equality Between Subsets of Coefficients in Two Linear Regressions', *Econometrica*.
Christainsen, G. B. & R. H. Harveman (1981). 'Public Regulations and the Slowdown in Productivity Growth', *American Economic Review Papers and Proceedings*, vol. 71, no. 2, May pp. 320–5.
Clark, Colin (1980). 'Materials–Labour Substitution in US Construction', *Economic Analysis and Policy*, new series, vol. 10, nos 1–2, March/September, pp. 44–51.
Coase, R. H. (1975). 'Marshall on Method', *Journal of Law and Economics*, vol. 18, pp. 25–31.
Coutts, Kenneth, Wynne Godley & William Nordhaus (1978). *Industrial Pricing in the United Kingdom*. Cambridge University Press, Cambridge.
Cowling, Keith (1981). 'Oligopoly, Distribution and the Rate of Profit'. *European Economic Review*, vol. 15, February, pp. 195–224.
Cowling, Keith (1982). *Monopoly Capitalism*. Macmillan, London.
Cramer, J. S. (1969). *Empirical Econometrics*. North-Holland, Amsterdam.
Davidson, Paul (1983). 'The Dubious Labour Market Analysis in Meltzer's Restatement of Keynes' Theory'. *Journal of Economic Literature*, vol. 21, March, pp. 52–6.
Davidson, Paul (1983). 'The marginal product curve is not the demand curve for labour and Lucas's supply function is not the supply curve for labour in the real world', *Journal of Post Keynesian Economics*, vol. 6, no. 1, Fall, pp. 105–117.
Dennison, Stanley R. (1984). 'Economics without Prices: A critique of the Low Pay Unit', *Institute of Economic Affairs*.

Dimsdale, N. H. (1984). 'Employment and Real Wages in the Inter-war Period', *National Institute Economic Review*, no. 110, November, pp. 94–103.

Dow, Sheila C. (1985). *Macroeconomic Thought. A Methodological Approach*. Basil Blackwell, Oxford.

Drazen, A. (1980). 'A Quantity-constrained Macroeconomic Model with Price Flexibility'. Department of Economics, University of Michigan, Working Paper.

Dufour, J. M., M. J. I. Gaudry & T. G. Liem (1980). 'The Cochrane Orcutt Procedure. Numerical Examples of Multiple Admissible Minima', *Economics Letters*, vol. 6, no. 1, pp. 43–8.

Duhem, Pierre (1954). *The Aim and Structure of Physical Theory*. Princeton University Press, Princeton, NJ. Translated by Phillip P. Wiener from *La theorie physique, son objet et sa structure*, 1906.

Dunlop, John (1938). 'The Movement of Real and Money Wage Rates', *Economic Journal*, vol. 48, September, pp. 413–34.

Durbin, J. &. G. S. Watson (1950). 'Testing for Serial Correlation in Least Squares Regression', *Biometrika*.

Fay, Jon A. & James L. Medoff (1985). 'Labor and Output over the Business Cycle: Some Direct Evidence', *American Economic Review*, vol. 75, no. 4, September, pp. 638–55.

Feinstein, C. H. (1972). *National Income, Expenditure and Output of the United Kingdom 1855–1965*. Cambridge University Press Cambridge.

Flinn, M. W. (1974) 'Trends in Real Wages, 1750–1850', *Economic History Review*, 2nd series, vol. 27, pp. 395–413.

Foss, M. F. (1981). 'Long-Run Changes in the Workweek of Fixed Capital', *American Economic Review Papers and Proceedings*, vol. 71, no. 2, May, pp. 58–63.

Friedman, Milton & Anna Schwartz (1982). *Monetary Trends in the United States and the United Kingdom: Their Relation to Income, Prices and Interest Rates, 1867–1975*. University of Chicago Press, Chicago and London.

Gayer, Arthur D., W. W. Rostow & Anna Jacobson Schwartz (1953). *The Growth and Fluctuations of the British Economy, 1790–1850: An Historical, Statistical and Theoretical Study of Britain's Economic Development*, Clarendon Press, Oxford.

Geary, P. T. & John Kennan (1982a). 'The Employment–Real Wage Relationship: An International Study', *Journal of Political Economy*, vol. 90, no. 4, August, pp. 854–71.

Geary, P. T. & John Kennan (1982b). 'Some International Evidence on Cyclical Fluctuations in Product and Labour Markets'. University of Iowa, Working Paper Series number 82-2, January.

Geary, P. T. & John Kennan (1984). 'International Substitution and the Phillips Curve: International Evidence'. Unpublished paper presented to the European Meetings of the Econometric Society, Madrid, September.

Geweke, John (1981). 'The Approximate Slopes of some Tests used in Time Series Analysis', *Econometrica*, vol. 49, November, pp. 1427–42.

Godfrey, L. G. (1982). 'A Note on the Estimation of Dynamic Regression Models with Autoregressive Errors by Means of the Cochrane–Orcutt Procedure', *Economics Letters*, vol. 10, no. 1–2, pp. 81–5.

Goldfeld, S. M. & R. E. Quandt (1965). 'Some Tests for Homoscedasticity', *Journal of the American Statistical Association*, vol. 60, pp. 539–47.
Gordon, David M. (1981). 'Capital–Labour Conflict and the Productivity Slowdown', *American Economic Review Papers and Proceedings*, vol. 71, no. 2, May, p. 30–5.
Gordon, David M., Thomas E. Weisskopf & Samuel Bowles (1983). 'Long Swings and the Nonreproductive Cycle', *American Economic Review Papers and Proceedings*, vol. 73, no. 2, May, pp. 152–7.
Gordon, R. J. (1979). 'The "End-of-Expansion" Phenomenon in Short-Run Productivity Behaviour', *Brookings Papers on Economic Activity*, pp. 447–61.
Haberler, Gottfried (1964). *Prosperity and Depression, A Theoretical Analysis of Cyclical Movement*. Fifth Edition, George Allen & Unwin, London.
Hamermesh, D. (1976). 'Econometric Studies of Labour Demand and their Applications to Policy Analysis', *Journal of Human Resources*, vol. 11, Fall, pp. 507–25.
Harding, Sandra G. ed. (1976). *Can Theories be Refuted? Essays on the Duhem–Quine Thesis*. D. Reidel Publishing Co, Dordrecht-Holland and Boston-USA.
Hart, Oliver D. (1983). 'Optional Labour Contracts under Asymmetric Information: An Introduction', *Review of Economic Studies*, vol. 50, pp. 3–35.
Hart, R. A. (1983). 'The Phillips Curve and Cyclical Manhour Variation', *Oxford Economic Papers*, vol. 35, no. 1, March, pp. 186–201.
Hatton, Timothy J. (1982). 'The British Labour Market 1855–1939: A Quantitative Approach'. Unpublished PhD thesis. Warwick.
Haugh, L. D. (1976). 'Checking the independence of 2 Covariance-Stationary Time Series: A Univariate Residual Cross-Correlation Approach', *American Statistical Association*, vol. 71, June, pp. 378–85.
Hendricks, W. (1981). 'Unionism, Oligopoly and Rigid Wages', *Review of Economics and Statistics*, vol. 63, no. 2, May, pp. 198–205.
Hendry, David F. &. N. R. Ericson (1983). 'Assertion without empirical basis: An econometric appraisal of Friedman & Schwartz, *Monetary trends in the United States and the United Kingdom*' in Bank of England (1983).
Hendry, David F. & N. R. Ericson (1984). Part II and Appendix B to Hendry & Ericson (1983). Supplement to *Bank of England* (1983).
Hendry, David F. & Kenneth F. Wallis (1984). *Econometrics & Quantitative Economics*. Basil Blackwell, Oxford.
Hildreth, C. & J. Y. Lu (1960). 'Demand Relations with Autocorrelated Disturbances'. *Research Bulletin 276*, Michigan State University Agricultural Experiment Station.
Hirsch, Barry T. & William J. Hausman (1983). 'Labour Productivity in the British and South Wales Coal Industry, 1874–1914', *Economica*, vol. 50, no. 198, March, pp. 145–57.
Hodrick, R. J. & E. C. Prescott (1980). *Post-war US Business Cycles: An Empirical Investigation*. Center for Mathematical Studies in Economics and Management Science, Northwestern University, Evanston, IL.
Hoffman, Walter G. (1965). *British Industry 1700–1950*. Basil Blackwell, Oxford.

BIBLIOGRAPHY

Hopcroft, M. & J. Symons (1983). 'A demand for Labour Schedule in the Road Haulage Industry'. LSE CLE Discussion Paper no. 169.

Hultgren, T. (1960). *Changes in Labour Cost during Cycles in Production and Business*. National Bureau of Economic Research, New York.

Hultgren, T. (1965). *Cost, Price and Profits: Their Cyclical Relations*. National Bureau of Economic Research, New York.

Hutton, J., H. Stamler and J. Stern (1978). 'Employment in Manufacturing in a Vintage Capital Model'. Government Economic Service Working Paper number 10, November.

Ireland, N. J. & D. J. Smyth (1970). 'Specification of Short-run Employment Functions', *Review of Economic Studies*, vol 37, pp. 281–5.

Kaldor, Nicholas (1956). 'Alternative Theories of Distribution', *Review of Economic Studies*, vol. 23, pp. 83–100.

Kalecki, Michal (1943). 'Costs and Prices' in *Studies in Economic Dynamics*. George Allen & Unwin, London.

Kalecki, Michal (1952). *Theory of Economic Dynamics*. 2nd edn. 1965. George Allen & Unwin, London.

Kalecki, Michal (1969). *Studies in the Theory of Business Cycles*. Basil Blackwell, Oxford.

Kalecki, Michal (1971). *Selected Essays on the Dynamics of the Capitalist Economy*. Cambridge University Press, Cambridge.

Katouzian, Homa (1980). *Ideology and Method in Economics*. Macmillan, London.

Kendall, M. G. & A. Stuart (1979). *The Advanced Theory of Statistics*, Vol. 2, 4th edn. Griffin, London.

Kennan, John (1979). 'Real Wages and Employment in Canadian Manufacturing: A Time Series Analysis'. Unpublished paper, March.

Keynes, John Maynard (1936). *The General Theory of Employment, Interest and Money*. 1973 edn, Volume VII of *The Collected Writings of John Maynard Keynes*, Macmillan Press, for the Royal Economic Society.

Keynes, John Maynard (1937a). 'Notes on Ohlin's Final Section' in Keynes (1973), pp. 187–91.

Keynes, John Maynard (1937b). 'Professor Pigou on Money Wages in Relation to Unemployment', *Economic Journal*, vol. 47, December.

Keynes, John Maynard (1939). 'Relative Movements of Real Wages and Output', *Economic Journal*, vol. 49, March, pp. 34–51.

Keynes, John Maynard (1940). *How to Pay for the War: A Radical Plan for the Chancellor of the Exchequer* in *Collected Writings*, vol. 9 (pp. 367–439). See also vol. 22, Chapter 2, for correspondence and articles.

Keynes, John Maynard (1973). *The Collected Writings of John Maynard Keynes*, Vol. 14. *The General Theory and After: Part II. Defence and Development*, ed. Donald Moggridge. Macmillan, London.

Keynes, John Maynard (1979). *The Collected Writings of John Maynard Keynes*, Vol. 23. *The General Theory and After. A Supplement*, ed. Donald Moggridge. Macmillan, Cambridge University Press for the Royal Economic Society.

Klant, Johannes J. (1984). *The Rules of the Game: the Logical Structure of Economic Theories*. Cambridge University Press, Cambridge.

Koutsoyiannis, A. (1977). *Theory of Econometrics*. Macmillan, London.

Kuh, E. (1966). 'Unemployment, Production Functions and Effective Demand', *Journal of Political Economy*, vol. 74, pp. 238–49, June.

Lakatos, I. (1970). 'Falsification and the Methodology of Scientific Research Programmes' in Lakatos & Musgrave (1970).

Lakatos, I. & A. Musgrave, eds (1970). *Criticism and the Growth of Knowledge*. Cambridge University Press, Cambridge.

Lawson, Tony & Hashem Pesaran, eds (1985). *Keynes' Economics: Methodological Issues*. Croom Helm, Beckenham.

Layard, P. R. G. & Steve J. Nickell (1980). 'The Case for Subsidising Extra Jobs', *Economic Journal*, vol. 90, March, pp. 51–73.

Layard, P. R. G. & Steve J. Nickell (1983). 'Marginal Employment Subsidies Again: A Brief Response to Whitley and Wilson', *Economic Journal*, vol 93, no. 372, December, pp. 881–2.

Layard, P. R. G. & Steve J. Nickell (1984). 'The Determination of Unemployment', LSE CLE Working Paper no. 609 (cited in Wadhwani 1985).

Layard, P. R. G. & Steve J. Nickell (1985a). 'The Causes of British Unemployment', *National Institute Economic Review*, 1/85, no. 11 (February), pp. 62–85.

Layard, P. R. G. & Steve J. Nickell (1985b). 'Unemployment, Real Wages, and Aggregate Demand in Europe, Japan and the US', LSE CLE Discussion Paper no. 214, March.

Lewis, W. A. (1978). *Growth and Fluctuations 1870–1913*. George Allen & Unwin, London.

Lindert, Peter H. & Jeffrey G. Williamson (1983). 'English Workers' Living Standards During the Industrial Revolution: A New Look', *The Economic History Review*, 2nd series, vol. 36, no. 1, February, pp. 1–25.

Lipsey, R. G. (1960). 'The Relation between Unemployment and the Rate of Change of Money Wage Rates in the UK 1862–1957', *Economica*, vol. 41, February, pp. 62–70.

Loomes, G. (1981). 'Why Oligopoly Prices Don't Stick', *Journal of Economic Studies*, vol. 8, no. 1, pp. 37–46.

Lucas, R. E. (1970). 'Capacity, Overtime and Empirical Production Functions', *American Economic Review*, vol. 60, no. 2, May.

Maddala, G. S. (1979). *Econometrics*, McGraw-Hill Kogakusha, Ltd, Tokyo.

McCombie, J. S. L. (1981). 'What Still Remains of Kaldor's Laws?', *Economic Journal*, vol. 91, March, pp. 206–16.

McIntosh, J. (1981). 'Aggregate Productivity Change in a Vintage Model—Canada 1946–1979', *Essex Economic Papers*. Department of Economics, University of Essex, no. 169, March.

Malcomson, J. M. & M. J. Prior (1979). 'The Estimation of a Vintage Model of Production for UK Manufacturing', *Review of Economic Studies*, vol. 46, pp. 719–36.

Malinvaud, E. (1977). *The Theory of Unemployment Reconsidered*. Basil Blackwell, Oxford.

Malinvaud, E. (1980). *Profitability and Unemployment*. Cambridge University Press, Cambridge.

Marris, Robin (1964). *The Economics of Capital Utilisation*. Cambridge University Press, Cambridge.

Marshall, Alfred (1885). *The Present Position of Economics*. Reprinted in Pigou (1925).
Marshall, Alfred (1899). 'Evidence Before the Indian Currency Committee' in Marshall (1926, pp. 263–326).
Marshall, Alfred (1926). *Official Papers*, edited by John Maynard Keynes, Macmillan for the Royal Economic Society.
Matthews, R. C. O., C. H. Feinstein & Odling-Smee (1982). *British Economic Growth 1856–1973*, Clarendon Press, Oxford.
Maynard, G. W. (1978). 'Keynes and Unemployment Today', *Three Banks Review*, no. 120, December, pp. 3–20.
Meade, J. E. (1938). *League of Nations World Economic Survey 1937–8*.
Meltzer, Allen H. (1981). 'Keynes' General Theory: A Different Perspective', *Journal of Economic Literature*, vol. 19, March, pp. 34–64.
Merrick, John (1984). 'The Anticipated Real Interest Rate, Capital Utilisation and the Cyclical Pattern of Real Wages', *Journal of Monetary Economics*, vol. 13, no. 1, January, pp. 17–30.
Michie, Jonathan (1985). 'The Cyclical Behaviour of Wages'. DPhil thesis. Bodleian Library, Oxford.
Miller, R. L. (1971). 'The Reserve Labour Hypothesis: Some Tests of its Implications', *Economic Journal*, vol. 8, no. 321, March, pp. 17–35.
Mintz, Ilse (1969). *Dating Postwar Business Cycles*. National Bureau of Economic Research, New York.
Mises, Ludwig von (1933). *Epistemological Problems of Economics*. Van Nostrand, Princeton, NJ.
Mises, Ludwig von (1962). *The Ultimate Foundation of Economic Science*. Van Nostrand, Princeton, NJ.
Mitchell, B. R, with the collaboration of Phillis Deane (1971). *Abstract of British Historical Statistics*, Cambridge University Press, Cambridge.
Modest, David M. & Bruce D. Smith (1983). 'The Standard of Living Debate, Rational Expectations, and Neutrality; Some Evidence from the Industrial Revolution', *Journal of Monetary Economics*, vol. 12, no. 4, November, pp. 571–93.
Munley, F. (1981). 'Wages, Salaries, and the Profit Share: A Reassessment of the Evidence', *Cambridge Journal of Economics*, vol. 5, no. 2, June, pp. 159–73.
Nadiri, M. I. & M. A. Schankerman (1981). 'Technical Change, Returns to Scale, and the Productivity Slowdown', *American Economic Review Papers and Proceedings*, vol. 71, no. 2, May, pp. 314–19.
National Institute (1984). *Economic Review*, 4/84, number 110, November.
Neftci, S. N. (1978). 'A Time Series Analysis of the Real Wages–Employment Relationship', *Journal of Political Economy*, vol. 86, no. 2, part 1, April, pp. 281–91.
Newell, A. & J. S. V. Symons (1985). 'Wages and Employment in the O.E.C.D. Countries'. Centre for Labour Economics, London School of Economics, Discussion Paper no. 219, May.
Nickell, Steve J. (1978). 'Fixed Costs, Employment and Labour Demand Over the Cycle', *Economica*, vol. 45, pp. 329–45.
Nickell, Steve J. (1981). 'An Investigation of the Determinants of Manufacturing Employment in the United Kingdom'. LSE CLE DP, no. 105,

November. Published in *Review of Economic Studies*, 1984, vol. 51, pp. 529–57.
Nickell, Steve J. (1982). 'Wages and Unemployment: A General Framework', *Economic Journal*, vol. 92, March, pp. 51–5.
Nickell, Steve J. (1984). 'The Modeling of Wages and Employment' in Hendry & Wallis (1984).
Nickell, Steve J. (1985). 'Unemployment and Pay', *Financial Times*, 6 February (and talk to Centre for Economic Policy Research, 19 February).
OECD (various dates). *Main Economic Indicators*.
OECD (1980). *Main Economic Indicators Historical Statistics 1960–1979*.
Oi, Walter Y. (1962). 'Labour as a Quasi-Fixed Factor', *Journal of Political Economy*, vol. 70, December, pp. 538–55.
Oi, Walter Y. (1981). 'Slack Capacity: Productive or Wasteful', *American Economic Review Papers and Proceedings*, vol. 71, no. 2. May, pp. 64–9.
Okun, Arthur M. (1981). *Prices and Quantities: A Macroeconomic Analysis*. Basil Blackwell, Oxford.
Oster, G. (1980). 'Labour Relations and Demand Relations: A Case Study of the "Unemployment effect"', *Cambridge Journal of Economics*, vol. 4, no. 4, December.
Otani, I. (1978). 'Real Wages and Business Cycles Revisited', *Review of Economics and Statistics*, vol. 60, May, pp. 301–4.
Otani, I. (1981). 'Real Wages, Business Cycles, and the Speed of Adjustment: A Reply', *Review of Economics and Statistics*, vol. 63, no. 2, May, pp. 312–13.
Panic, M. (1978). *Capacity Utilisation in UK Manufacturing Industry*. National Economic Development Office, London.
Pheby, John (1985). 'Are Popperian Criticisms of Keynes Justified?' in Lawson & Pesaran (1985), pp. 99–115.
Phillips, A. W. (1958). 'The Relation Between Unemployment and the Rate of Change of Money Wages in the UK 1861–1957', *Economica*, vol. 25, November, pp. 283–99.
Pigou, A. C., ed. (1925). *Memorials of Alfred Marshall*. Macmillan, London.
Pigou, A. C. (1933). *The Theory of Unemployment*. Macmillan, London.
Pigou, A. C. (1937). 'Real and Money Wages in Relation to Unemployment', *Economic Journal*, vol. 47, September, pp. 405–22.
Pitchford, J. D. (1981). 'Taxation, Real Wage Rigidity and Employment: the Flexible Price Case', *Economic Journal*, vol. 91, pp. 716–20, September.
Popper, K. (1959). *The Logic of Scientific Discovery*. Harper, New York.
Popper, K. (1963). *Conjectures and Refutations*. Routledge & Kegan Paul, London, (4th edition: 1972).
Popper, K. (1972). *Objective Knowledge. An Evolutionary Approach*, Oxford University Press, London.
Qualls, P. D. (1981). 'Cyclical Wage Flexibility, Inflation, and Industrial Structure: An Alternative View and some Empirical Evidence', *Journal of Industrial Economics*, vol. 29, no. 4, June.
Ragan, J. F. (1976). 'Measuring Capacity Utilisation in Manufacturing', *Federal Reserve Bank of New York Quarterly Review*, vol. 1, Winter.
Raisian, John (1983). 'Contracts, Job Experience, and Cyclical Labour Market Adjustments', *Journal of Labour Economics*, vol. 1, no. 2, April, pp. 152–70.

Ricardo, David (1817). *The Principles of Political Economy and Taxation*. 1973 edition. Everyman, London.
Richardson, J. H. (1939). 'Real Wage Movements', *Economic Journal*, vol. 49, September.
Robbins, Lionel C. R. (1935). *An Essay on the Nature & Significance of Economic Science*. 2nd edition, Macmillan, London.
Robinson, J. (1979). *Collected Economic Papers V*. Basil Blackwell, Oxford.
Rostow, W. W. (1947). *British Economy of the Nineteenth Century*. Clarendon, Oxford.
Rueff, Jacques (1925). 'Les variations du chomage en Angleterre', *Politique et Parlementaire*, vol. 125, no. 373, December, pp. 425-36.
Ruggles, R. (1940). 'Relative Movements of Real and Money Wage Rates', *Quarterly Journal of Economics*, vol. 54, November, pp. 130-49.
Sachs, J. D. (1979). 'Wages, Profits and Macroeconomic Adjustment: A Comparative Study', *Brookings Papers on Economic Activity*, vol. 2, pp. 269-319.
Sachs, J. D. (1980). 'The Changing Cyclical Behaviour of Wages and Prices: 1890-1976', *American Economic Review*, vol. 70, no. 1, pp. 78-90.
Sachs, J. D. (1983). 'Real Wages and Unemployment in the OECD Countries', *Brookings Papers on Economic Activity*, no. 1, pp. 255-89.
Salter, W. E. G. (1969). *Productivity and Technical Change*. 2nd edn. Cambridge University Press, Cambridge.
Sargent, T. J. (1978). 'Estimation of Dynamic Labor Demand Schedules Under Rational Expectations', *Journal of Political Economy*, vol. 86, December, pp. 1009-44.
Sargent, T. J. and N. Wallace (1974). 'The Elasticity of Substitution and Cyclical Behaviour of Productivity, Wages and Labor's Share', *American Economic Review*, vol. 44, May.
Saul, S. B. (1969). *The Myth of the Great Depression*. Macmillan, London.
Schelling, Thomas C. (1946). 'Raise Profits by Raising Wages?', *Econometrica*, vol. 14, no. 3, July, pp. 227-34.
Schor, Juliet B. (1982). 'Changes in the Cyclical Variability of Wages: Evidence from Nine Countries, 1955-1980'. Unpublished PhD dissertation, University of Massachusetts.
Schor, Juliet B. (1985). 'Changes in the Cyclical Pattern of Real Wages: Evidence from Nine Countries, 1955-80', *Economic Journal*, vol. 95, no. 378, June, pp. 452-68.
Schwartz, Anna Jacobson (1975). 'Preface' (with W. W. Rostow) to Arthur D. Gayer, W. W. Rostow & Anna Jacobson Schwartz, *The Growth and Fluctuations of the British Economy, 1790-1850, An Historical, Statistical, and Theoretical Study of Britains Economic Development*, Harvester Press, Hassocks.
Sedgwick, P. N. (1984). 'Economic recovery in the 1930s' in Bank of England (1984a), pp. 29-56.
Simon, Herbert A. (1984). 'On the behavioural and rational foundations of economic dynamics'. *Journal of Economic Behaviour and Organisation*, vol. 5, pp. 33-55.
Sims, Christopher (1974). 'Seasonality in Regression', *Journal of American Statistical Association*, vol. 69, no. 347, September, pp. 618-26.

Sims, Christopher (1980). 'Macroeconomics and Reality', *Econometrics*, vol. 48, no. 1, January, pp. 1–48.

Smith, Adam (1776). *The Wealth of Nations*, 1976 edition. University of Chicago Press, Chicago.

Smyth, D. J. (1981). 'Real Wages, Business Cycles and the Speed of Adjustment of Employment in Manufacturing Sectors of Industrialised Countries', *Review of Economics and Statistics*, vol. 63, no. 2, May, pp. 311–12.

Solow, Robert M. (1980). 'Theories of Unemployment', *American Economic Review*, vol. 70, no. 1, March, pp. 1–11.

Solow, Robert M. (1985). 'Economic History and Economics', *American Economic Review Papers and Proceedings*, vol. 75, no. 2, May, pp. 328–31.

Solow, Robert M. & Joseph E. Stiglitz (1968). 'Output Employment and Wages in the Short-run', *Quarterly Journal of Economics*, vol. 82, no. 4, November, pp. 537–60.

Sraffa, Piero (1926). 'The Laws of Returns under Competitive Conditions', *Economic Journal*, vol. 36, no. 144, December, pp. 535–50.

Stegmuller, W., W. Baker & W. Spohn, eds (1982). *Philosophy of Economics*. Springer-Verlag, Berlin.

Stewart, I. G. (1958). 'Input-Output Table for the United Kingdom', *Times Review of Industry, London and Cambridge Bulletin*, no. 28, pp. vii–ix, December.

Stewart, Ian M. T. (1979). *Reasoning and Method in Economics*. McGraw-Hill, London.

Symons, J. (1981). 'The Demand for Labour in British Manufacturing'. LSE CLE Discussion Paper, no. 91.

Symons, J. (1984), 'Is the Real Wage Still too High?', Centre for Labour Economics, London School of Economics, Working Paper, no. 623.

Symons, J. (1985), 'Relative Prices and the Demand for Labour in British Manufacturing', *Economica*, vol. 52, no. 205, pp. 37–49, February.

Symons, J. &. R. Layard (1984). 'Neoclassical Demand for Labour Functions for Six Major Economies', *Economic Journal*, vol. 94, no. 376, December, pp. 788–99.

Tarshis, Lorie (1939). 'Changes in Real and Money Wages', *Economic Journal*, vol. 49, March, pp. 150–4.

Tatom, John A. (1980). 'The "Problem" of Procyclical Real Wages and Productivity', *Journal of Political Economy*, vol. 88, no. 2, April, pp. 385–94.

Taylor, John B. (1984). 'Improvements in Macroeconomic Stability: The Role of Wages and Prices'. Working Paper no. 1491, November, National Bureau of Economic Research, New York.

Tinbergen, J. (1937). *An Econometric Approach to Business Cycle Problems*. Herman, Paris.

Tinbergen, J. (1939). 'A Method and its Application to Investment Activity. Statistical Testing of Business Cycle Theories I'. League of Nations.

Tobin, James (1947). 'Money, Wage Rates and Employment' in Seymour E. Harris, ed. *The New Economics; Keynes' Influence on Theory and Public Policy*. 1947, Knopf, New York.

Tobin, James, ed. (1983). *Macroeconomics, Prices, and Quantities*. Basil Blackwell, Oxford.

Treasury (1985). *The Relationship Between Employment and Wages. Empirical Evidence for the UK*. HMSO, London.
Tucker, Rufus S. (1936). 'Real Wages or Artisans in London, 1729–1935', *Journal of the American Statistical Association*, vol. 31, pp. 73–84.
Turvey, Ralph (1980). Demand and Supply. George Allen & Unwin, London.
US Department of Labor (1983a). 'Output per Hour, Hourly Compensation and Unit Labor Costs in Manufacturing. Eleven Countries. 1950–1982. Index Tables'. Bureau of Labor Statistics, Office of Productivity and Technology, May. Unpublished.
US Department of Labor (1983b). 'Underlying Data for Indexes of Output per Hour, Hourly Compensation and Unit Labor Costs in Manufacturing, Eleven Countries, 1950–1982'. Bureau of Labor Statistics, Office of Productivity and Technology, May.
Vany, A. de & N. G. Frey, (1981). 'Stochastic Equilibrium and Capacity Utilisation', *American Economic Review Papers and Proceedings*, vol. 71, no. 2, May, pp. 53–7.
Vicarelli, Fausto, ed. (1985). *Keynes's Relevance Today*. Macmillan, London.
Wadhwani, Sushil B. (1984). 'Inflation, Bankruptcy and Employment', LSE CLE Discussion Paper no. 195, March.
Wadhwani, Sushil B. (1985a). 'The Effects of Aggregate Demand Inflation, Real Wages and Uncertainty on Manufacturing Employment', LSE CLE Discussion Paper, no. 210, February.
Wadhwani, Sushil B. (1985b). 'Wage Inflation in the United Kingdom', *Economica*, vol. 52, no. 206, May, pp. 195–207.
Wallis, K. F. (1973). *Topics in Applied Econometrics*. Gray-Mills, London.
Wallis, K. F. (1974). 'Seasonal Adjustment and Relations Between Variables', *Journal of the American Statistical Association*, vol. 69, no. 345, March, pp. 18–31.
Ward, Benjamin (1972). *What's Wrong with Economics*, Macmillan, London.
Weisskopf, T. E. (1981). 'Wages, Salaries and the Profit Share: A Rejoinder', *Cambridge Journal of Economics*, vol. 5, no. 2, June, pp. 175–82.
Whitley, J. D. &. R. A. Wilson. (1983). 'The Macroeconomic Merits of a Marginal Employment Subsidy', *Economic Journal*, vol. 93, no. 372, December, pp. 862–80.
Wilber, Charles K. with Robert S. Harrison (1978). 'The Methodological Basis of Institutional Economics: Pattern Model, Storytelling, and Holism', *Journal of Economic Issues*, vol. 12, no. 1, March, pp. 61–89.
Wood. G. H. (1909). 'Real Wages and the Standard of Comfort since 1850', *Journal of the Royal Statistical Society*, pp. 99–103.
Worswick, David (1984a). 'The Recovery in Britain in the 1930s' in Bank of England (1984a), pp. 5–28.
Worswick, David (1984b). 'The Sources of Recovery in UK in the 1930s', *National Institute Economic Review*, 4/84, November, no. 110, pp. 85–93.
Worswick, David (1984c). 'Two Great Recessions: the 1980s and the 1930s in Britain', *Scottish Journal of Political Economy* vol. 31, no. 3, November, pp. 209–28.
Worswick, David (1985). 'Jobs for All?' *Economic Journal*, vol. 95, 377, March, pp. 1–14.

Wren-Lewis, Simon (1985), 'Expectations in Keynesian Econometric Models' in Lawson & Pesaran (1985), pp. 66–79.
Yeomans, K. A. (1979). *Applied Statistics*. Penguin, Harmondsworth.
Zarnowitz, Victor (1985). 'Recent Work on Business Cycles in Historical Perspective: A Review of Theories and Evidence, *Journal of Economic Literature*, vol. 23, no. 2, June, pp. 523–80.

Author Index

Ackley, Gardner 18
Alogoskoufis, George S. 48

Barna, T. 168
Barro, Robert J. 18, 21, 30
Beenstock, Michael 123
Bernanke, Ben S. 11, 33, 40, 43, 49–50, 53, 55, 111, 133
Beveridge, William 42
Blaug, Mark 4–5, 8
Boddy, Raford 19
Bodkin, R. G. 32, 38–40, 43–4, 46–52, 54–5, 87–8. 127, 134
Boschan, Charlotte 176
Bowers, John 18
Bowles, Samuel 112
Bowley, A. L. 116, 166, 166 n
Branson, W. H. 20
Breusch, T. S. 142, 146
Brittan, Samuel 3
Broadberry, Stephen N. 121–2
Bry, Gerhard 176
Burda, Michael C. 49–50, 54
Burns, Arthur F. 11–12

Callaghan, James 131
Canzoneri, Matthew B. 132
Capie, Forrest 123
Carr, E. H. 12
Chow, G. C. 73, 73 n
Coase, R. H. 125
Coutts, Kenneth 28–9, 137–9
Cowling, Keith 29, 137

Deane, Phyllis 167, 172–4
Deaton, David 18
Dennison, Stanley 2–3
Dimsdale, N. H. 123
Duhem, Pierre 4–6
Dunlop, John vii, 1, 6, 32–5, 37, 48, 51, 54, 112, 115 8, 124, 133, 166–7

Ebanks, Walter 176

Fay, Jon A. 19
Feinstein, C. H. 113 n, 165–8, 170–1, 175
Friedman, Milton 176

Geary, P. T. 32–3, 40, 43–50, 52–6, 72, 88, 91, 99, 102, 131–2, 135
Godley, Wynne 137–9
Goldfeld, S. M. 141
Gordon, David M. 112
Griffiths, Brian 123
Grossman, H. 21, 30

Harrod, Roy 8
Hart, Oliver 20
Hendry, David 10
Hultgren, T. 38

Kalecki, Michal v, 23–30, 34, 45, 132
Katouzian, Homa 4
Kennan, John 32–3, 40, 43–56, 72, 88, 91, 99, 102, 131–2, 135
Keynes, John Maynard v, vii, 1–3, 5–9, 12–13, 15, 26, 32–7, 42, 51, 54, 87, 112–8, 124–5, 127–34, 166–7
King, Robert G. 18
Klant, Johannes J. 7, 12
Koutsoyiannis, A. 9
Kuh, E. 38

Lakatos, I. 5
Lawson, Nigel 3
Layard, P. R. G. 11, 25, 33, 40, 44, 46, 49, 52–3, 55–6, 62, 71–3, 88–9
Lipsey, R. G. 123
Lucas, R. E. 18, 28

Maddala, G. S. 73 n
Malinvaud, E. 30
Marris, Robin 28
Marshall, Alfred 10, 13, 34, 113 n, 113–8, 121, 124–5, 165
Matthews, R. C. O. 113 n
Maynard, G. W. 137
Meade, J. E. 34–5
Medoff, James L. 19

Michie, Jonathan 57, 81
Mintz, Ilse 176
Mises, Ludwig von 4, 7, 12
Mitchell, B. R. 9, 11–12, 167, 172–4

Neftci, S. N. 32, 47, 49–56, 131
Newell, A. 128
Nickell, Steven J. 3, 10–11, 25, 33, 48, 53, 72
Nordhaus, William 137–9

Odling-Smee, J. C. 113n
Ohlin, Bertil 87
Okun, Arthur M. 32, 38
Otani, I. 3, 33, 43, 47–51, 55–6, 71–2

Pagan, A. R. 142, 146
Panic, M. 18
Pheby, John 125
Phillips, A. W. 122
Pigou, A. C. 35
Popper, Karl 4–6, 9, 12
Powell, James L. 11, 33, 40, 43, 49–50, 53, 55, 111, 133

Quandt, R. E. 141

Richardson, J. H. 6, 37
Robbins, Lionel C. R. 7–9, 12
Rostow, W. W. 113n
Rueff, Jacques 35
Ruggles, R. 6, 32, 37–8

Sachs, J. D. 33, 46, 50–1, 111, 135
Sargent, T. J. 32, 47, 49–52, 55–6, 88, 99, 128, 131
Schor, Juliet 53–4, 112
Schwartz, Anna Jacobsen 176
Sims, Christopher 177
Solow, Robert M. 28, 30, 112
Sraffa, Piero 23, 129
Stewart, I. G. 168
Stewart, Ian M. T. 7
Stiglitz, Joseph E. 28, 30
Symons, J. 3, 11, 33, 40, 44–56, 62, 71–3, 88–9, 128

Tarshis, Laurie 6, 32–5, 37, 48, 51, 54, 112, 132–3
Tatom, John A. 5, 18–20, 56, 109, 132–3
Taylor, John B. 112
Tinbergen, J. 8
Tobin, James 6, 32, 37
Turk, Jeremy 18
Turvey, Ralph 137

Wadhwani, Sushil B. 33, 52
Wallis, K. F. 10, 177
Ward, Benjamin 130–2
Weisskopf, T. E. 112
Whitley, J. D. 11
Wilson, R. A. 11
Wood, G, H. 166
Worswick, David 111, 123, 126
Wren-Lewis, Simon 131

Zarnowitz, Victor 41

Subject Index

aggregation effects, 99, 102, 110
analytical school, 7
apriorism, 4, 7, 10
   empirical, 7
   rationalistic, 7
average product of labour, 15, 25-7

business cycles, 1, 13, 15, 18, 27, 36, 41-3, 127
   long-swings, 112

Canada, 50-1, 57-89
Capacity utilization, 13, 18-20, 23-7, 36, 132
capital stock, 18-20, 33
cost curves, 23, 36
   shape of cost curves, 3, 36

demand for labour, 3, 21-3, 40, 42-5, 53
   labour demand schedules, 16, 44, 51-2, 72, 88-90, 128-31
   notional and effective, 16-17, 21-2
descriptive statistics, 11-12, 31, 128, 133
detrending, 2, 38, 47-9, 57, 127, 176
direct costs, 45, 64-71, 78, 83, 120-1, 130, 135-6, 137-9; *see also* material input prices
disaggregate data, 99-110
Duhem's irrefutability hypothesis, 4-6

effective demand, 22, 41, 59, 62, 122, 129
empiricism, 12
employment, 2-3, 13, 20, 43-4, 79-90
   conditional on output, 80, 83-7
   hours per worker and number of workers, 87

falsification, 4-6, 130-1
France, 57-88

General Theory of Employment, 34, 112, 127, 130
government policy, 60, 126, 131-4

heteroscedasticity, 141-2, 145-6
higher-order serial correlation, 142-3, 146-7

implicit contracts, 20-1
induction, 7, 34-5, 125
inference, 6, 9, 12, 112, 124, 128, 132-3
imperfect competition, 16; *see also* monopoly

Japan, 57-87

Kaleckian assumptions, 23-30, 36, 103, 131-3

lags, 46-7, 51-2, 59-63, 78
   and leads, 60-3, 78
Lakatosian response, 5
law of diminishing returns, 7

Macro econometric models, 11-12, 131-2
marginal cost, 23, 34-6, 132
   marginal user cost, 35-6
marginal product of labour, 2-3, 5-6, 13, 15-30, 32, 36, 43, 47, 56, 127-33
micro foundations of macro relations, 108-110
monopoly: degree of, 16, 25; *see also* Price mark-up
multicollinearity, 104-8
   orthogonalizing the explanatory variables, 106-7

neoclassical assumptions, 15-30, 34, 42, 60, 78, 108-110, 124, 127-33
new classical theory, 42, 129
nineteen thirties, 6, 15, 35, 111-12, 121-3, 126, 128, 130-2

output, 13, 21-2
   cyclical output, 2-3, 12-13, 15, 42
overhead costs, 23-7, 102-3, 132
   overhead labour, 23-7

parameter stability, 73–7, 143–5
Phillips curve, 122–3
post-war boom, 57, 126–7
   breakdown, 74, 127
prices, 26
   'cost determined' and 'demand determined', 25
   material input prices, 17, 25, 30, 45, 52, 62–8, 83, 95, 135–6; *see also* direct costs
   price deflator: CPI, WPI, VAP, 15 n, 46, 135–6
   Price mark-up, 23–5, 28–30, 34, 36, 63–5; *see also* monopoly: degree of
   'price taking' assumptions, 129
   'price-theoretic' approach, 18
   pro-cyclical movement of, 18, 43, 62
Productivity, 18, 23, 28–30, 32
Profits, 23–30, 38, 43, 132

Quantity rationing, 16, 21–3, 30

Realization of profits, 28
reduced form correlations, 9, 11, 41–3

scatter diagrams, 81–2
seasonal adjustment, 95, 177

structural models, 11, 123; *see also* Reduced form correlations
'stylized fact' of cyclical wage behaviour, 1–2, 13, 127–30

technology shocks, 17–20, 23
time series plots, 56
treasury, 15, 41, 52, 131

unemployment, 3, 21–3, 43–4
United Kingdom, 48, 57–88, 91–124
United States, 48, 50–4, 57–89, 111, 126

verification, 12, 131, 134
vintage model, 20

wages: nominal, real and product, 15 n, 35, 135–6
   cyclical pattern, 1–3, 9, 13–14, 23, 27–31, 134
   cyclical wage debate, 1–3, 32–3, 50–6, 127–33
   wage bargaining, 60, 103, 108
   wage cuts, 21, 41, 60–2, 129, 131, 133
   wage equations, 11, 39–41
West Germany, 57–89